Rising Tide

Gender Equality and Cultural Change around the World

The twentieth century gave rise to profound changes in traditional sex roles. But the force of this "rising tide" has varied among rich and poor societies around the globe, as well as among younger and older generations. *Rising Tide* sets out to understand how modernization has changed cultural attitudes toward gender equality and to analyze the political consequences of this process. The core argument suggests that women's and men's lives have been altered in a two-stage modernization process consisting of (1) the shift from agrarian to industrialized societies and (2) the move from industrial to postindustrial societies. This book is the first to systematically compare attitudes toward gender equality worldwide, comparing almost seventy nations that run the gamut from rich to poor, from agrarian to postindustrial. *Rising Tide* is essential reading for those interested in understanding issues of comparative politics, public opinion, political behavior, political development, and political sociology.

Ronald Inglehart is Professor of Political Science and Program Director at the Institute for Social Research at the University of Michigan. His research deals with changing belief systems and their impact on social and political change. He helped found the Euro-Barometer surveys and directs the World Values Survey. His books include *Modernization and Postmodernization: Cultural, Economic and Political Change in 43 Societies* (1997).

Pippa Norris is the McGuire Lecturer in Comparative Politics at the John F. Kennedy School of Government, Harvard University. Her work analyzes comparative elections and public opinion, gender politics, and political communication. Companion volumes by this author, also published by Cambridge University Press, include *Democratic Phoenix* (2002), *Digital Divide* (2001), and *A Virtuous Circle* (2000).

Rising Tide

Gender Equality and Cultural Change around the World

RONALD INGLEHART
University of Michigan

PIPPA NORRIS
Harvard University

CAMBRIDGE
UNIVERSITY PRESS

PUBLISHED BY THE PRESS SYNDICATE OF THE UNIVERSITY OF CAMBRIDGE
The Pitt Building, Trumpington Street, Cambridge, United Kingdom

CAMBRIDGE UNIVERSITY PRESS
The Edinburgh Building, Cambridge CB2 2RU, UK
40 West 20th Street, New York, NY 10011-4211, USA
477 Williamstown Road, Port Melbourne, VIC 3207, Australia
Ruiz de Alarcón 13, 28014 Madrid, Spain
Dock House, The Waterfront, Cape Town 8001, South Africa

http://www.cambridge.org

First published 2003

Printed in the United States of America

Typeface Sabon 10/13.5 pt.   *System* LATEX 2$_\varepsilon$ [TB]

A catalog record for this book is available from the British Library.

Library of Congress Cataloging in Publication data
Inglehart, Ronald.
Rising tide : gender equality and cultural change around the world / Ronald Inglehart,
Pippa Norris.
    p. cm.
Includes bibliographical references and index.
ISBN 0-521-82203-3 – ISBN 0-521-52950-6 (pb.)
1. Sex role – Cross-cultural studies.   2. Women's rights – Cross-cultural studies.
3. Social change – Cross-cultural studies.   4. Social values – Cross-cultural studies.
5. Women in politics – Cross-cultural studies.   I. Norris, Pippa.   II. Title.
HQ1075 .I53   2003
305.3 – dc21   2002031077

ISBN 0 521 82203 3 hardback
ISBN 0 521 52950 6 paperback

Contents

Tables

viii   *Tables*

Figures

Preface and Acknowledgments

The rise of more egalitarian attitudes toward the roles of women and men, documented in this book, the transformation of lifestyles, families, the workplace, and the public sphere, has been experienced as part of our lives during the last quarter-century. Both of the authors started to explore these trends many years ago; an integral part of *The Silent Revolution* (1977) was an attempt to explain the underlying causes of the social movements and new politics fermenting among the younger generations in North America and Western Europe, including the rise of environmentalism, civil rights in the United States, countercultural community groups, and the second wave women's movement. A decade later, *Politics and Sexual Equality* (1987) took up the issues of how women's lives were being transformed in Western nations and what had caused the substantial disparities in economic resources and political power. Subsequent work by both authors has returned to these themes on many occasions, but given the substantial political developments and social changes that have occurred during recent decades, it seemed time for a more direct examination of the state of gender equality around the world, in terms of both causes and consequences.

This book owes many debts to friends and colleagues. Some preliminary ideas were first sketched out in articles published in the *International Political Science Review* and the *Journal of Democracy*. The theme of the book received encouragement in conversations over the years with many colleagues, including Jane Bayes, Karen Beckwith, Victoria Budson, Ivor Crewe, Mark Franklin, Peter Hall, Swanee Hunt, Jane Jacquette, Elaine Kamarck, Jyette Klytte, Joni Lovenduski, Jane Mansbridge, Wilma Rule, Gina Sapiro, Aili Tripp, and Sharon Wolchik. We are also most grateful to all those who went out of their way to provide feedback on initial ideas or to read through draft chapters and provide chapter-and-verse comments, especially Karen Beckwith. The support of Cambridge University Press has proved invaluable, particularly the help of our editor, Lewis Bateman.

The analysis draws upon a unique database – the World Values Survey (WVS) and the European Values Surveys (EVS). These surveys provide data from more than seventy societies containing more than 80 percent of the world's population and covering the full range of variation, from societies with per capita incomes as low as $300 per year to societies with per capita incomes 100 times that high, and from long-established democracies with market economies to authoritarian states and ex-socialist states. We owe a large debt of gratitude to the following WVS and EVS participants for creating and sharing this invaluable data: Anthony M. Abela, Q. K. Ahmad, Rasa Alishauskene, Helmut Anheier, W. A. Arts, Jose Arocena, Soo Young Auh, Taghi Azadarmaki, Ljiljana Bacevic, Olga Balakireva, Josip Balobn, Miguel Basanez, Elena Bashkirova, Abdallah Bedaida, Jorge Benitez, Jaak Billiet, Alan Black, Sheila Bluhm, Ammar Boukhedir, Rahma Bourquia, Fares al Braizat, Pavel Campeanu, Augustin Canzani, Marita Carballo, Henrique Carlos de O. de Castro, Pi-Chao Chen, Pradeep Chhibber, Mark F. Chingono, Hei-yuan Chiu, Margit Cleveland, Russell Dalton, Andrew P. Davidson, Herman De Dijn, Jamie Diez Medrano, Juan Diez Nicolas, Karel Dobbelaere, Peter J.D. Drenth, Javier Elzo, Yilmaz Esmer, P. Estgen, T. Fahey, Nadjematul Faizah, Georgy Fotev, James Georgas, C. Geppaart, Renzo Gubert, Linda Luz Guerrero, Peter Gundelach, Jacques Hagenaars, Loek Halman, Mustafa Hamarneh, Sang-Jin Han, Stephen Harding, Mari Harris, Bernadette C. Hayes, Camilo Herrera, Virginia Hodgkinson, Nadra Muhammed Hosen, Kenji Iijima, Ljubov Ishimova, Wolfgang Jagodzinski, Aleksandra Jasinska-Kania, Fridrik Jonsson, Stanislovas Juknevicius, Jan Kerkhofs SJ, Johann Kinghorn, Dieter Klingemann, Hennie Kotz, Zuzana Kusá,

Marta Laqos, Bernard Lategan, Dr. Abdel-Hamid Abdel-Latif, M. Legrand, Dr. Carlos Lemoine, Noah Lewin-Epstein, Ola Listhaug, Jin-yun Liu, Brina Malnar, Mahar Mangahas, Mario Marinov, Carlos Matheus, Robert B. Mattes, Rafael Mendizabal, Felipe Miranda, Mansoor Moaddel, Jose Molina, Alejandro Moreno, Gaspar K. Munishi, Neil Nevitte, Elone Nwabuzor, F. A. Orizo, Dragomir Pantic, Juhani Pehkonen, Paul Perry, Thorleif Pettersson, Pham Thanh Nghi, Pham Minh Hac, Gevork Pogosian, Bi Puranen, Ladislav Rabusic, Angel Rivera-Ortiz, Catalina Romero, David Rotman, Dr. Rajab Sattarov, Sandeep Shastri, Shen Mingming, Renata Siemienska, John Sudarsky, Toru Takahashi, Tan Ern Ser, Farooq Tanwir, Jean-Francois Tchernia, Kareem Tejumola, Larissa Titarenko, Miklos Tomka, Alfredo Torres, Niko Tos, Jorge Vala, Andrei Vardomatskii, Malina Voicu, Alan Webster, Friedrich Welsch, Christian Welzel, Ephraim Yuchtman-Yaar, Josefina Zaiter, Brigita Zepa, and P. Zulehner.

Most of these surveys were funded by sources inside the given country, but the surveys in many of the developing countries were made possible by support from the Bank of Sweden Tercentenary Foundation, the Swedish International Development Agency, and the U.S. National Science Foundation. We are grateful for their support.

For more information about the World Values Survey, see the WVS websites <http://wvs.isr.umich.edu/> and <http://www. worldvaluessurvey.com>. Most of the European surveys used here were gathered by the European Values Survey group. For detailed EVS findings, see Loek Halman, *The European Values Study: A Sourcebook Based on the 1999/2000 European Values Study Surveys* (Tilburg: EVS, Tilburg University Press, 2001). For more information, see the EVS website, <http://evs.kub.nl>. We thank Karen Long for assistance in cleaning and coding the WVS data. We would also like to thank the panel discussants and colleagues who commented as draft papers were presented at professional meetings and seminars, including the International Political Science Association meeting in Quebec in 2000; the American Political Science Association annual meeting in 1998; the Gender, Politics and Society group at the Minda de Gunzberg Center for European Studies; and the Women and Public Policy Program at the John F. Kennedy School of Government. Lastly, this book would not have been possible without the encouragement and stimulation provided by many colleagues and students at the John F. Kennedy School of Government, Harvard University, and the Department of Political Science and the Institute for Social Research at the University of Michigan.

Ann Arbor, Michigan
Cambridge, Massachusetts
May 2002

PART I

THE CAUSES OF THE RISING TIDE

I

Introduction

Explaining the Rising Tide of Gender Equality

During the late twentieth century, the issue of gender equality once again became a major issue on the global agenda. The UN Decade for Women, which ended in 1985, initiated the integration of women into development, triggering the formation of thousands of women's organizations and networking them across the world.[1] The trend accelerated during the following decade. In 1993, the Vienna World Conference proclaimed that women's rights were human rights; in 1994, the Cairo International Conference on Population and Development placed women's empowerment and health at the center of sustainable development programs. Two years later, the Beijing Fourth World Conference on Women adopted a platform seeking to promote and protect the full enjoyment of human rights and fundamental freedoms for all women.[2] Although there has been substantial progress toward gender equality in much of the world, great disparities persist, as systematic indicators demonstrate.[3]

In many places, most women's lives remain wretched. Afghanistan was among the most oppressive regimes, with women and girls living under an extreme version of Islamic law introduced by the Taliban. They were denied education, barred from the workplace, and unable to venture out in public without a male companion and the full head-to-toe covering of the *burqa*. They suffered from limited access to health care, including laws forbidding treatment of women by male doctors, and pervasive threats of domestic and state-legitimated violence.[4] Few regimes are so draconian, but women in many societies face endemic

3

and substantial gender gaps in the division of household responsibilities, limited access to educational opportunities and economic resources, as well as legal and political barriers to positions of political
power. Indicators of well-being ranging from literacy and longevity to
labor force participation, poverty rates, and child mortality and schooling all reveal persistent disparities between women and men.[5] Some
societies have experienced a mixture of progress and regression, as
new entrepreneurial opportunities arose for women following market
liberalization in post-Communist Europe, along with weakened social safety nets for poorer families.[6] By contrast, other countries have
achieved major gains in legal, economic, and political gender equality that are probably irreversible. Sweden exemplifies a society where
women experience the highest level of parliamentary representation
of any nation in the world, along with gender parity in secondary
schooling and paid employment and extensive parental rights and
childcare facilities.[7] Although such contrasts in women's lives around
the globe are well established, the reasons for them are not. What
explains the disparities between the leaders and laggards in gender
equality?

Economic Growth and Human Development

One approach common the 1960s and early 1970s emphasized economic growth as the most effective strategy for achieving human development and improvements in the living conditions and status of
women. After World War II, optimism abounded that the world could
be rebuilt to end poverty, injustice, and ignorance, improving women's
lives as an inevitable part of development. Walt Rostow's influential
book *The Stages of Economic Growth* (1960) suggested that human
progress was driven by a dialectic that could be accelerated.[8] The end
of colonial rule in many parts of Africa, Asia, and the Caribbean was
seen as a major opportunity to promote prosperity and democracy in
these societies. Greater affluence was expected to facilitate freedom
from want and fear due to an expansion of health care and adequate
nutrition, schools and housing, jobs and basic social protections, increasing the urban middle classes and laying the social foundations for
the consolidation of democratic institutions and civic society. Growth
was seen as the panacea that would lift all boats, and it was often

implicitly assumed that this included endemic problems of women's literacy and education, their poverty, low pay, and occupational segregation in the workforce, their care-giving responsibilities in the home and family, and their participation and representation in the political system. The hope that economic development will automatically benefit women in poorer societies continues to be voiced.[9] At its most simple, this proposition is often taken for granted as self-evident. After all, in the examples we have cited, Sweden is one of the richest societies in the world, with a per capita income of $26,000 per year; the figure for Afghanistan is around $800. Do these countries' striking differences in gender equality simply reflect their differing degrees of development?

But by the end of the twentieth century, the limitations of growth alone were clear. Numerous anomalies are obvious even to the casual observer. Kuwait, Saudi Arabia, and Quatar, for instance, are about as rich as Sweden in per capita GDP, but women in these societies cannot stand for office or even vote, and they have narrowly restricted rights and opportunities outside the home. It is illegal for women to drive in Saudi Arabia, and the Middle East and North Africa have the lowest rates of female labor force participation in the world.[10] Conditions for women are more favorable in some poorer nations. In India, for example, although women's rights are also limited in many important ways, about 800,000 women serve in local government, with one-third of all local council seats reserved for them.[11] Broader experience confirms that gender equality in elected office continues to lag behind in the transitional "Asian tiger" nations, as well as in many high-growth states in Latin America.[12] Even in the most affluent societies around the world, such as the United States, France, and Japan, where women have made substantial gains in access to universities, company boardrooms, and the professions, there has been minimal progress for women in government – while in South Africa, by contrast, women comprise almost one-third of all parliamentarians, ranking this nation eleventh worldwide in the proportion of women in the lower house.[13] It has become apparent that problems of gender equality are more complex and intractable than the early developmental theorists assumed.[14] Growing affluence does tend to generate the expansion of literacy and schooling, the establishment of a social protection safety net, and the rise of white-collar jobs in the service sector, but this process is not inevitable, nor does it necessarily automatically benefit women's lives.

The Role of the State: Human Rights, Legal Reforms, and Political Institutions

During the 1980s and 1990s, recognizing the limitations of economic strategies alone, the international women's movement and official bodies such as the United Nations and European Union turned their attention increasingly toward the role of the state in reinforcing or alleviating institutional barriers to women's progress, and toward the need to establish political, social, and economic rights in order to secure gender equality through legal reform and the courts.[15] There was also a shift in the literature around this period, from focusing on the problems facing women's well-being toward emphasizing the active role of women's agency and voice in helping women to attain equal rights: to earn an independent income, to find employment outside the home, to have ownership rights, to become literate, to participate in community decision making.[16] The independence and empowerment of women became understood as an integral part of the development process, so that women could articulate their own wants and needs.

In many countries legal rights for women remain limited; a comprehensive review of legislation in over 100 countries by Humana found that in the early 1990s women still lacked many basic rights, such as the right to own land, to manage property, to conduct business, and even to travel without spousal consent.[17] In much of sub-Saharan Africa, women have land rights through their husbands as long as the marriage endures, but lose this property when divorced or widowed. In Turkey, until a recent reform of the civil code, a wife needed her husband's consent to work outside the home; women were not entitled to sue for divorce, to claim alimony, or to retain their maiden names. In Egypt and Jordan, women need their husband's permission to travel. In Ireland, it remains illegal to have an abortion except in extremely limited circumstances (where the mother's life is in danger). In established democracies, women have had the legal franchise for many decades – since the 1920s in most Protestant countries, and since the 1950s in most Catholic ones. But in newer democracies, such as Namibia and South Africa, most women have only recently acquired voting rights.

And laws restricting women's rights to vote and to run for office persist in a handful of Middle Eastern countries, including Kuwait, Qatar, Saudi Arabia, Oman, and the United Arab Emirates.[18]

The United Nations has encouraged states to recognize women's rights, most importantly through the Convention on the Elimination of All Forms of Discrimination against Women (CEDAW), adopted by the UN General Assembly in 1979 and subsequently signed by 165 nation-states. This convention emphasizes the importance of women's equal participation with men in public life. The women's movement in many nations has emphasized the need for equal opportunity and affirmative action strategies through reforming institutional barriers, removing structural biases, and altering the rules of the game to get women into positions of elected office. A particularly effective means to do this has been the use of quotas in the selection of female parliamentary candidates – which has recently been adopted in many Western European, Asian, and Latin American countries – and the parity program adopted in France.[19] Policies designed to prevent sex discrimination, to secure equal pay, maternity, and reproductive rights, and to increase opportunities for women in the workforce and education have been adopted in many countries, and the role of the state is now widely understood to be central in actively consolidating and reinforcing gender equality.[20]

These strategies have secured concrete gains for women in many nations, particularly when government agencies or the courts have effectively implemented legal reforms and policy initiatives. Changing the "rules of the game" can have a dramatic impact on women's lives, accelerating progress and opening new opportunities. Yet at the same time there can be a substantial gap between the recognition of de jure formal rights and actual practice. Many governments have signed international conventions pledging themselves to support equal opportunity in political representation; and political leaders, official bodies, and administrative agencies have often declared themselves in favor of this principle, along with groups in civic society such as trade unions and parties. Yet in the world as a whole, women remain far from parity at the apex of power – as heads of state at the prime ministerial and presidential level, in the executive branch as ministers and as senior public officials, and in national parliaments.[21] In the same way, CEDAW recognizes the importance of equality in the paid labor force.

Yet although many governments have signed on to this principle, in practice women are disproportionately likely to have low-wage jobs because of persistent occupational segregation and wage discrimination by sex, as well as lack of child care for working mothers; and in most countries women in management and corporate boardrooms continue to encounter a glass ceiling.[22] Even in liberal countries such as Sweden and Norway, segregation in jobs typically held by women and men remains common. Statutory reform and formal recognition of women's rights in international bodies are symbolic gains, an important advance in itself, but they are seldom sufficient to effect substantial social change if the capacity or the political will to implement these reforms remains weak.

Cultural Barriers

Economic growth and legal-institutional reforms are both important in any long-term comprehensive strategy to promote gender equality. But in addition, as this book will demonstrate, *culture matters*, and indeed it matters a lot.[23] Perceptions of the appropriate division of roles in the home and family, paid employment, and the political sphere are shaped by the predominant culture – the social norms, beliefs, and values existing in any society, which in turn rest on levels of societal modernization and religious traditions. 'Gender' refers to the socially constructed roles and learned behavior of women and men associated with the biological characteristics of females and males.[24] In many societies, rigid gender roles determine the rights, resources, and powers of women and men, notably the division of labor in the home and workplace. In others, men's and women's roles are more interchangeable, and innate biological differences lead to fewer social expectations. Where a culture of gender equality predominates, it provides a climate where de jure legal rights are more likely to be translated into de facto rights in practice; where institutional reforms are implemented in the workplace and public sphere; where women embrace expanded opportunities to attain literacy, education, and employment; and where the traditional roles of women and men are transformed within the household and family. Moreover, the critical importance of culture is that women as well as men adopt the predominant attitudes, values, and beliefs about the appropriate division of sex roles within any society.

Where traditional values prevail, women are not only limited by society in terms of the opportunities they seek, but also choose to limit themselves. Cultural change is not *sufficient* by itself for gender equality – a limitation not always sufficiently recognized by the consciousness-raising individualistic focus of the women's movement of the 1960s. But we argue that cultural change is a *necessary* condition for gender equality: women first need to change themselves before they can hope to change society. In turn, cultural change lays the basis for the mass mobilization of women's movements and broad support for public policies that reinforce, consolidate, and accelerate the process of gender equality.

At one level, there is nothing particularly new or startling about this claim. A mainstream tradition in sociology, anthropology, history, and social psychology has long theorized that there are great cross-cultural differences in beliefs about gender roles among societies around the globe, even among societies at similar levels of socioeconomic development – such as Sweden, Britain, and the United States, on one hand, and India, the Philippines, and Indonesia, on the other.[25] Feminist movements in many countries have long emphasized cultural differences in family and sex roles, and the critical importance of changing traditional patriarchal norms for transforming relationships between the sexes.[26] Most support for this thesis has come from qualitative evidence, often based on personal interviews, participant observation, and case studies. Comparative analysis of aggregate indicators has also revealed the substantial contrasts between the lives and roles of women and men worldwide. Nevertheless, systematic survey evidence monitoring cultural attitudes toward gender equality across many societies remains scattered and inconclusive, with most studies limited to a handful of affluent postindustrial societies and established democracies in Western Europe and North America.[27] While it is widely assumed that culture matters, it remains unclear *how much* it matters as compared to levels of societal development and legal-institutional structures; and we know even less about how these factors interact in the long-term process of value change. This book will demonstrate that cultural traditions are remarkably enduring in shaping men's and women's worldviews; nevertheless, glacial shifts are taking place that move systematically away from traditional values and toward more egalitarian sex roles. This shift is intimately related to the processes of societal modernization and to generational replacement. Moreover, we will demonstrate that culture matters: where there are more egalitarian attitudes, these are systematically related to the actual conditions of women's and men's lives. We acknowledge that this is not a simple one-way direction of causality; rather, it is an interactive process, because changes in our lives affect our underlying attitudes and values. But we also demonstrate that cultural change is not an ad hoc and erratic process; rather, patterns of human development and societal modernization underpin attitudinal shifts. The broad direction of value change is predictable, although the pace is conditioned by the cultural legacy and institutional structure of any given society, as exemplified by the role of an Islamic heritage in the Middle East, the legacy of Communism in Central Europe, and the egalitarian tradition in Scandinavia.

To develop these arguments, this book examines evidence of a rising tide of support for gender equality in over seventy societies around the world. It then explores the causes of this cultural shift and its conse-quences for women's political power, including their civic engagement, support for the women's movement, and political representation. This introductory chapter first develops the core theoretical argument and outlines the research design, providing details about (1) the four waves of the World Values Survey / European Values Survey carried out from 1981 to 2001, (2) the comparative framework and societal classifica-tion used here, and (3) the time period used for trend analysis. The final section of the chapter outlines the book and summarizes the contents of subsequent chapters.

Societal Modernization and Cultural Change

The revised version of modernization theory developed in this book hy-pothesizes that human development brings changed cultural attitudes toward gender equality in virtually any society that experiences the various forms of modernization linked with economic development. Modernization brings systematic, *predictable* changes in gender roles. The impact of modernization operates in two key phases:

1. Industrialization brings women into the paid workforce and dramatically reduces fertility rates. Women attain literacy and greater educational opportunities. Women are enfranchised

and begin to participate in representative government, but still have far less power than men.

2. The postindustrial phase brings a shift toward greater gender equality as women rise in management and the professions and gain political influence within elected and appointed bodies. Over half of the world has not yet entered this phase; only the more advanced industrial societies are currently moving on this trajectory.

These two phases correspond to two major dimensions of cross-cultural variation that will be described in more detail in the final chapter: (1) a transition from traditional to secular-rational values, and (2) a transition from survival to self-expression values. The decline of the traditional family is linked with the first dimension. The rise of gender equality is linked with the second. Cultural shifts in modern societies are not sufficient by themselves to guarantee women equality across all major dimensions of life; nevertheless, through underpinning structural reforms and women's rights, they greatly facilitate this process.

Modernization theories suggest that economic, cultural, and political changes go together in coherent ways, so that industrialization brings broadly similar trajectories even if situation-specific factors make it impossible to predict exactly what will happen in a given society. Certain changes become increasingly likely to occur, but the changes are probabilistic, not deterministic. Modernization theories originated in the work of Karl Marx, Max Weber, and Emile Durkheim. These ideas were revived and popularized during the late 1950s and early 1960s by Seymour Martin Lipset, Daniel Lerner, Walt Rostow, and Karl Deutsch.[28] These writers argued that the shift from agrarian agriculture towards industrial production leads to growing prosperity, higher levels of education, and urbanization, which in turn lay the social foundations for democratic participation in the political system. Traditional societies are characterized by subsistence economies largely based on farming, fishing, extraction, and unskilled work, with low levels of literacy and education, predominately agrarian populations, minimum standards of living, and restricted social and geographic mobility. Citizens in agrarian societies are strongly rooted to local communities through ties of "blood and belonging," including those of kinship, family, ethnicity, and religion, as well as through

long-standing cultural bonds. The shift from traditional agrarian
society toward industrialized society involves the move from agricultural production to manufacturing, from farms to factories, from
peasants to workers. Social trends accompanying these developments,
as shown in Table 1.1, include migration to metropolitan conurba-
tions, the rise of the working class and urban bourgeoisie, rising living
standards, the separation of church and state, increasing penetration
of the mass media, the growth of Weberian bureaucratization and
rational-legal authority in the state, the foundations of the early welfare state, and the spread of primary schooling. This phase occurred
in the Industrial Revolution in Britain during the mid to late eigh-
teenth century and spread throughout the Western world during the
nineteenth and early twentieth centuries. The early developmental theorists emphasized a range of social trends that commonly accompany
the process of industrialization, including changes in traditional sex
roles, the family, and marriage.

During the early 1970s, Daniel Bell popularized the view that after a certain period of industrialization, a further distinct stage of development could be distinguished, as a nonlinear process, in the rise
of postindustrial societies.[29] For Bell, the critical tipping point was
reached when the majority of the workforce moved from manufacturing into the service sector, working as lawyers, bankers, financial
analysts, technologists, scientists, and professionals employed in the
knowledge industries. The now-familiar social and economic shifts
characterizing postindustrial societies are listed in Table 1.1 They include the rise of a highly educated, skilled, and specialized workforce;
population shifts from urban to suburban neighborhoods and greater
geographic mobility, including immigration across national borders;
rising living standards and growing leisure time; rapid scientific and
technological innovation; the expansion and fragmentation of mass
media channels, technologies, and markets; the growth of multilay-
ered governance, with power shifting away from the nation-state toward global and local levels; market liberalization and the expansion
of nonprofit social protection schemes; the erosion of the traditional
nuclear family; and growing equality of sex roles within the home,
family, and workforce.

There is a broad consensus that certain socioeconomic developments have been sweeping across many societies, although alternative

TABLE I.I. *Typology of stages of societal modernization*

	From Agrarian to Industrial Societies	From Industrial to Postindustrial Societies
Population	The population shift from agrarian villages to metropolitan conurbations.	The diffusion from urban areas to suburban neighborhoods. Greater social geographic mobility, including immigration across national borders, generating the rise of more multicultural societies.
Human capital	Growing levels of education, literacy, and numeracy and the spread of basic schooling.	Rising levels of education, especially at secondary and university levels, generating increased levels of human capital and cognitive skills.
Workforce	The shift from extraction and agriculture toward manufacturing and processing.	The rise of the professional and managerial occupations in the private and public sectors and greater occupational specialization.
Social status	The rise of the working class and the urban bourgeoisie, and the decline of peasant society and traditional landed interests.	The move from ascribed occupational and social roles assigned at birth toward achieved status derived from formal educational qualifications and careers.
Living conditions	Growing standards of living, rising longevity and expanding leisure time.	Economic growth fueling an expanded middle class, rising living standards, improved longevity and health, and growing leisure time.
Science and religion	The industrial revolution in manufacturing production. Growing division of church and state. The diversification of religious sects and denominations.	Rapid technological and scientific innovation. The process of secularization weakening religious authority.

(continued)

TABLE I.I *(continued)*

	From Agrarian to Industrial Societies	From Industrial to Postindustrial Societies
Mass media	The wider availability of mass-circulation newspapers and periodicals and, during the twentieth century, access to electronic mass media.	The shift in the mass media from mass broadcasting toward more specialized narrowcasting, with the fragmentation of media outlets across markets and technologies.
Government	The expansion of the franchise, the growth of Weberian bureaucratization and reliance on legal-rational authority in government.	The growth of multilayered governance at the global and local levels, as well as the expansion in the nonprofit sector.
Social protection	The development of the early foundations of the welfare state and the elements of social protection for illness, unemployment, and old age.	Market liberalization and the contraction of the state, displacing social protection increasingly to the nonprofit and private sectors.
Family structures	The shift from extended to nuclear families, the gradual reduction in the fertility rate.	The erosion of the nuclear family, the growth of nontraditional households, and changing patterns of marriage and divorce.
Sex roles	The entry of more women into the paid workforce.	Growing equality of sex roles in the division of labor within the home, family, and workplace, and the rise of women (especially married women) in the paid labor force.
Cultural values	Material security, traditional authority, and communal obligations.	Quality of life issues, self-expression, individualism, and postmaterialism.

interpretations dispute their exact nature and periodization and the appropriate weight to be given to different components. There remains considerable controversy, however, concerning the consequences of these changes, and in particular concerning the probable impact of the modernization process on gender equality. Why would we expect these changes in socioeconomic conditions to go hand in hand with cultural shifts? In a series of works, Inglehart has demonstrated how the evolution from agrarian to industrial to postindustrial societies brings about two coherent, predictable, and interrelated dimensions of change: (1) socioeconomic changes in the process of production, as Bell claimed; and (2) a transformation in societal cultures, including rising emphasis in postindustrial societies on the pursuit of quality-of-life values rather than material concerns.[30] We see economic, political, and cultural changes as evolving together in coherent trajectories, without claiming, as Marx did, that the changes in the processes of economic production drive the superstructure of value change, or that, conversely, cultural processes such as the rise of Protestantism cause the socioeconomic developments, as Weber argued. We view these causal processes as reciprocal.

People living near the subsistence level tend to be primarily concerned with the basic struggle for survival when facing the unpredictable risks of disease, illiteracy, malnutrition, infant mortality, ethnic conflict and civil war, unsafe drinking water, and the spread of AIDS/HIV. Women and children are among the most vulnerable populations in these societies, not only because they are high-risk populations but also because they are usually dependent on a male breadwinner. Of the world's 6 billion people, the World Bank estimates that 1.2 billion live on less than $1 a day.[31] Global poverty fell substantially during the 1990s, mainly driven by high economic growth in some larger nations such as China and India, but extreme poverty in sub-Saharan Africa worsened. Levels of infant mortality have been reduced around the globe, but the problem remains substantial; in 1998, there were 105 deaths per 1,000 live births in societies with low human development.[32] Basic problems of survival are starkly illustrated by average life expectancy; in agrarian societies, on average people can expect to live for fifty-nine years, twenty years less than in postindustrial societies. Opportunities for social and geographic mobility are limited by minimal literacy and schooling, which is especially common for girls and women.

In this context, Inglehart argues, poorer people in low-income societies tend to give top priority to meeting subsistence and survival needs. In richer countries, public policies provide subsistence-level incomes, adequate housing, and effective health care. In preindustrial societies, without state services to cushion unpredictable blows, most people's lives are highly vulnerable to such risks as unemployment, ill health, poor crops, and violent crime, as well as to disasters such as floods, earthquakes, and famine. Societies whose people live with high levels of insecurity tend to develop cultures mistrustful of rapid change, emphasizing the values of traditional authority and strong leadership, inherited social status, and communal ties and obligations, backed up by social sanctions and norms derived from religious authorities. In these societies, the traditional two-parent family, with its division of sex roles between male breadwinner and female caregivers, is crucial for the survival of children, and therefore of society. Social norms buttress traditional family values and patriarchal norms of male dominance, strongly discouraging divorce, abortion, and homosexuality and instilling negative attitudes toward an independent economic role for women outside of the household. The legal structure involving property, marital, and citizenship rights for women reflects these traditional norms. Preindustrial societies emphasize childbearing and child rearing as the central goal of any woman, her most important function in life, and her greatest source of satisfaction and status. Given their very high rates of infant and child mortality, high rates of reproduction are emphasized in preindustrial societies; large extended families provide a source of subsistence and protection for the parents in old age, as well as a means for the transmission of land and property. In peasant societies, women usually work within the home, primarily in the production and preparation of food, and in child care. Even in these societies, there may be conflicts between the social norms shaping the appropriate division of sex roles and the actual life experiences of women and men, particularly if the male loses the capacity to act as the major breadwinner of the household, or if the woman heads a single-parent family.[33]

The rise of capitalism and the Industrial Revolution brought challenges to traditional values and a worldview that encouraged achieved rather than ascribed status, individualism rather than community, innovation instead of continuity with tradition, and increasingly secular rather than religious social beliefs. The traditional roles of women – taking prime responsibility for care of children and the elderly – continued, but during the nineteenth and early twentieth centuries more and more women in industrial societies entered the paid labor force, mainly in factories and white-collar clerical and retail jobs, and attained greater legal rights to own property, to divorce, and to vote. Fertility rates and the size of the average family fell, reflecting the availability of safe contraception, improvements in health care that reduced the risks of infant mortality, and the fact that large extended families were no longer so crucial for protection in old age. People's lives became less vulnerable to sudden disaster, as savings and insurance schemes were developed to hedge against economic risks. The rise of local cooperatives, unions, building societies, and savings and loan schemes, and the development of social protection by philanthropic voluntary organizations and the state, helped to cover the worst problems of sickness, ill health, unemployment, and old age.

In the period following World War II, postindustrial societies developed unprecedented levels of prosperity and economic security, with rising standards of living fuelled by steady economic growth, despite occasional cyclical downturns. Governments in these societies expanded the role of the welfare state to provide greater social protection for the worst-off citizens; more recently, health care, pensions, and care of the elderly have been contracted out to the nonprofit and private sectors, under state regulation. Under conditions of greater existential security, Inglehart theorizes, public concern about the material issues of unemployment, health care, and housing no longer necessarily takes top priority. Instead, in advanced industrial societies the public has given increasingly high priority to quality-of-life issues, individual autonomy and self-expression, the need for environmental protection, and direct participation in political decision making through petitions, protests, and demonstrations. Cultural shifts have transformed not only political life but also personal life, and nowhere more so than in the erosion of the traditional two-parent nuclear family; in liberalizing patterns of sexual behavior, marriage, and divorce; and in the wider acceptance among both women and men of greater gender equality in the home, the workforce, and the public sphere. Women are less restricted to attaining status and fulfillment through the traditional route of family, marriage, and children, as alternative opportunities for self-expression and financial autonomy have become available. These changing norms have given rise to political demands, fuelling support for the second-wave feminist movement, and legal reforms associated with securing equal opportunities and women's rights. In short, the rising tide of support for gender equality in postindustrial societies is part of a broad and coherent cultural shift that is transforming economically developed societies. Although the broad outlines of this shift are predictable, not every society responds to these developments in the same way: as we will demonstrate, traditional cultural heritages help to shape contemporary social change. A society's values and religious beliefs, its institutions and leaders, and the structure of the state all help to shape this process in ways that differ from one society to another. Moreover, even in rich societies, some groups fall through the social safety net, producing disparities between rich and poor.

If this theory is correct, and cultural shifts are coherent and predictable, then five specific propositions follow – each of which can (and will) be tested in this study.

1. *Cross-national comparisons*: First, if coherent cultural patterns tend to be associated with specific levels of socioeconomic development, then postmodern values of gender equality will be most widespread in the most affluent and secure societies; conversely, the publics of poorer preindustrial societies will systematically be most likely to emphasize traditional gender roles. The fact that we have data from more than seventy countries, covering the full range of variance from low-income societies to affluent postindustrial societies, will make it possible to test this hypothesis in a more conclusive fashion than has ever before been possible.

2. *Sectoral comparisons*: Within any given society, postmodern values of gender equality will be most evident among the most secure, that is, the wealthier, better-educated sectors of the public. The less secure strata will prove more traditional in their attitudes toward women.

3. *Gender comparisons*: Women and men are expected to differ in their values and attitudes toward gender equality, with women proving more supportive of gender equality, especially

in postindustrial societies. In traditional societies, both men and women often accept substantial gender inequalities. But societal modernization is transforming everyone's life experience, *especially* women's, reducing their vulnerability, generating greater financial autonomy, expanding literacy and educational opportunities, and strengthening the social safety net, especially for maternal and child care, reproductive control, and provision for the elderly.

4. *Generational comparisons*: In societies that have experienced sustained periods of economic growth and increasing physical security (such as Germany, the United States, and Japan) or very rapid economic growth (such as South Korea and Taiwan), we expect to find substantial differences in the values held by older and younger generations. The young should be more egalitarian in their attitudes toward sex roles, while the older cohorts should believe in more traditional roles for women and men; and the generation gap should be particularly large for women. We predict that the younger generation of women will hold the most egalitarian gender values within a given society, while the older generation of women will prove the most traditional. But societal values do not change overnight; instead, there is a substantial time lag, because adults tend to retain the norms, values, and beliefs that were instilled during their preadult years. Since, according to our hypotheses, these generational differences are linked to economic growth, we do not expect to find equally large generational differences in societies that have not experienced major increases in real GNP per capita over the last several decades (for example, Nigeria and Zimbabwe).

5. *Religious legacies*: Finally, we anticipate that religious legacies will leave a strong imprint on contemporary values. In particular, controlling for a society's level of GNP per capita and the structure of the workforce, we expect that the publics of Islamic societies will be less supportive of gender equality than the publics of other societies.

In considering patterns of trends over time in changing values with respect to gender equality, the "convergence model" suggests that the changes in men and women's lives in the home, the workforce, and the political sphere occurred first in postindustrial societies, driven by structural shifts in the workforce and educational opportunities, generating the women's movement of the 1960s and 1970s, but that in the long term laggard societies will gradually catch up as the culture shift ripples around the globe. The process of globalization has accelerated the recognition of women's rights, as well as the process of democratization. In the short term, however, value change has widened the cultural differences between postindustrial and agrarian societies, including the differences between women living in these types of societies.

The Comparative Framework

In order to examine the evidence for these predictions, this study follows Prezeworski and Teune's "most different systems" research design, seeking to maximize contrasts among a wide range of societies and thereby to distinguish systematic clusters of characteristics associated with different dimensions of gender equality.[34] Some important trade-offs are involved in this approach, notably the loss of contextual depth that can come from focusing on one nation or studying a few similar countries. But the strategy of carrying out broad comparisons has major advantages. Most importantly, it allows us to examine whether, as theories of societal modernization claim, basic values seem to shift along with the shift from traditional agrarian societies, with largely illiterate and poor populations, through industrial economies based on manufacturing and a growing urban working class, to postindustrial economies based on a large service-sector middle class. And since it allows us to compare societies with sharply differing religious legacies, political systems, and democratic traditions, it enables us to analyze the role of these other, conceivably very important, factors.

Human development is also a complicated, multifaceted process of social transformation, including changes in the economy, with the shift from agricultural production and extraction to industrial production and the rise of the service sector; changes in society, with the growth of education, affluence, and leisure, life expectancy and health, urbanization and suburbanization, the spread of the mass media, and changes in family structures and community social networks; and changes in politics, with the process of democratization. Not all of these developments necessarily go hand in hand in advancing the position of women in every society. The early stages of industrialization, for example, may expand literacy and educational opportunities for women, and yet may simultaneously weaken the informal extended family support networks available in agrarian communities. Structural adjustments in developing countries may produce efficiency gains in the longer term, but may also disproportionately hurt women's interests.[35] The democratic transition in the post-Communist world opened up new opportunities for gains in political rights and civic liberties, but the abandonment of gender quotas for elected office simultaneously sharply reduced the number of women in parliament.[36] In affluent nations such as the United States, Japan, and France, women have advanced in management and the professions further and faster than in legislatures and cabinets. One difficulty is that the abstract concept of "societal modernization" encompasses many complex dimensions of social change, including crosscutting developments, some of which, like the growth of white-collar occupations and education, expand opportunities for women, while others, such as privatization and the contraction of social protection, create new inequalities.

Types of Societies

Before moving on to consider the evidence, we need to clarify the core typologies used to classify types of societies and states. Overall, for the global comparison 191 nation-states were classified according to levels of societal modernization. The Human Development Index produced annually by the United Nations Development Program (UNDP), provides the standard 100-point scale of societal modernization, combining levels of knowledge (adult literacy and education), health (life expectancy at birth), and standard of living (real per capita GDP). This measure is widely used in the development literature, and it has the advantage of providing a broader and more reliable indicator of societal well-being than monetary estimates based on levels of affluence.[37] Using the 1998 Human Development Index (HDI), *postindustrial* societies are defined as the 20 most affluent states around the world, with an HDI score over .900 and mean per capita GDP of $29,585. *Industrial* societies are classified as the 58 nations with a moderate HDI (ranging from .740 to .899) and a moderate per capita GDP of $6,314. Lastly, *agrarian* societies are the 97 nations with lower levels of development (HDI of .739 or below) and mean per capita GDP of $1,098.[38]

TABLE 1.2. *Indicators of societal modernization*

Type of Society	% GNP from Services, 1998	% Urban Population, 2000	Life Expectancy (Years), 1998	% Adult Literacy, 1998	% Gross Educational Enrollment Ratio, 1998
Postindustrial	65.5	79.1	78	99.0	93.5
Industrial	59.2	67.2	73	93.3	75.3
Agrarian	45.6	40.9	59	67.0	54.1
All	51.7	53.8	66	79.2	65.5

Note: Mean social indicators in 172 nations. See Appendix A for the classification of nations and Appendix B for concepts and measures.
Source: Calculated from UNDP. *UNDP Human Development Report 2000.* New York: UNDP/Oxford University Press.

To see how far this classification predicts broader patterns of development, Table 1.2 illustrates some of the contrasts in the most common indicators of social well-being. The classic definition of postindustrial societies emphasizes the shift in production from fields and factories to the service sector. Almost two-thirds of GNP in the societies classified as postindustrial derives from the service sector, but this figure falls to only 45 percent in agrarian societies. Table 1.2 shows how levels of urbanization, literacy, education, and life expectancy systematically vary across classifications of different types of society. Perhaps the clearest contrast is in life expectancy: a person living in the average postindustrial society can expect to live seventy-eight years, as compared to only fifty-nine years in agrarian societies. Table 1.3 summarizes two basic indicators of change in levels of societal development from 1980 to 1998. The Human Development Index shows that there have been some gains in all societies during the last twenty years. Nevertheless, the disparities in levels of human development between societies currently classified as postindustrial and agrarian have scarcely closed at all. The per capita GDP in postindustrial societies has grown far faster than that of industrial societies, and agrarian nations have made no gains. In the next chapter, this initial classification is discussed further, and comparisons are drawn between this measure of societal modernization and the UNDP Gender-related Development Index (GDI), which takes into account the overall level of societal modernization and the disparities that can exist between women and men even in

TABLE 1.3. *Trends in societal modernization, 1980–98*

Type of Society	Human Development Index			Per Capita GDP		
	1980	1998	Change	1980	1998	Change
Postindustrial	.860	.918	+.058	20,932	29,585	+8,653
Industrial	.742	.802	+.060	6,155	6,314	+159
Agrarian	.486	.564	+.078	1,099	1,098	−1
All	.625	.681	+.056	5,506	6,162	2,565

Note: Real per capita GDP is measured in U.S. dollars estimated at purchasing power parity. See Appendix A for the classification of nations and Appendix B for concepts and measures.

Source: Calculated from UNDP. *UNDP Human Development Report 2000*. New York: UNDP/Oxford University Press.

affluent societies, as well as the Dikkstra and Hanmer Relative Status of Women (RSW) index, which measures gender equality within Countries.[39]

Type of States

Over the years, numerous attempts have been made to develop effective measures of a given society's level of democracy. It should be noted that alternative measures emphasize different components, and that all the alternative indices suffer from certain conceptual or methodological flaws. Nevertheless, one recent review concluded that, despite these differences, in practice there is considerable similarity in the rank order correlations of nations across different indices.[40] The Gastil index, a seven-point scale used by Freedom House, has become widely accepted as a standard measure providing a basic classification of political rights and civil liberties. We adopt this measure because it has the advantage of comprehensive coverage, including all nation-states and independent territories around the globe, as well as the ability to be used for time-series analysis, since the index has been published every year since the early 1970s. We have reversed the Gastil scale in the analysis for ease of interpretation, so that a higher score represents higher levels of democracy. We are also interested in how long democracy has endured in given societies. To obtain a measure of length of democratic stability, we use the annual Freedom House ratings produced from 1972 to 2000.[41] We define as *older democracies* the thirty-nine states

TABLE 1.4. *Classification of societies and states in the pooled World Values Surveys / European Values Surveys, 1981–2001*

Type of Society	Type of State				
	Older Democracy	Newer Democracy	Semi-democracy	Non-democratic	Total
Postindustrial	21				21
Industrial	3	16	10	3	32
Agrarian	1	3	9	8	21
Total	25	19	19	11	74

Note: The number of nations in each category. For details about the classifications, see Appendix A.

around the world with at least twenty years' continuous experience of democracy from 1980 to 2000 and a Freedom House rating of 5.5 to 7.0 in the most recent estimate. We classify as *newer democracies* the forty-three states with less than twenty years' experience with democracy and a current Freedom House rating of 5.5 to 7.0. Another forty-seven states were classified as *semi-democracies* (Freedom House describes them as "partly-free"; others call them "transitional" or "consolidating" democracies); these states have been democratic for less than twenty years and have current Freedom House ratings of 3.5 to 5.5. *Non-democracies* are the remaining sixty-two states, with a Freedom House score for 1999–2000 from 1.0 to 3.0; they include military-backed dictatorships, authoritarian states, elitist oligarchies, and absolute monarchies. Appendix A lists the classifications of nations used throughout the book, based on these measures. Clearly there is considerable overlap between human and democratic development at the top of the scale; many older democracies are also affluent postindustrial societies. But the pattern of states among industrial and agrarian societies shows a far more complex pattern, with newer democracies, semi-democracies, and non-democracies at different levels of socioeconomic development.

The World Values Survey
The analysis of cultural attitudes is based upon the World Values Surveys (WVS), a global investigation of socio-cultural and political change. The study has carried out representative national surveys of

the basic values and beliefs of publics in more than seventy nation-states on all six inhabited continents (see Figure 1.1), containing in total 4.7 billion people or over 80 percent of the world's population. It builds on the European Values Surveys, first carried out in twenty-two countries in 1981. A second wave of surveys, in forty-three nations, was completed in 1990–91; a third wave was carried out in fifty-five nations in 1995–96; and a fourth wave with fifty-five nations took place in 1999–2001 (see Table A.2).[42] The pooled survey used in this book includes almost a quarter-million respondents, facilitating subgroup analysis even for minority groups. The survey includes some of the most affluent market economies in the world, such as the United States, Japan, and Switzerland, with per capita annual incomes as high as $40,000 or more, together with middle-level industrializing countries, such as Taiwan, Brazil, and Turkey, and poorer agrarian societies, such as Uganda, Nigeria, and Vietnam, with per capita annual incomes of $300 or less. Some smaller nations, such as Malta, Luxembourg, and Iceland, have populations below one million; at the other extreme, almost one billion people live in India and well over one billion in China. The pooled survey with all waves contains older democracies such as Australia, India, and the Netherlands; newer democracies such as El Salvador, Estonia, and Taiwan; semi-democracies such as Russia, Brazil, and Turkey; as well as eleven non-democracies, exemplified by Zimbabwe, Pakistan, and Egypt. The transition process also varies markedly. Some nations have experienced a rapid consolidation of democracy during the 1990s; today the Czech Republic, Latvia, and Argentina currently rank as high in political rights and civil liberties as nations with long traditions of democracy such as Belgium, the United States, and the Netherlands.[43] The survey includes some of the first systematic data on public opinion in many Islamic states, including Jordan, Iran, Algeria, Egypt, Indonesia, and Morocco. The most comprehensive coverage is available for Western Europe, North America, and Scandinavia, where public opinion surveys have the longest tradition, but countries are included from all world regions, including five sub-Saharan African nations and six Middle Eastern states. The four waves of this survey took place from 1981 to 2001, although the same countries were not always included in each wave, so comparisons over the full period can be carried out only in twenty societies. Data drawn from the Eurobarometer surveys, conducted biannually

FIGURE 1.1. The societies contained in the pooled World Values Surveys / European Values Surveys, 1981–2001.

since 1970, and from the Political Action Study of the mid-1970s facilitates longer-term comparisons.

The Plan of the Book

Based on these considerations, **Chapter 2** goes on to analyze *indirect* attitudinal evidence of support for gender equality, including comparisons among different types of societies. With remarkable consistency, we find that the publics of richer, postindustrial societies are much more likely to support gender equality than the publics of agrarian or industrial countries. Intergenerational differences, which are largest in postindustrial societies and relatively minor in agrarian societies, suggest that the former are undergoing intergenerational changes. Women in postindustrial societies, in particular, are deeply divided by generation in their support for gender equality. Lastly, support for gender equality in the political sphere, in the workplace, and in the home is also explained by many of the standard factors commonly associated with cultural shifts, including education, religiosity, marital status, and postmaterialism.

Chapter 3 considers the role of religion in more depth. In particular, the process of societal modernization is path-specific and is conditioned by the cultural heritage and structural context of a given society. This chapter demonstrates that the cross-sectional differences in support for gender equality vary even among societies at similar levels of human development, being shaped by factors such as the strength of religiosity and the type of religious values. Multivariate analysis probes these factors in more depth, and the chapter considers whether an Islamic religious heritage is the most powerful barrier to change.

Part II of the book examines the political consequences of the rising tide of gender equality. **Chapter 4** examines evidence of the shift from the traditional to the modern gender gap in voting behavior. The chapter compares cross-national support for parties across the left-right spectrum among women and men and considers how far these differences reflect the same modernization and cultural factors that shape attitudes toward traditional gender roles. The study also examines generational patterns in the size of the gender gap.

One of the most intractable problems of gender equality concerns continuing male predominance in traditional political elites, such as parties and parliaments. **Chapter 5** goes on to compare gender differences in three dimensions of political participation: traditional activism via elections and parties; civic activism through voluntary organizations, new social movements, and community associations; and protest activity, such as signing petitions and taking part in boycotts and demonstrations. The study shows how the major forces of modernization and cultural heritage affect these differences.

Chapter 6. Do similar factors lead to the familiar gender gap in political leadership, in terms of women as heads of state, cabinet ministers, and parliamentary representatives? This chapter compares women and men in national parliaments around the world. The analysis considers the reasons for the persistence of gender differences and the roles of societal modernization and cultural legacies in explaining levels of female representation.

Chapter 7. The conclusion examines how far attitudes toward gender equality form part of a larger cultural shift towards self-expression values. The conclusion draws together the major findings from all of the chapters and considers their implications for the transformation of women's and men's lives and for cultural change worldwide.

2

From Traditional Roles toward Gender Equality

Developmental theory is based on the assumption that traditional societies are characterized by sharply differentiated gender roles that discourage women from working outside the home. An extensive literature in demography, sociology, anthropology, and social psychology has documented the familiar yet profound transformation of sex roles associated with the process of societal modernization.[1] Virtually all preindustrial societies emphasize childbearing and child rearing as the central goal for women and their most important function in life, along with tasks like food production and preparation at home; jobs in the paid workforce are predominately male. In postindustrial societies, gender roles have increasingly converged because of a structural revolution in the paid labor force, in educational opportunities for women, and in the characteristics of modern families.[2] In most affluent countries, people are marrying later than in previous generations and having fewer children.[3] A rapid increase in premarital cohabitation is challenging the once-privileged position held by marriage. More and more women, especially those who are married, have entered the paid labor force, creating the transition from male breadwinner to dual-earning families.[4] Although the gender gap in rates of economic participation is narrowing, women's and men's roles in the labor force continue to differ. Women still have to juggle the demands of family responsibilities and market work, and they hold different jobs than men do, often with lower status and rewards. These social trends raise questions about long-established moral values and attitudes toward the family and gender roles that were once taken for granted. Traditional family values have by no means disappeared, but they appear to be under greater strain in postmodern societies. Not all consequences of these sweeping developments can be examined here, but this account leads four major predications that are open to empirical investigation – namely, we expect to find systematic differences in cultural indicators of gender equality:

- between societies based on their level of economic development,
- within societies based on generational cohorts,
- between women and men, and
- within societies based on structural and cultural factors such as education and class.

In order to examine these propositions, this chapter analyses *indirect* attitudinal evidence, including comparisons among different types of societies. It demonstrates that richer, postindustrial societies support the idea of gender equality more than agrarian and industrial societies. Intergenerational differences, which are largest in postindustrial societies and relatively minor in agrarian societies, suggest that the former are undergoing intergenerational changes. Lastly, support for gender equality in the political sphere, in the workplace, and in educational opportunities is strongly related to patterns of education, religiosity, marital status, and postmaterialism, following familiar patterns of cultural attitudes.

Measuring Attitudinal Support for Gender Equality

How do we best measure attitudes toward gender equality? If this is a multidimensional phenomenon, then inconsistent trends could be apparent in different arenas, such as the home, the workforce, and the public sphere. The entry of married women into the paid labor market, for example, which expands pooled household incomes, may prove more socially acceptable to men than equality in the division of common domestic chores, such as routine house care and care of children and the elderly.[5] Women working in sectors such as education, health, and voluntary organizations, reflecting traditional sex roles of women as caregivers, may encounter fewer barriers than those challenging conventional sexual stereotypes in military, political, and religious institutions. Equal opportunity policies reflecting common classical liberal beliefs may prove more popular than strategies designed to achieve affirmative action, gender parity, or positive discrimination for women.[6] Feminist philosophy contains multiple complex strands of thought, as reflected in deep-seated divisions among socialist, liberal, and cultural perspectives within the women's movement. Before examining the evidence, we first need to establish if attitudes toward gender equality fall into a single coherent ideological dimension.

Since the early 1970s, an extensive literature in social psychology has developed and tested reliable and valid multidimensional scales of attitudes toward the division of sex roles in the home and workplace, including attitudes toward gender equality, feminism, the status of women, and support for the women's movement.[7] Although useful, these comprehensive scales have usually been tested among small convenience samples of college students, often in the United States, restricting the generalizability of the results outside of that particular context. Cross-national comparisons have commonly used a more limited range of survey items available from sources such as the Eurobarometer and the International Social Survey Programme.[8] This study develops a Gender Equality Scale by combining a battery of five items from the pooled 1995–2001 World Values Surveys / European Values Surveys.

- MENPOL Q118: "On the whole, men make better political leaders than women do." (Agree coded low) (1990–2001 WVS/EVS).
- MENJOBS Q78: "When jobs are scarce, men should have more right to a job than women." (Agree coded low) (1990–2001 WVS/EVS).
- BOYEDUC Q.119: "A university education is more important for a boy than a girl." (Agree coded low) (1990–2001 WVS/EVS).
- NEEDKID Q110 "Do you think that a woman has to have children in order to be fulfilled or is this not necessary?" (Agree coded low) (1981–2001 WVS/EVS)
- SGLMUM Q112 "If a woman wants to have a child as a single parent but she doesn't want to have a stable relationship with a man, do you approve or disapprove?" (1981–2001 WVS/EVS)

These five items are similar to those commonly contained in the more comprehensive psychological scales of gender equality, tapping

TABLE 2.1. *Factor analysis of the Gender Equality Scale (five-item)*

	Component
Men make better political leaders than women.	.710
Men should have more right to a job than women.	.672
University education is more important for a boy.	.641
Necessary for woman to have children to be fulfilled	.556
Woman wants to have children as single parent	.395
% of total variance	36.6

Note: Principal component factor analysis.
Source: Pooled WVS/EVS, 1995–2001.

attitudes toward politics, the workforce, education, and the family. Three items use statements with Lickert-style four-point agree-disagree responses, while two use dichotomies; these items were all recoded so that higher values consistently represent greater support for gender equality. Principal component factor analysis revealed that all five items tap a single dimension (see Table 2.1), with a Cronbach's Alpha of 0.54.[9] The Gender Equality Scale was summed across the items and standardized to 100 points for ease of interpretation. The full five-item scale is available for the 1995–2001 waves of the WVS/EVS in sixty-one societies. Two items (NEEDKID and SINGLEMUM) are available in twenty societies for time-series analysis over all four waves since the early 1980s.

Cross-national Comparisons

If there are coherent and predictable value shifts associated with societal modernization, then the most egalitarian attitudes toward the division of sex roles should be found in the most affluent societies. This is certainly what we would expect given other major cultural shifts documented in previous work, including the transition from traditional to secular-rational values and the transition from survival to self-Expression values.[10] The distribution of sixty-one nations on the gender equality scale for 1995–2001, shown in Figure 2.1, provides preliminary support for the proposition that attitudes toward traditional or egalitarian roles for women and men vary systematically according to levels of economic development. The countries ranking as most egalitarian include some of the most affluent in the world, such as Finland,

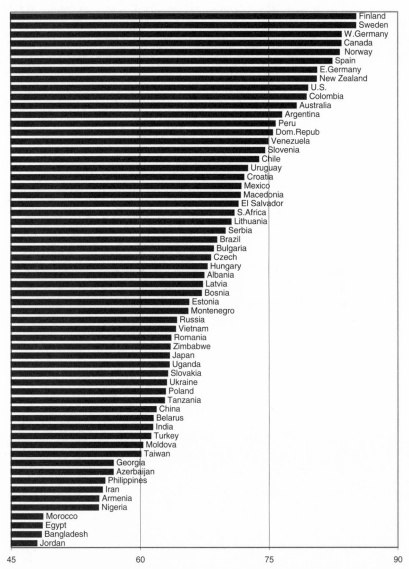

45	60	75	90

FIGURE 2.1. Gender Equality Scale by nation. Combined 100-point scale of the following 5 items: MENPOL Q118: "*On the whole, men make better political leaders than women do.*" (Agree coded low); MENJOBS Q78: "*When jobs are scarce, men should have more right to a job than women.*" (Agree coded low); BOYEDUC Q119: "*A university education is more important for a boy than a girl.*" (Agree coded low); NEEDKID Q110 "*Do you think that a woman has to have children in order to be fulfilled or is this not necessary?*" (Agree coded low); SGLMUM Q112 "*If a woman wants to have a child as a single parent but she doesn't want to have a stable relationship with a man, do you approve or disapprove?*" (Disapprove coded low). *Source*: WVS/EVS, pooled 1995–2001.

Sweden, Canada, and West Germany, each scoring over 80 percent. Many moderate-income industrialized nations, such as Brazil, Mexico, and Bulgaria, rank in the middle of this scale, while some of the poorest societies fall at the bottom, including Nigeria, Armenia, Morocco, Bangladesh, and Jordan, all ranked with GDP per capita of $1,500 or less in 1998 and gender equality scores below 60 percent.[11] Overall, the mean score on the 100-point scale was 80 percent for postindustrial societies, compared to 68 percent for industrial nations and 60 percent for agrarian societies.

To analyze the pattern more systematically, the degree of support for gender equality in each country was compared to levels of economic development, measured by logged per capita GDP (in purchasing power parity U.S. dollars). The result, shown in the scattergram in Figure 2.2, confirms the consistency and strength of the association between gender equality and development ($R^2 = 0.54$). All of the postindustrial

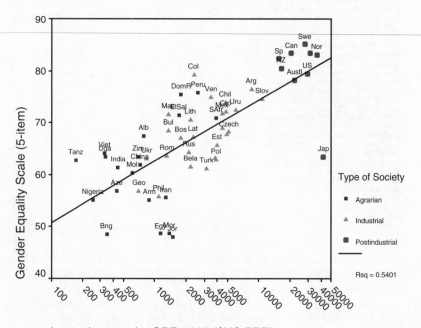

Logged per capita GDP 1998 ($US PPP)

FIGURE 2.2. Gender Equality Scale and economic development. *Gender Equality Scale*: see Figure 2.1. *Logged per capita GDP 1998*: see UNDP. *Human Development Report 2000*. New York: Oxford University Press/UNDP. *Source*: Pooled WVS/EVS, 1995–2001.

nations, with the important exception of Japan, are clustered in the top right-hand corner, as most strongly in favor of gender equality and also most affluent. A range of industrial societies cluster in the middle of the distribution, with Latin American nations such as Colombia and Venezuela more egalitarian in their attitudes toward sex roles than post-Communist societies such as Poland, Belarus, and Russia. This suggests that other factors are also influential, beyond economic development, such as the historical role of the state under Communist regimes and the religious legacy that predominates in certain areas of the world. Lastly, agrarian societies proved to be least egalitarian, although again there were important differences among these poorer nations that deserve further exploration in the next chapter, such as the contrasts apparent between Vietnam and Bangladesh, or between India and Azerbaijan. These results suggest that although economic prosperity is *one* of the factors most strongly associated with the existence of an ethos of equality between women and men in a society, it is far from the whole story.

Amartya Sen has drawn an important and influential distinction between the acquisition of income and wealth and the broader notion of human development, with the latter containing many other important indicators of societal well-being, such as the ability to enjoy clean water and sanitary facilities, to obtain sufficient nutrition, and to get adequate shelter and warmth, as well as conditions of freedom from conflict and crime and social exclusion, all of which shape prospects for survival into old age.[12] Economic growth can influence these conditions, but even in affluent nations there can still be many pockets of social inequality and inadequate safety nets. There are sharp contrasts between high-growth economies such as South Korea that have had considerable success in raising the quality of life, and others such as Brazil that have a history of severe social inequality, unemployment, and neglect of public health care. To explore these contrasts further, the UNDP defines and measures human development by factors such as longevity, education, and literacy as well as GDP; they have collected a wide variety of statistics that can be used to assess and compare progress in societal modernization during the 1990s.[13] Many of these indicators, such as estimates of the average daily supply of calories, per capita electricity consumption, and the percentage of GNP derived from agriculture, are essentially gender-neutral. Others are more closely related to the conditions of women's lives and inequalities between the sexes, such as the ratio of women to men at different educational levels, the proportion of births to young mothers, and the contraception rate.

The comparison of many nations in Table 2.2 shows that across a wide range of selected indicators, the attitudes on the gender equality scale are strongly and significantly related to both the societal and the gender-related indicators, in the predicted direction. Of course, there could be an interaction effect at work with some of these indicators, if cultures favorable to gender equality are the ones that most facilitate equal opportunities for women in education or employment. But even those developmental indicators demarcating poorer nations that are not directly related to gender relations, such as basic levels of food aid, energy use, and the debt service ratio, prove to be strongly associated with egalitarian beliefs regarding sex roles. This supports the contention that societal modernization leads to more secure lives, primarily through increasing personal incomes and wealth and facilitating effective public sector and nonprofit programs for social protection, which in turn gradually create a climate conducive to more liberal views of social roles, including those determined by sex, class, and ethnicity. When life is no longer "nasty, poor, brutish and short," restricted by widespread fears and insecurities based on life-threatening challenges, then women and men gradually develop greater willingness to adopt interchangeable roles within the family and workforce. Correlations cannot prove causation, and indeed, there could in theory be an alternative 'X' factor (as there is in Weberian theories of the Protestant ethic) that simultaneously drives *both* support for gender equality and levels of societal development.[14] But it is clear from this wide range of evidence from many nations, and consistent with our theoretical interpretation, that where societal modernization and human development have progressed furthest, traditional conceptions of a strict demarcation between the roles of women and men have broken down most fully.

Generational Change and Cohort Analysis

So far we have established differences between rich and poor nations, but not whether attitudes toward women have become more liberal

TABLE 2.2. *Gender Equality Scale and indicators of societal modernization*

	Year	Correlation	Sig.	Number of Nations
Societal indicators				
Per capita GDP (PPP $US)	1998	.608	.000	55
Human Development Index (HDI)	1998	.666	.000	55
% Urban population	1998	.538	.000	51
% GNP from services	1998	.389	.000	47
% GNP from agriculture	1997	−.587	.000	45
Average life expectancy (years)	1998	.505	.000	52
Daily supply of calories	1996	.482	.000	51
Per capita commercial energy use (oil equivalent)	1996	.611	.000	48
Per capita electricity consumption (kw-hours)	1996	.635	.000	51
Debt service ratio	1997	.415	.007	41
Dependency ratio (%)	1997	−.271	.054	51
Food aid in cereals (thou. metric tons)	1994–5	−.609	.003	22
Drug crimes (per 100,000 people)	1994	.616	.000	32
Level of democratization (Freedom House Index)	2000	.537	.000	58
Gender-related indicators				
Gender-related development index (GDI)	1997	.709	.000	52
Gender empowerment measure (GEM)	1997	.843	.000	41
Female administrators and managers (% of total)	1997	.493	.001	41
Female professional and technical workers (% of total)	1997	.420	.006	41
Female primary net educational enrolement, as % of male enrollment	1997	.556	.000	42
Female secondary net educational enrolement, as % of male enrollment	1997	.566	.000	41
Female tertiary students, per 100,000 women	1996	.623	.000	34
Female adult literacy rate, as % of male rate	1997	.677	.000	37
Births to mothers under 20 (%)	1991–7	−.469	.003	39
Contraceptive prevalence rate (%)	1990–8	.498	.001	39

Note: The figures represent correlation coefficients between national scores on the Gender Equality Scale (from the pooled WVS/EVS, 1995–2001) and selected indicators of societal modernization, without any controls.

For the 100-point standardized Gender Equality Scale (5-item), see Table 2.1.

For the definitions, measures, and sources of the social indicators, see Appendix B.

Source: UNDP. 2000. *Human Development Report 2000.* New York: Oxford University Press/UNDP.

over the years. For indirect evidence of long-term trends, cohort analysis can be used to examine whether, as predicted, the younger generations are more in favor of equal roles in the home, the workplace, and the public sphere than their parents' and grandparents' generations. The theory of value change argued here suggests that secular social trends have only a glacial effect on cultural norms but that, through the socialization process, the conditions experienced during the formative years of childhood and early adolescence make an indelible impression on people. As a result, the values held in later life continue to be shaped by these seminal early experiences. Certain decisive historical events and common experiences also leave an imprint on a generation. Those growing up during the interwar era in Western nations experienced the dramatic collapse of stocks and savings, mass unemployment, and soup kitchens during the 1930s triggered by the Great Depression, followed by a military conflict that engulfed the world at the end of the decade. Given these conditions, the interwar generation in postindustrial societies is likely to prioritize materialist social goals, such as the importance of secure and full employment, low inflation, and the underlying conditions for economic growth, and to hold traditional views toward the division of household and parental responsibilities and support for authorities. By contrast, the postwar generation in these nations, coming of age during periods of unprecedented affluence, domestic peace, and social stability, are more likely to adhere to postmaterialist values, including equality between the sexes in sharing household tasks and equal opportunities in the labor market. Using only cross-sectional survey evidence, it is difficult to disentangle generational effects from life-cycle effects that may alter attitudes and values as people move from youth to middle age and then to retirement. The experience of education, entry into the labor force, child rearing, and old age can all be expected to shape beliefs about appropriate sex roles in the home and workplace. Cultural messages conveyed by the mass media and contact with organizations such as the women's movement can also color perceptions about appropriate attitudes and behavior for women and men. Significant changes in the lives of women and men may also generate a period effect, exemplified during the 1960s by the availability of safer contraception and wider access to abortion in many countries. Nevertheless, we assume that the acquisition of sex roles and core values of gender equality learned early in life in

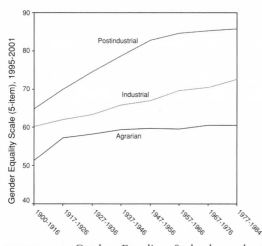

FIGURE 2.3. Gender Equality Scale by cohort and type of society. *Gender Equality Scale*: see Figure 2.1. *Source*: Pooled WVS/EVS, 1995–2001.

the family, school, and community are part of the primary socialization process, so that the enduring values of different birth cohorts can be attributed mainly to their formative experiences in childhood and adolescence.

In order to examine the evidence supporting these propositions, support for gender equality can be analyzed both by type of society and by ten-year birth cohorts. The results, presented in Figure 2.3, illustrate the substantial generational gaps in cultural values in affluent nations. In postindustrial societies, members of the interwar generations, born between the 1920s and the 1940s, prove far more traditional in their beliefs about the appropriate division of sex roles. By contrast, the postwar baby boom generations display far more egalitarian attitudes. This generation that grew up during the affluent fifties and came of age during the sixties and seventies witnessed the rise of the second-wave women's movement, expanded educational opportunities for women, and growing female participation in the paid workforce, in routine white-collar jobs, and in careers as managers, administrators, and professionals. Moreover, in these societies, after a rapid rise among the interwar generations, there is a plateau evident among the postwar generations, so that cohorts born in the 1950s, 1960s, and 1970s share similar egalitarian attitudes. The cultural changes in affluent nations have therefore proved enduring and stable. Within postindustrial societies, there is a ten-point gap on the gender equality scale between the interwar and postwar generations. By contrast, the line illustrating cohort change in industrialized nations is far flatter, and there is a six-point gap between the pre-war and postwar generations. Lastly, in the poorer, agrarian societies there is an almost flat line across cohorts, except for the oldest group, and there is only a one-point gap between the interwar and postwar generations.

But has this shift mainly affected women, or have men changed along with women? Some survey evidence comparing attitudes toward marriage and the family in Britain, Ireland, the United States, and West Germany found greater contrasts between men and women than across countries.[15] Yet other studies have documented important generational shifts in male sex-role attitudes in America.[16] To explore these issues, Figure 2.4 shows the generational gap for men and women in support for gender equality. This analysis confirms that the growing belief in equal sex roles evident in affluent nations is strongest among the postwar generation of women; nevertheless, the rising tide is not simply confined to this group, as in these nations younger men have also gradually come to favor equal opportunities for women and men. Interestingly, both women and men in affluent societies seem to have reached a "plateau" in support for gender equality, as there appears to be little difference between postwar baby boomers born in the late 1950s and subsequent cohorts. Most importantly, the patterns show that the key contrast, and indeed the growing gap in values and attitudes, is between types of societies rather than between women and men. This pattern is particularly marked on three issues – women's leadership in politics, equal opportunities in the paid workplace, and the need for women to have children in order to be fulfilled.

These findings have implications that can be interpreted in two alternative ways. It is often assumed in the West that claims for women's rights are universal, and that men in patriarchal societies have restricted women's opportunities for secondary education, employment, and empowerment, and their rights to divorce, reproductive freedom, and property. In this perspective, the legal, political, and social system in traditional societies reflects and buttresses men's interests. This argument assumes that women in these countries, lacking empowerment and silenced in the public sphere, are unable to express their real

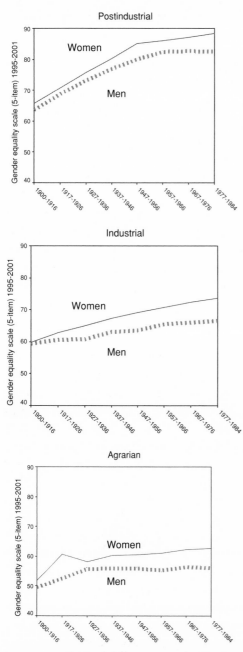

FIGURE 2.4. Societal differences on the Gender Equality Scale.

dissatisfaction with the status quo. In this view also, where women's voices are silenced, a coalition of international agencies such as the United Nations, working with multiple transnational feminist networks, women's organizations, and NGOs, can legitimately intervene on behalf of these women to demand that governments introduce equal opportunities. But the results of this analysis suggest an alternative proposition, namely, that common, deeply engrained belief systems in poorer developing societies mean that both men and women willingly adhere to the traditional division of sex roles in the home, family, and workplace. In this regard, men in these societies are not actively restricting and silencing women's demands; instead, both sexes believe that women and men should have distinct roles, as primary breadwinners and caregivers. It is true that due to the hegemonic grip of patriarchal ideology pervasive throughout such societies, and reinforced by the socialization process in the family, schools, religious organizations, and the media, women in these nations may be suffering from problems of "false consciousness" about their "real" interests, as many Western feminists might argue. Younger generations of educated professional women in these societies may become increasingly dissatisfied with traditional beliefs, creating coalitions with feminists elsewhere. Nevertheless, the evidence suggests that, if given a free choice, most women in these societies would still willingly opt for traditional roles in the home and family, leaving men predominant in the public sphere. In this regard, women may be prisoners, but they are willing prisoners, with the limits to their roles set by their socialization as much as by society's laws. Egalitarian ideas common among feminists in North America and Western Europe may eventually prove universally applicable, but these beliefs may be less widely shared than is commonly recognized. The evidence, therefore, suggests that in affluent Western nations more egalitarian beliefs have gradually become predominant among both women and men, reflecting the changed lifestyles and experiences of the postwar generation. In agrarian societies, by contrast, traditional attitudes continue to prevail among both men and women. This statement needs qualifying, since women favor gender equality slightly more strongly than men within every society. Nevertheless, it appears that, despite claims for the universalism of women's rights, there is a growing gap between the egalitarian beliefs and feminist values of Western societies and the traditional beliefs in poorer societies. Possible consequences of this widening cultural cleavage will be explored further in the conclusion.

Comparisons within Societies

What individual-level factors best explain support for gender equality? Previous studies comparing feminist attitudes in the fifteen EU member states have reported that at the individual level, the social background of women has often proved important, including their labor force participation, age, education, religiosity, and partisanship.[17] A regression model was used to examine predictors of support for the gender equality scale in the pooled WVS/EVS surveys across all fifty nations for 1995–2001, including social background variables that are often found to be associated with modern and traditional attitudes (age, gender, income, religiosity, work status, marital status, and children), as well as family savings, taken as a proxy measure of household economic security. Controls were included for the level of human development and democratization of society, and global regions were included as an indicator of residual cultural factors around the world.

The results in Table 2.3 show that all of these factors proved to be significant, with coefficients in the expected direction. Among these variables, levels of human development proved to be one of the strongest predictors of attitudes. Comparing just the social and demographic factors, with societal controls, support for gender equality was strongest, as expected, among the younger generation, women, the better educated, and the less religious. But marked regional coefficients remained, suggesting that levels of societal modernization and the social backgrounds of respondents were insufficient to account for the remaining contrasts among those living in Asia and Central and Eastern Europe (who were less supportive of gender equality than average) and among Scandinavians (who were the most egalitarian). This suggests that social groups with similar characteristics living in different regions, such as professional women or older home workers in New York and New Delhi, or in Stockholm and Santiago, would still display divergent values. The next chapter will go on to explore these contrasts in more detail, including the imprint of cultural legacies produced by different religious traditions, state regimes, and national histories.

TABLE 2.3. *Social characteristics and support for the Gender Equality Scale*

	Unstandardized Coefficients (B)	Standard Error	Standardized Beta Coefficients	Sig.
(Constant)	44.589	.875		.000
Societal development				
Human Development Index, 1998	37.176	.947	.234	.000
Level of democratization, 1999–2000	1.416	.073	.104	.000
Social background				
Age (years)	−.147	.004	−.139	.000
Gender (men = 1, women = 0)	−5.102	.138	−.137	.000
Educational (three categories)	2.947	.096	.116	.000
Income	.000	.000	.021	.000
Frequency of church attendance (seven-point scale)	−.817	.036	−.090	.000
Work status (paid work = 1, else = 0)	.551	.094	.022	.000
Married or living as married (1, else = 0)	−.800	.154	−.021	.000
With at least one child (1, else = 0))	−1.125	.235	−.020	.000
Family savings in past year (four-point scale)	−.424	.073	−.022	.000
Region				
Asia	−11.506	.224	−.246	.000
Central and Eastern Europe	−10.121	.213	−.234	.000
Middle East	−8.991	.298	−.130	.000
North America	−1.979	.278	−.032	.000
Africa	−.830	.381	−.011	.029
Western Europe	1.474	.394	.015	.000
Scandinavia	1.988	.379	.023	.000
Adjusted R^2	.28			

Note: OLS Regression models with the Gender Equality Scale, 1995–2001 (five item) as the dependent variable. Regional dummy variables (0/1) exclude South America. For the coding of variables, see Appendix B.

Source: Pooled WVS/EVS, 1995–2001.

TABLE 2.4. *Mean scores on the Gender Equality Scale*

	Agrarian	Industrial	Postindustrial	Total
All	60	68	81	67
Gender				
Women	65	70	81	70
Men	59	66	77	64
Diff.	6	4	4	6
Education				
High	63	69	83	69
Moderate	60	69	80	68
Low	56	65	76	63
Diff.	7	4	7	6
Age group				
Under 30	63	72	84	69
30–59	61	67	81	67
60+	59	62	71	64
Diff.	4	10	13	5
Postmaterialism (four-item)				
Postmaterialist	69	75	85	80
Mixed	63	68	78	68
Materialist	59	63	72	62
Diff.	10	12	13	18
R's occupational class (V230)				
Manager/professional	63	69	80	70
Lower middle	66	71	81	73
Skilled working	61	66	79	67
Unskilled working	61	65	78	65
Diff.	2	4	2	5
Work status				
Women in paid work	64	70	82	72
Men in paid work	59	66	77	65
Women looking after home	61	70	76	66
Diff. among women	3	0	6	6
Marital status				
Separated	69	74	83	75
Cohabiting	66	71	85	73
Divorced	69	70	82	73
Single	66	72	84	71
Married	61	66	77	66
Widowed	62	63	71	64
Diff.	7	11	12	13

(continued)

TABLE 2.4 *(continued)*

	Agrarian	Industrial	Postindustrial	Total
Children				
No children	65	72	84	70
At least one child	62	67	79	67
Diff.	3	5	4	3

Note: For coding, see Appendix B. For the 100-point Gender Equality Scale, see Table 2.1.
Source: Pooled WVS/EVS, in sixty-one societies, 1995–2001.

Table 2.4 breaks down the mean gender equality scale by social group and type of society. In addition, the influence of postmaterialism was also examined, as one of the best-established indicators of cultural change, using the standard four-part scale that divides people into materialists, mixed, and postmaterialists.[18] The results confirm our expectations, with the highest scores on gender equality (over 80 percent) found in postindustrial societies among women, those under thirty, those who were unmarried or widowed, those without children, and among adherents of postmaterialist values. Among affluent nations, the generation gap proved a stronger predictor of egalitarian attitudes than sex, class, or education, strongly supporting the thesis of long-term secular cohort change in these fundamental values.

Conclusions

Early accounts emphasized the importance of economic growth for promoting gender equality, and subsequent decades saw a strong focus on establishing effective legal, social, and political rights for women. Cultural accounts have often claimed that values are equally important, but it has been difficult to examine that proposition systematically, in large part because, without cross-national surveys, the predominant approach has been to compare social norms and behavior through qualitative techniques such as personal interviews, participant observation, and textual exegesis, usually covering one or a few societies. Cultural relativists argue that such an approach is appropriate, because subtle differences can be detected in attitudes toward women even among relatively similar nations with different cultural histories, such as Germany and France, or Canada and the United States. This chapter has compared systematic survey evidence in many nations at different levels of societal modernization. Survey questions may fail to catch some of the more nuanced aspects of complex social relations; nevertheless, the WVS data provides a broad map of the state of beliefs and values about sex roles in many societies around the globe. The results, based on analysis of the 100-point Gender Equality Scale, suggest five main conclusions:

1. Far from being a random distribution, attitudes toward gender equality form coherent and predictable patterns.

2. In particular, there are clearly established contrasts among countries at different levels of societal modernization, with agrarian nations the most traditional in their perceptions of sharply divided sex roles, industrial societies in the early stages of transition, and postindustrial societies the most egalitarian in their beliefs about the roles of women and men.

3. Moreover, this is not just a matter of *economic* development, because a wide range of non-gender-related indicators of human development, from levels of energy use to average life expectancy, are equally good predictors of support for gender equality.

4. The analysis of generational differences also showed predictable patterns, with younger generations in postindustrial societies being far more egalitarian than their parents and grandparents. This generational change was less evident in industrialized nations, and within poorer agrarian societies there was no evidence of significant generational shifts.

5. Within societies, there are significant differences between women and men, but in postindustrial nations younger men have also shifted their values along with younger women. Support for gender equality was also stronger among the well educated, the less religious, the unmarried, and among postmaterialists. But perhaps the most important finding is that the gap that has emerged *between* traditional agrarian societies and egalitarian postindustrial societies is far greater than the gap that exists between women and men *within* each type of society.

Despite the role of human development, attitudes toward gender equality were still found to vary even among societies at similar levels of human development, according to factors such as religious traditions, type of state, and level of democratization. Among rich nations, there are substantial contrasts between Japan and Norway, for example, just as there are between poorer societies such as Jordan and Columbia. We will attempt to understand these factors in more depth in the next chapter.

3

Religion, Secularization, and Gender Equality

We have established the existence of systematic and predictable differences in cultural attitudes toward gender equality that vary across nations according to their level of human development, within societies based on generational differences, and among social groups according to factors such as education and marital status. Building on this foundation, this chapter demonstrates that the process of societal modernization in any given society is conditioned by cultural legacies and religious traditions. We hypothesize that (1) a process of secularization has gradually accompanied societal modernization, weakening the strength of religious values in postindustrial societies, particularly among the younger generation, and fuelling the rising tide of gender equality. (2) Postindustrial societies have experienced a parallel liberalization of attitudes toward sexuality, exemplified by the issues of abortion, homosexuality, prostitution, and divorce. (3) Yet religiosity continues to exert a strong influence on social norms about the appropriate division of sex roles in the home, the workforce, and the public sphere, especially in agrarian societies. (4) Moreover, attitudes toward women vary among adherents of different religious sects and denominations; in particular, an Islamic religious heritage is one of the most powerful barriers to the rising tide of gender equality.

The literature suggests multiple reasons why religion can be expected to exert a major influence over prevalent attitudes and practices regarding sex roles.

- An extensive body of work in sociology, social psychology, anthropology, and theology studies suggests that religion has functioned as one of the most important agencies of socialization determining social norms and moral values with regard to gender equality in all societies, and influencing support for feminism and attitudes toward the second-wave women's movement. The role of the church in this process is similar to that of other important socialization agencies, including the family, community, school, workplace, and the mass media.[1]
- Religious organizations, particularly the Catholic Church and the evangelical movement among fundamentalist Christians in the West, and Islamic fundamentalist leaders in Muslim nations, have often actively sought to reinforce social norms of a separate and subordinate role for women as homemakers and mothers, buttressing traditional policies and the legal framework regulating marriage and divorce, abortion and contraception, family and childcare policy.[2]
- Research on electoral behavior and public opinion, influenced by Duverger's seminal work on women and politics in Western Europe in the 1950s, has long regarded women's greater religiosity as an important influence on patterns of partisanship and voter choice, including greater female support for parties of the center-right, such as Christian Democrats and Conservatives.[3]
- Studies of political representation, legislative elites, and leadership recruitment have established that the type of religious culture acts as an important contextual factor inhibiting women's entry into elected office. In particular, recent cross-national studies have found that fewer women enter legislatures in predominately Catholic and Islamic societies, controlling for many other common factors such as levels of economic development, democratization, and types of electoral systems.[4]
- Lastly, in recent years considerable research in the human rights literature has focused attention on the problems facing women in Muslim societies, and the question of whether rights such as citizenship can be regarded as universal if they conflict with pervasive religious beliefs, social norms, and Islamic law governing the role of women in the Middle East.[5]

If traditional religious beliefs and practices are eroding in many affluent nations, with the growing secularization of the modern world, this could help explain the increasing support for gender equality in the home and workplace that we have already observed in postindustrial nations, especially among younger generations.[6] This is a plausible proposition that deserves analysis; but so far, little systematic cross-national survey data has been available to examine how religious beliefs and practices vary around the globe, or how they may ebb and flow in response to the processes of societal modernization and broader shifts in the cultural zeitgeist. Moreover, even the basic contention of growing secularization remains under challenge. Some divinity scholars point to evidence of religious revivals and countersecular movements, such as the vigorous resurgence of Orthodox Judaism in Israel, as well as to fundamentalist Islamic movements in many countries in the Middle East and North Africa and the development of new religious movements and evangelical revivals in the West.[7] In particular, Samuel Huntington has claimed that following the end of the Cold War, civilizational cultures, based largely on religious values, are playing a larger role in domestic and international conflict.[8] We therefore need to compare the evidence to see whether there has been growing secularization, as commonly assumed, before then examining the relationships among the strength of religious beliefs, the type of religious faith, and support for the values of gender equality.

The Loss of Religious Faith?

The theory that modernization has led to secularization was emphasized in the work of Max Weber and was popularized among sociological and theological writers during the 1950s and 1960s.[9] At its simplest, secularization theories suggest that modernization leads to the decline of religious beliefs, as indicated by the erosion of church attendance, denominational allegiance, and faith in religious authorities; the loss of prestige and influence of religion's symbols, doctrines, and institutions; and the growing separation between church and state.[10] Modernization theories suggest that growing levels of literacy and education, and wider sources of information, have strengthened rational belief in scientific knowledge, expert authorities, and technological know-how, with priests, ministers, rabbis, and mullahs regarded as only one source of authority, and not necessarily the most important one, competing with the expertise of experts and professionals such as psychologists, physicists, and physicians.[11]

The evidence supporting secularization is strongest for Western Europe, where many people have ceased to be regular churchgoers outside of special occasions such as Christmas and Easter, weddings and funerals, a pattern particularly marked among the younger generations.[12] Evidence from the Eurobarometer surveys conducted since 1970 suggests a consistent erosion in church attendance experienced across the fifteen Europe Union member states during the last three decades, with a fairly steep fall found in Belgium, Luxembourg, and the Netherlands and a relatively shallow decline over the years in Germany, France, and Ireland.[13] Nevertheless, despite gradually emptying pews, the disparities in religiosity within European societies remain marked, depending upon historical traditions and the power of the church, producing contrasts such as the continuing hegemonic grip of the Catholic Church in Ireland and the far more secular society evident in Protestant Denmark. Even within Europe, however, a distinction needs to be drawn between behavioral indicators such as habitual attendance at church services, which has fallen, and religious values and beliefs, which may persist.[14] Among affluent nations, the United States provides an interesting anomaly, with church attendance almost as high today among Americans as it was sixty years ago. According to Gallup polls, in 1939 about four out of ten Americans reported attending church or synagogue every week; almost the same proportion persisted, with minor fluctuations, in the most recent (2001) polls.[15] Some erosion is evident in other indicators of religiosity in the Gallup series; for example, about two-thirds of Americans (65%) currently count themselves members of a church or synagogue, down from almost three-quarters (73%) in 1937. The salience of religion has also fallen slightly: today about two-thirds of Americans (64%) report that religion is "very important" in their own life, down from three-quarters (75%) in 1952.[16]

Elsewhere in the world the picture remains complex, and it is difficult to establish reliable data on longitudinal trends and cross-national comparisons in churchgoing and religious affiliation. The *World Christian Encyclopedia* compares churches and religions around the globe and provides the most comprehensive estimates of secularization

TABLE 3.1. *Factor analysis of the Strength of Religiosity Scale (six-item)*

	Component
Importance of God	.883
Comfort in religion	.846
Belief in God	.836
Religious identity	.797
Attend religious services	.716
Life after death	.653
% of total variance	62.8

Note: Principal component factor analysis.
Importance: V196. *"How important is God in your life."* (% "Very," scaled 6–10)
Comfort: V.197. *"Do you find that you get comfort and strength from religion?"* (% Yes)
Believe: V191. *"Do you believe in God?"* (% Yes)
Identify: V186. *"Independently of whether you go to church or not, would you say you are... a religious person, not a religious person, or a convinced atheist?"* (% Religious)
Attend: V185. *"Apart from weddings, funerals and christenings, about how often do you attend religious services these days?"* (% Once a week or more)
Life: V192. *"Do you believe in life after death?"* (% Yes)
Source: WVS/EVS, pooled sample 1981–2001.

during the twentieth century, based on an annual religious "mega-census" completed by ten million church leaders, clergy, and other Christian workers.[17] The study suggests that the proportion of "non-religionists," defined as including agnostics, atheists, and other nonreligious groups, grew from an estimated 3.2 million in 1900 (0.2% of the globe's population) to about 19% in 1970 and peaked at 21% of the world's population in 1980, before falling back to 15% by 2000, following the collapse of Communism and the revival of organized religion in Central and Eastern Europe.

Cross-national survey evidence is needed for more reliable comparisons, using multiple indicators of religiosity to take account of diverse religious practices among different sects and denominations. To develop a systematic Strength of Religiosity Scale, Table 3.1 presents the results of factor analysis using six indicators from the pooled WVS/EVS for 1981–2001, namely, the proportion of the population in different

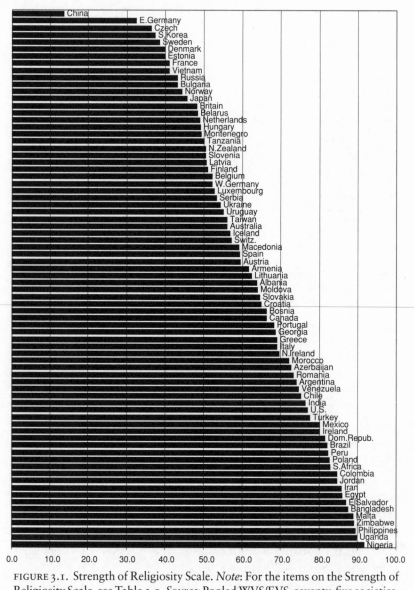

FIGURE 3.1. Strength of Religiosity Scale. *Note*: For the items on the Strength of
Religiosity Scale, see Table 3.1. *Source*: Pooled WVS/EVS, seventy-five societies,
1981–2001.

societies: (1) who say that religion is "very important" in their lives,
(2) who find comfort in religion, (3) who believe in God, (4) who identify themselves as religious, (5) who believe in life after death, and
(6) who attend religious services regularly. All of these items tap values

and beliefs common throughout the world's religions, and they were carried in all four waves of the WVS, making possible comparison over time. Factor analysis showed that all of the items tapped a common dimension and formed a consistent and reliable Strength of Religiosity Scale (Cronbach's Alpha = 0.48). After recoding, the scale was standardized to 100 points, for ease of interpretation, where higher scores represent stronger religiosity.

The comparison shows substantial contrasts in the strength of religiosity worldwide (see Figure 3.1). Low-income societies in Africa and Asia, exemplified by Nigeria, Uganda, the Philippines, and Zimbabwe, emerge as the most religious according to this scale, while at the other end of the spectrum, some of the post-Communist societies are among the most secular, including the Czech Republic and East Germany as well as postindustrial societies in Northern Europe, such as Sweden and Denmark. Nevertheless, although development is related to religiosity, there are many important exceptions to this pattern, above all the continuing strength of religiosity in the United States and, by contrast, the lower-than-expected levels in South Korea, Vietnam, and Tanzania. When broken down by type of society (see Table 3.2), agrarian

TABLE 3.2. *Strength of religiosity by type of society (percent)*

	Agrarian	Industrial	Postindustrial	Total
Believe in God	97	80	79	83
Believe in life after death	83	62	68	69
Religion "very important"	87	60	55	64
Identify as religious	73	58	59	61
Comfort from religion	74	51	46	54
Attend religious service regularly	47	45	21	28
Mean religiosity, 100-point scale	73	54	53	58

Believe: V191. *"Do you believe in God?"* (%Yes)
Life: V192. *"Do you believe in life after death?"* (% Yes)
Importance: V196. *"How important is God in your life."* (% "Very," scaled 6–10)
Identify: V186. *"Independently of whether you go to church or not, would you say you are . . . a religious person, not a religious person, or a convinced atheist?"* (% Religious)
Comfort: V.197. *"Do you find that you get comfort and strength from religion?"* (%Yes)
Attend: V185. *"Apart from weddings, funerals and christenings, about how often do you attend religious services these days?"* (% Once a week or more)
Source: WVS/EVS, pooled sample 1981–2001.

societies are clearly the most religious: in these nations, almost half of the public regularly attend church, while three-quarters or more regard themselves as religious, see religion as very important in their lives, and believe in life after death; and there is an almost universal belief in God. By contrast, postindustrial societies prove to be far less religious across all the different indicators, but especially on the behavioral item of church attendance, where only a fifth remain regular churchgoers. The industrialized societies prove to be moderately religious, but far closer to the rich than to poor nations.

To examine the cross-national pattern more systematically, and to identify any important outliers, the scatter plot in Figure 3.2 compares strength of religiosity to indicators of societal modernization, measured by the country's rank on the standard UNDP Human Development Index, incorporating life expectancy, education and adult literacy, and GDP per capita. The results confirm that modern societies tend to be more secular in orientation. Simple economic development provides part of the explanation here, but an even stronger relationship is evident with human development; societies with widespread literacy, education, affluence, security, and access to multiple sources of information from the mass media tend to be the most secular. By contrast, the poorest and least developed nations, such as Bangladesh, Zimbabwe, Nigeria, Ghana, and India are the most religious in their values, beliefs, and behavior. The wide scatter of countries in the middle of the graph shows the continued impact of historical legacies of Orthodox faith in the post-Communist world in Central and Eastern Europe compared to the stronger role of the church in Latin America, where Catholicism has traditionally predominated. The comparison also confirms that the United States and Ireland are outliers on both measures, along with Italy, as countries that remain far more religious than most other comparable affluent postindustrial societies, with Scandinavian societies with a Lutheran background proving to be the most secular. China also remains a striking outlier, a pattern that may reflect both the confucian tradition and communist constraints on the open expression of religious feelings in that country.

Moreover, as before, we can break down these patterns by cohort of birth and gender to see whether it is the younger generations in postindustrial societies who prove to be least religious, and whether cohorts of women differ more than cohorts of men, as indirect evidence

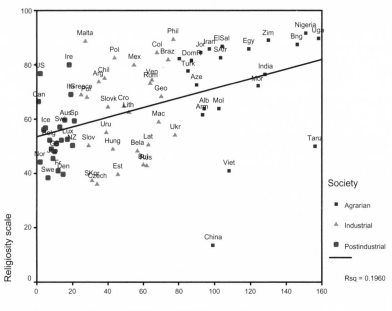

FIGURE 3.2. Religiosity and human development. *Note*: For the 100-point Strength of Religiosity scale, see Table 3.1. *Source*: The rank on the Human Development Index, 1998, including measures of longevity, adult literacy and education, and per capita GDP, is from the UNDP. *Human Development Report, 2001*. New York: UNDP/Oxford University Press.

of long-term culture shifts. The graph in Figure 3.3 vividly confirms these propositions. In affluent nations, there is a steady fall in religious adherence among successive cohorts of women and men, so that the youngest generation is about fifteen points less religious on this scale than the interwar generation. But it is women in these affluent societies who have been transformed most by this process: the oldest cohort of women in postindustrial societies is more religious than similar cohorts in industrialized nations, yet the younger generation of women in postindustrial nations is by far the least religious. This suggests that the transformation in women's lives in modern societies during the twentieth century, generated by widening opportunities in education, the workforce, and public affairs and changes in families, the home, and modern lifestyles, has contributed to this dramatic decline in religiosity, along with broader trends in societal modernization

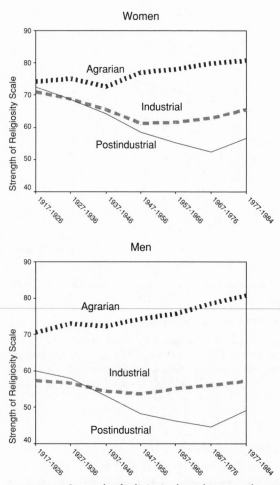

FIGURE 3.3. Strength of religiosity by cohort, gender, and type of society. *Note*:
The combined 6-item Strength of Religiosity Scale, standardized to 100 points,
consists of the following items: Identify: V186. *"Independently of whether you go
to church or not, would you say you are . . . a religious person, not a religious person,
or a convinced atheist?"* (% Religious) Attend: V185. *"Apart from weddings,
funerals and christenings, about how often do you attend religious services these
days?"* (% Once a week or more) Importance: V196. *"How important is God
in your life?"* (% Very, scaled 6–10) Believe: V191. *"Do you believe in God?"*
(% Yes) Life: V192. *"Do you believe in life after death?"* (% Yes) Comfort: V.197.
"Do you find that you get comfort and strength from religion?" (% Yes) *Source*:
Pooled WVS/EVS, 1995–2001.

that have affected both sexes equally. Interestingly, industrialized nations show a modest slide in religiosity among the interwar generations of women, before a fairly stable pattern emerges among postwar cohorts. Lastly, in agrarian societies, aside from an early "blip" that is probably due to the limited number of respondents in the 1900–1916 cohort, there is a steady high level of religiosity. Many observers, such as Samuel Huntington, suggest that there has been a religious revival in many poorer societies in recent decades, especially among fundamentalist sects in Muslim societies, perhaps as a backlash against the perceived threats of modern Western values to traditional social norms and sexual mores.[18] The cohort analysis suggests that agrarian societies remain largely unchanged, so that the younger generations are as fully religious as their parents and grandparents but not more so. But this results in a widening cultural gap, as affluent Western nations have become progressively more secular in orientation.

Although some scholars of religions have disputed growing secularization, Weber's thesis - that modernization leads to less religious societies – is supported by analysis of age differences and by cross-national comparison of the survey evidence, although it is clear that the different historical legacies of different faiths continue to shape their worldviews. The churches, sects, and faiths founded centuries ago have left an indelible imprint on each society that remains evident in religious practices, beliefs about God, and patterns of religious attendance around the globe.

The Values of Sexual Liberalization

Just as societal modernization has affected beliefs in God, churchgoing habits, and the authority of religious leaders, so we would expect parallel developments to be evident in support for traditional moral values governing sexuality. We will examine four issues that have been an important part of the feminist debate, the women's movement, and sexual liberalization: approval or disapproval of abortion, divorce, homosexuality, and prostitution. Abortion involves the core claim that women should have control over their reproductive rights, the issue most hotly debated between liberals and the Christian Right in the United States, although one less contentious today in many European

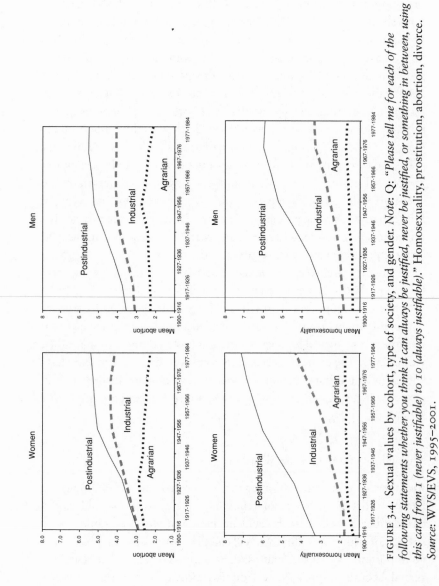

FIGURE 3.4. Sexual values by cohort, type of society, and gender. *Note: Q: "Please tell me for each of the following statements whether you think it can always be justified, never be justified, or something in between, using this card from 1 (never justifiable) to 10 (always justifiable)." Homosexuality, prostitution, abortion, divorce. Source: WVS/EVS, 1995–2001.*

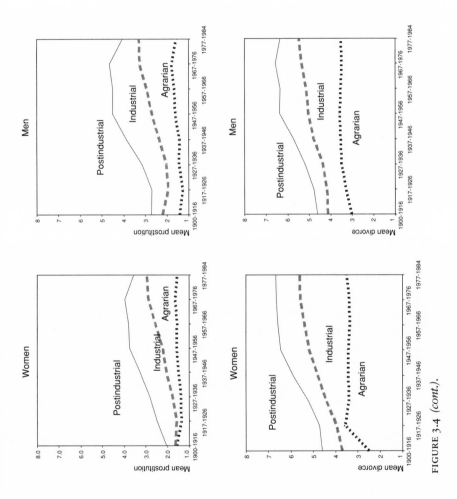

FIGURE 3.4 (cont.).

societies. Divorce is an important issue, especially in a few Catholic and many Muslim societies, where women have limited or no legal rights to dissolve the marriage. Tolerance of homosexuality, including gay and lesbian rights, has also been a central part of the sexual liberalization that began during the early 1960s. And the issue of prostitution is one that divides the women's movement, although liberals have argued for greater sexual tolerance, and indeed for legalization and unionization to protect the rights of sex workers. If traditional religious values have eroded on a consistent basis, along with patterns of church attendance, then this should become clear through cohort analysis of approval of these forms of sexual liberalization, divided by type of society and by gender to see whether women and men agree on these values. On each issue, people were asked to use ten-point scales to show how far they believed abortion, prostitution, homosexuality, and divorce were justified, ranging from low (never justified) to high (always justified).

Figure 3.4 shows the dramatic changes in sexual values evident among the older and younger cohorts in postindustrial societies, with steadily increasing tolerance for nontraditional sexual values across all four dimensions (with the exception of a modest conservative reversal among the youngest cohort on the issue of prostitution). The liberalization of sexuality in modern nations is particularly dramatic on the issues of abortion, divorce, and homosexuality, affecting the attitudes of both women and men, although women are slightly more tolerant of homosexuality *and* divorce. The pattern in industrialized nations shows broadly parallel shifts, although at a lower level of support, and there remain some important differences in the trends, for example, unlike the trend in more affluent countries, there is no "backlash" yet on tolerance of prostitution in these societies. By contrast, traditional sexual values are evident in agrarian societies, and there is usually little difference between younger and older cohorts, with the interesting exception of abortion, where there is evidence of a shift toward greater disapproval among younger generations. The overall pattern shows that the decline of religiosity we have found in postindustrial societies is not simply confined to replacing of spiritual beliefs and reliance upon religious authorities with a more rational and secular orientation, but that this change in the cultural outlook is closely associated with major shifts in core sexual and moral values. The consistency of the generational differences across various indicators in each type of society strongly suggests that these shifts are not simply ephemeral phenomenon, responding to temporary fashions and fads, but instead represent enduring developments, so that younger women and men in affluent nations differ in many basic values from their parents' and grandparents' generations. Despite the common observation that the sexual revolution started in 1964, the patterns of moral values that became evident then are part of a far longer-term development with a momentum that continues to move younger generations in a more liberal direction.

The Impact of Religiosity and Denomination on Gender Equality

Does strength of religiosity and type of religious faith help to predict beliefs about sex roles as well as about gender equality in education, the workforce, and the public sphere – the issues at the heart of this study? If so, it suggests that increasing secularization, which, as we have seen, is consistently associated with societal modernization, may play an important part in explaining the rising tide of gender equality. Most work on this issue has compared the impact of religious cultures by classifying societies based on the predominant faith in each nation, drawing on common worldwide reference sources and almanacs. For the global picture, we can compare 190 nations based on the CIA's *World Factbook 2001*, with data supplemented by the estimates of religious populations drawn from the *World Christian Encyclopedia*.

Figure 3.5 maps the classification of predominant religions in each nation based on these sources. Overall, nation-states divide into three major blocs: the largest number, fifty-seven nations, are classified as Roman Catholic, while forty-nine are Muslim and forty-six are Protestant, with the remainder Orthodox (twelve), Buddhist (twelve), other (including indigenous religions), Hindu, and Jewish. In terms of populations living under different majority religions, however, there is a different picture, as the largest group, representing over one billion people, live in Muslim states, and almost as many live in Hindu states (mainly India). Further analysis of how these denominations divide by type of society, shown in Table 3.3, demonstrates the strong

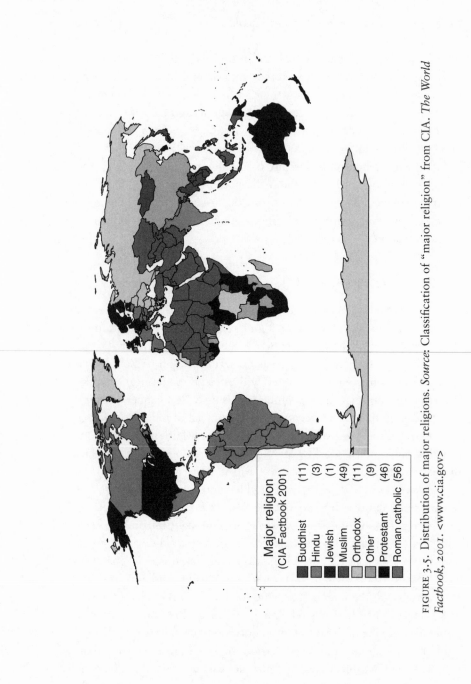

Major religion
(CIA Factbook 2001)

■	Buddhist (11)
	Hindu (3)
■	Jewish (1)
	Muslim (49)
	Orthodox (11)
	Other (9)
■	Protestant (46)
	Roman catholic (56)

FIGURE 3.5. Distribution of major religions. *Source*: Classification of "major religion" from CIA. *The World Factbook, 2001.* <www.cia.gov>

TABLE 3.3. *Major religion by type of society, 190 nation-states worldwide*

Major Religion	Type of Society			
	Agrarian	Industrial	Postindustrial	Total
Roman Catholic	19	29	9	57
Muslim	39	10		49
Protestant	28	9	10	47
Orthodox	2	10		12
Buddhist	8	3	1	12
Other	9			9
Hindu	2	1		3
Jewish		1		1
Total number of nation-states	*107*	*63*	*20*	*190*

Classification of types of society: See Appendix B.
Classification of major religion (adhered to by the largest population) in 190 nation-states around the world based on CIA. *The World Factbook, 2001*. Washington, DC: Central Intelligence Agency. "Other" includes "indigenous beliefs."
Source: <http://www.cia.gov/cia/publications/factbook>

relationship between modernization and Christianity (including Roman Catholicism and Protestantism), with all of the postindustrial societies around the world drawing on a Christian heritage, with the single exception of Japan. Nevertheless, it is apparent that there is a wide variety of sects and faiths among industrialized and agrarian societies, including Catholic, Protestant, Muslim, and Buddhist, as well as indigenous local religions.

One important limitation of these classifications is that they take no account of pluralistic societies that are deeply and fairly evenly divided into many minority religious faiths, none of which includes a third or more of the population. There are important minority groups in societies such as Israel, Northern Ireland, and Bosnia-Herzegovina that are deeply divided by ethno-religious conflict. The categorization of "predominant religion" often measures nominal adherence to "official" denominations, reflecting birth certificates, practices of baptism, and census records, rather than the proportion of active practitioners or true believers. Moreover, other than estimates of regular religious attendance, based on the annual "mega-survey" published in the *World Christian Encyclopedia*, there are few reliable measures of the strength of adherence to religious beliefs and practices. The global comparisons of the impact on gender equality of the predominant religion in

TABLE 3.4. *Mean scores on the Gender Equality Scale by denomination, religiosity, and type of society*

	Agrarian	Industrial	Postindustrial	*Total*
Denomination				
No denomination	67	69	80	72
Catholic	69	70	81	71
Protestant	64	66	81	71
Jewish	72	64	85	67
Orthodox	64	62	77	63
Hindu	62	74	70	63
Buddhist	70	60	61	61
Muslim	57	59	76	57
Religiosity				
Weak	63	67	81	70
Moderate	63	68	79	68
Strong	61	67	77	65
All	60	68	81	67

Note: For the coding, see Appendix B. For the 100-point Gender Equality Scale, see Table 2.1.
The 100-point Strength of Religiosity Scale in Table 3.1 is recoded to produce the categories.
Source: Pooled WVS/EVS, 1995–2001.

190 nations therefore need to be supplemented by more detailed analysis of the wide range of religious beliefs and practices in over 70 nations included in the pooled 1981–2001 World Values Surveys / European Values Surveys. Since we assume that basic religious values such as faith in God, attendance at church services, and denominational identities evolve only at a glacial pace, in response to long-term social and economic developments, the comparison of all societies across the pooled dataset is appropriate for cross-national comparisons.

In order to analyze the impact of religion, Table 3.4 first describes the mean scores on the Gender Equality Scale used in the previous chapter broken down by adherence to different denominations and by strength of religiosity, without any prior controls. But for a more systematic understanding, we need to turn to multivariate regression analysis models, since we have already established that levels of human development and many social factors such as age, education, and gender affect both religiosity and support for gender equality. Table 3.5 provides the results of OLS regression models for the impact of denomination and

TABLE 3.5. *Religion and support for the Gender Equality Scale*

	Model 1	Model 2			
	Correlation (R)	Unstandardized Coefficients (B)	Std. Error	Standardized Beta Coefficients	Sig.
(Constant)		31.519	.782		.000
Religious denomination					
Catholics	.13	7.75	.307	.194	.000
Protestants	.07	4.43	.309	.110	.000
No denomination	.10	4.41	.337	.090	.000
Hindu	−.04	13.2	2.76	.018	.000
Jewish	−.01	6.14	1.36	.017	.000
Orthodox (e.g. Greek or Russian)	−.10	0.66	.349	.012	.057
Buddhist	−.04	−4.47	.688	−.026	.000
Muslim	−.20	−1.41	.626	−.010	.024
Strength of religiosity					
Religiosity	−.19	−.008	.004	.011	.062
Adjusted R²		.24			

Model 1: Simple correlations without any prior controls; all results are significant at the .01 level. Model 2: OLS regression models with the Gender Equality Scale, 1995–2000 (five-item) as the dependent variable, controlling for *societal modernization* (Human Development Index, 1998; level of democratization, 1999) and *social background* (age, gender, education, income, frequency of religious attendance, work status, marital status, children, and family savings). For details of the full model and the control variables, see Table 2.3 and Appendix B. The religious denominations are coded as dummy (0/1) variables.
Source: Pooled WVS/EVS, 1995–2001.

strength of religiosity on the 100-point Gender Equality Scale 1995–2000, as the dependent variable, controlling for *societal modernization* (the 1998 Human Development Index and the 1999 Freedom House level of democratization) as well as *social background* variables (age, gender, education, income, frequency of religious attendance, work status, marital status, children, and family savings), factors all found to be important when used earlier in Chapter 2. Given the large size of the sample, the usual tests of statistical significance are not helpful in interpreting the results of the analysis, so we focus on the strength of the standardized beta coefficients.

The results of this analysis demonstrate that the *type* of religion matters for beliefs about gender equality far more than the *strength* of religiosity. In Table 3.4, the strongest contrast in attitudes toward the appropriate division of sex roles among women and men is that between Western Christian and nondenominational populations living in affluent postindustrial societies, who adhere to the most egalitarian beliefs about the family, workforce, and politics, and Muslims living in poorer, agrarian nations, who are by far the most traditional group in their attitudes toward gender equality. Moreover, these patterns continue to prove significant in the multivariate analysis presented in Table 3.5, even after controlling for levels of societal and democratic development and the standard social variables such as age, gender, and education that we have already established as explanatory factors. This suggests that religious beliefs are not simply a by-product of the fact that many Muslims can be found living in poorer societies in North Africa, the Middle East, and Asia; instead, the evidence indicates that traditional religious values and religious laws have played an important role in reinforcing social norms of a separate and subordinate role for women as homemakers and mothers, and a role for men as patriarchs within the family and primary breadwinners in the paid workforce.[19] If we compare attitudes toward both gender equality and the indicators of sexual liberalization discussed earlier (including approval or disapproval of divorce, abortion, prostitution, and homosexuality) by predominant type of religion, rather than by type of socioeconomic development, the results confirm two striking and important patterns. First, there is a persistent gap in support for gender equality and sexual liberalization between the West (which is most liberal), Islamic societies (which are most traditional), and all other societies (which fall between these extremes). Another finding has very important implications: the gap between the West and Islam is usually narrowest among the oldest generation, but this gap has steadily widened across all the indicators as the younger generations in Western societies have become progressively more liberal and egalitarian, while the younger generations in Islamic societies remain as traditional as their parents and grandparents. This suggests that Islamic societies have not experienced a backlash against liberal Western sexual mores among the younger generations, as some popular accounts assume, but rather that young Muslims remain unchanged despite the transformation of lifestyles and beliefs experienced among their peers living in postindustrial societies.[20] But the result is a growing gap between the basic values of young people in Islamic societies and those in the West.

Moreover, these predominant beliefs and values matter not only for cultural attitudes, but also for the actual conditions of men and women's lives. Table 3.6 shows the relationship at the national level between the proportion of the population adhering to different religious denominations, the strength of religiosity, and a range of common social indicators of gender equality selected from the UNDP *Human Development Report 2001* as the dependent variables. The cross-national comparison is restricted to the ninty-three poorer, agrarian societies around the world, in order to isolate the impact of religious denominations by controlling for countries at similarly low levels of human development. The differences in the indicators cannot be explained simply as by-products of low per capita income or the restricted availability of educational opportunities or maternal health care, since all of the nations under comparison are classified with a Human Development Index of .739 or below and a per capita annual income of about $1,000 or less. The male/female ratio measures that are used also provide the fairest indicators, as this statistic focuses on relative disparities between women's and men's lives within each of these societies, rather than on absolute levels of education or development. The majority religion in each nation is classified based on the CIA *World Factbook, 2001*. The results of the analysis, shown in Table 3.6, confirm that religion matters, not only for cultural attitudes but also for the opportunities and constraints on women's lives, such as the ratio of females to males in educational enrolment, the female adult literacy rate, the use of contraception, and the UNDP Gender-Related Development Index, as well as for opportunities for women in the paid workforce and in parliamentary representation.

Conclusions and Discussion

An extensive literature in sociology, anthropology, social psychology, divinity studies, and women's studies has long argued that religion has exerted a decisive impact on the cultural perceptions of the appropriate division of labor between men and women, and that it has shaped social norms and sexual values. The influence of religious authorities

TABLE 3.6. *Type of religious culture and gender equality indicators in agrarian states*

	Year	Catholic	Protestant	Buddhist	Muslim	All
Women's empowerment						
Female professionals and administrators (%)	1997	25	15	18	10	15
Female administrators and managers (%)	1997	46	38	31	28	35
Women in the lower house (%)	2001	11	8	13	6	9
Women's education						
Female/male adult literacy, ratio	1997	88	84	80	65	75
Female/male economic activity rate, ratio	1997	57	76	81	62	68
Female/male primary education enrollment, ratio	1997	98	96	97	83	91
Female/male secondary education enrollment, ratio	1997	95	84	95	72	82
Female/male tertiary education enrollment, ratio	1997	93	71	89	58	69
Reproduction						
Contraceptive prevalence rate (%)	1990–98	42	27	39	31	33
Births to mothers under twenty (%)	1991–97	13	17	8	9	11
Composite UNDP indicators						
Gender-related development index (GDI), value	1997	.65	.52	.58	.53	.55
Gender empowerment measure (GEM), value	1997	.45	.35	.32	.28	.35
Total number of agrarian states worldwide		*16*	*26*	*7*	*36*	*93*

Note: The comparison includes all ninety-three agrarian states worldwide for which data is available. The classification of the major religion (adhered to by the largest population) in states around the world is based on CIA. *The World Factbook, 2001.* Washington, DC: Central Intelligence Agency.
Source: <http://www.cia.gov/cia/publications/factbook> For the classification of nations, see Appendix A. The gender-related social indicators are from UNDP. 2000. *Human Development Report, 2000.* New York: UNDP/Oxford University Press. It should be noted that UNDP data is missing in some indicators, making the total number of nations in each category less than the total.

70

has often served to limit opportunities for women outside the home, in education, at work, and in positions of authority. The results of this study confirm that religion plays an important role in this regard; in particular, the study establishes four key findings:

1. A process of secularization has gradually accompanied societal modernization, weakening the strength of religious values among the younger generation in postindustrial societies and fuelling the rising tide of gender equality.

2. Cohort analysis shows that postindustrial societies have experienced a parallel liberalization of moral values regarding sexuality among the younger generation, exemplified by attitudes toward the issues of abortion, homosexuality, prostitution, and divorce.

3. At the same time, religiosity continues to exert a strong influence on social norms about the appropriate division of sex roles in the home, the workforce, and in the public sphere, especially in agrarian societies.

4. Attitudes towards women vary among adherents of different religious sects and denominations; in particular, an Islamic religious heritage is one of the most powerful barriers to the rising tide of gender equality.

It remains to be seen how far the coherent cultural shifts in attitudes toward gender equality that we have uncovered matter for gender differences in public life, particularly among the electorate, in civic society, and in political leadership. It is to these matters that we now turn.

PART II

THE CONSEQUENCES OF THE RISING TIDE

There is a tide in the affairs of men
Which, taken at the flood, leads on to fortune.
Shakespeare, *Julius Caesar*

4

The Gender Gap in Voting and Public Opinion

We have explored the causes of the rising tide of gender equality, but not yet the consequences. During the postwar era, the conventional wisdom in political science held that women in Western democracies were politically more conservative than men. Gender differences in party preferences were never as marked as the classic electoral cleavages of class, region, and religion; there were no mass "women's parties" like those associated with trade unions, regions, and churches. Nevertheless, "women's conservatism" was seen as a persistent and well-established phenomenon. During the 1980s, this conventional wisdom came under increasing challenge. In many West European countries, a process of gender *dealignment* appeared, with studies reporting minimal sex differences in voting choice and party preference. And in the United States, the phenomenon of the gender gap manifested itself in the early 1980s, with women shifting their allegiance toward the Democratic Party while men moved toward the Republican Party on a stable and consistent basis, reversing the previous pattern of voting and partisanship.[1]

This gender realignment in the United States raises the question of whether similar developments are occurring elsewhere. If this phenomenon is caused by factors inherent in societal modernization, such as increased female participation in the paid workforce, the break-up of the traditional family, and the transformation of sex roles in the home, then we would expect to find similar gender gaps emerging in other postindustrial nations. On the other hand, if the gender gap is caused by factors that are distinctive to American politics, such as its lack of strong class cleavages, the centrist pattern of two-party competition, and the salience of issues such as abortion and affirmative action, then the modern gender gap in the United States might be still another example of American exceptionalism.[2] Answering this question is important in order to clarify whether the rising tide of gender equality is altering women's political power in many nations, and also to provide a clearer theoretical understanding of the underlying process of value change.

This chapter focuses on comparing gender differences in ideology, electoral preferences, and public opinion, the most common meaning of the term "gender gap," in more than seventy nations. Building on previous chapters, we hypothesize that (1) the process of societal modernization is reshaping the political values and attitudes of women and men, just as it has altered other basic values. (2) In particular, women are now moving to the left of men, even controlling for structural differences in men's and women's lives such as religiosity, education, and workforce participation. (3) Because this transition is still taking place, we would expect to find substantial variations in this pattern by age cohort in postindustrial societies, with older women remaining more conservative than men, while the younger generation of women move to the left of men. If this is indeed the case, these societies would seem to be experiencing an intergenerational ideological realignment in gender politics that is likely to persist, given the long-term process of generational replacement.

Theoretical Framework

The Orthodox Account of Female Conservatism

Research on gender differences in the electorate has been a recurrent theme in political science beginning with the earliest systematic surveys of voting behavior.[3] Many hoped, and others feared, that once women were enfranchised there would be a distinctive "women's vote." Gender was not regarded as a primary electoral cleavage, equivalent to class, region, and religion, because women and men experienced many cross-cutting forces, but the seminal account of European voting behavior by Lipset and Rokkan viewed gender as one of the secondary cleavages shaping the electoral base of party politics.[4]

TABLE 4.1. *The gender gap in the early 1970s*

	Men	Women	Gap
Italy	44	30	−14
Germany	60	47	−13
Britain	50	41	−9
Belgium	40	36	−6
France	54	49	−5
The Netherlands	47	45	−2
United States	32	37	+5

Note: Percentage supporting parties of the left.
Source: Ronald Inglehart. 1977. *The Silent Revolution: Changing Values and Political Styles among Western Publics.* Princeton, NJ: Princeton University Press.

The early classics of the 1950s and 1960s established the orthodoxy in political science: gender differences in voting were generally fairly modest, but women were likelier than men to support center-right parties in Western Europe and in the United States, a pattern that we can term the "*traditional* gender gap."[5] Most explanations of the traditional gender gap emphasized structural differences between men and women in religiosity, longevity, and labor force participation; for example, women in Italy and France were more likely to attend churches associated with Christian Democratic parties.[6] During this era, women were also commonly assumed to be more conservative in their political attitudes and values, producing an ideological gap underpinning their party preferences.[7] The conventional wisdom was summarized in *The Civic Culture*, first published in 1963: "Wherever the consequences of women's suffrage have been studied, it would appear that women differ from men in their political behavior only in being somewhat more frequently apathetic, parochial, [and] conservative.... Our data, on the whole, confirm the findings reported in the literature."[8] Inglehart confirmed that during the early 1970s, women remained more likely than men to support Christian Democratic and Conservative parties in Western Europe, particularly in Italy and Germany (see Table 4.1), although a new pattern seemed to be emerging in the United States, which he speculated might represent the wave of the future.[9] Nevertheless, the prevailing view was that the relative conservatism of women was a fixed, structural characteristic.

Theories of Gender Dealignment

This orthodoxy came under increasing challenge during the 1980s, when scholars in many Western countries found a pattern of gender dealignment among the electorate. Voting studies noted this pattern in Britain[10] as well as in Germany,[11] the Netherlands,[12] and New Zealand.[13] This literature suggested that the old pattern of female conservatism was apparently no longer evident; instead, the situation in the 1980s seemed contingent upon political circumstances: in some established democracies women seemed to lean to the right, in others to the left (particularly in Nordic societies),[14] and in others no significant differences could be detected.[15] Studies of ideological self-placement, rather than voting choice, found that during the mid-1980s women in Western Europe saw themselves as slightly more conservative than men, although this gap was reduced when controls were incorporated for labor force participation and religiosity.[16] The pattern seemed consistent with dealignment theories suggesting that the impact of traditional social-party linkages had weakened in many established democracies, notably the force of social class and religion.[17] These theories argued that voters had become more instrumental. Under these conditions, no party could expect to enjoy a persistent and habitual advantage among women or men; instead, contingent factors such as government performance, party policies, and leadership images would dominate voting decisions.

Theories of Gender Realignment

During the last decade, however, there has been much speculation, although little concrete evidence, that women were realigning to the left throughout postindustrial societies, a situation that we will term the "*modern* gender gap," replicating the pattern that first emerged in the United States. The process of "partisan realignment" is understood to produce an enduring and stable change in the mass coalitional basis of party politics. A classic example occurred in the United States when African-Americans moved toward the Democrats during the 1950s and 1960s, while Southern white conservatives shifted toward the Republicans, leading to a persistent and deep-rooted change in the racial basis of American party politics.[18] In the United States, the process of gender realignment meant that although women leaned toward the Republican Party in the 1952, 1956, and 1960 presidential elections, during the 1960s and 1970s traditional gender differences in the electorate faded, and from the 1980s onward the modern voting gap became apparent in successive presidential, gubernatorial, and state-level contests, as well as in levels of Democratic Party identification.[19] The modern gender gap in American elections has not been as large as cleavages based on race or religion; nevertheless, this pattern has proved consistent, stable, and decisive in many contests, representing a long-term shift in the mass basis of electoral competition in the United States.

The Developmental Theory of Gender Realignment

What might cause gender realignment to occur? We hypothesize that structural developments lead to, and interact with, cultural shifts that tend to reshape political values. The long-term trajectory of value transformation is generally predictable and coherent, although the pace of realignment within each country remains contingent upon institutional contexts, the political mobilization of major social cleavages, and other situation-specific conditions. Factors affecting this process include how far leaders respond strategically to shifts in public opinion, which groups are mobilized into politics, and patterns of party competition. Previous chapters have demonstrated how preindustrial and agrarian societies continue to be characterized by sharply differentiated gender roles that discourage women from taking jobs outside the home. As we have already seen, virtually all preindustrial societies emphasize traditional sex roles: childbearing and child rearing are regarded as the central goal for women and their most important function in life; careers in the paid workforce outside the home remain predominately male. Religiosity reinforces traditional sex roles. By contrast, we have shown how gender roles converge in postindustrial societies due to the cultural shift in attitudes toward women and the structural revolution in the paid labor force, in educational opportunities for women, and in the characteristics of modern families. This revolution occurred during the twentieth century in the most developed nations, producing contrasting experiences for the younger generation of women compared to their mothers and grandmothers. As women's lives change in postindustrial societies, we expect that this process will influence broader social values, political attitudes, ideological orientations, and ultimately partisan preferences.

This account emphasizes that structural and cultural trends common to postindustrial societies have led to secularization and to more egalitarian sex roles, both of which have realigned women's political values, particularly among the younger generation. These hypotheses generate certain testable propositions about how the size and direction of the differences between women and men in left-right political ideology and in left-right voting behavior should vary systematically, under four conditions:

1. First, if we analyze *trends over time*, we would expect to find that women in recent decades have gradually shifted to the left in their voting behavior and political ideology.

2. The transformation of sex roles in the paid labor force, in education, and in the family has gone much further in postindustrial than in preindustrial societies, as has the process of value change. Consequently, in *cross-national comparisons*, we would expect to find that the *modern* gender gap has advanced furthest in postindustrial societies.

3. If we compare *generational cohorts* within postindustrial societies, as indirect evidence of longitudinal change, we would also predict that the ideological gender gap would reverse by birth cohorts, given the way that changes in lifestyles and cultural trends have transformed the lives of older and younger groups of women in these nations. Previous studies in Britain have examined the pattern of the gender gap by generation, with younger women leaning left, while older women remain more conservative than their male counterparts.[20] Consequently, we would hypothesize that in these countries, the modern gender gap should be evident among the younger generation, and the traditional gap should remain relatively strong among the older cohorts. These generational patterns would not be expected in industrialized or developing societies, since structural and cultural changes in these societies have taken different pathways.

4. Finally, if we compare *social groups within societies*, we would expect to find that women today hold more left-oriented values than men, in terms of support for an active role for government in social protection and public ownership of business and industry, and in support for a variety of political issues. Support for

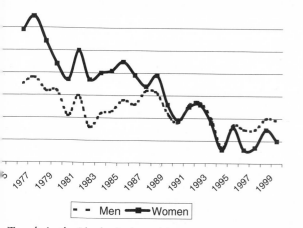

Trends in the ideological gender gap, 1973–99, EU-5. *Note*: This
rends in left-right ideological self-placement among the five coun-
ed in the surveys throughout this period (Italy, France, Germany,
nd the Netherlands). *Source*: Eurobarometer surveys, European

ehavior

l values can affect electoral behavior, especially where party
·n revolves around programmatic differences on economic
i as the role of public ownership or the welfare state; but
ountries other issues may prove more important. Direct evi-
·ends in the electoral gender gap can be compared in eleven
·rial societies where information about voting preferences is
·n successive waves of the WVS/EVS since the early 1980s.
·ts were asked: *"If there were a national election tomorrow,*
·arty on this list would you vote?" The parties are classified
·ft-right spectrum using the 1993 Huber and Inglehart scale
·xpert ratings of the positions of parties in forty-two coun-
·a ten-point left-right scale.[23] This measure allows compar-
·mean left-right positions of women and men voters within
·try, calculating the voting gap as the difference between
·ns, tested for significance with ANOVA.[24] The results in
·how a mixed pattern for the early 1980s: in four countries
·lands, the United States, Denmark, and Italy) women leaned
·while in six others they leaned rightward. But the pattern of
·r time is consistent: in countries where women were more

left-leaning values among women and men can be expected to
vary systematically according to *structural factors*, namely, participation in the paid labor force, class, education, marital status,
union membership, and religiosity, as well as according to *cultural factors*, including attitudes toward gender equality, general
beliefs about the role of government, and postmaterialist values.

Ideological Values and Voting Behavior

Attitudes toward the Role of Government

Does the evidence support these propositions? One can compare left-
right economic values using a variety of indicators, but perhaps the
most common measure suitable for cross-national analysis concerns
attitudes toward the role of the state and the marketplace. The classic
left-right issue cleavage, long dividing socialists and conservatives, concerns how far government should go in providing social protection and
an economic safety net via the welfare state, and how far the private
sector and the free market should be unconstrained by the state. The
World Values Surveys / European Values Surveys, 1990–2000, tap these
values with two items that form a single reliable indicator; here they
are recoded so that high scores represent the conservative position and
standardized to a 100-point Role of Government Scale, for ease of
interpretation. The items ask the following:

*"Now I would like you to tell me your views on various issues. How would you
place your views on this scale? 1 means you agree completely with the statement on
the left. 10 means you agree completely with the statement on the right, and if your
views fall in-between you can choose any number in-between.*

- *Private ownership of business and industry should be increased (10) – Government ownership of business ands industry should be increased (1).*
- *The government should take more responsibility to ensure that everyone is
provided for (1) – People should take more responsibilities to provide for
themselves (10)."*

Comparing the mean scores on the Role of Government Scale, as shown
in Figure 4.1, confirms the expectation that across most countries of
the world, women today hold more left-leaning views than men, with
the gender gap being particularly strong in poorer nations such as
Uganda, Ghana, and Bangladesh, as well as in some middle-income

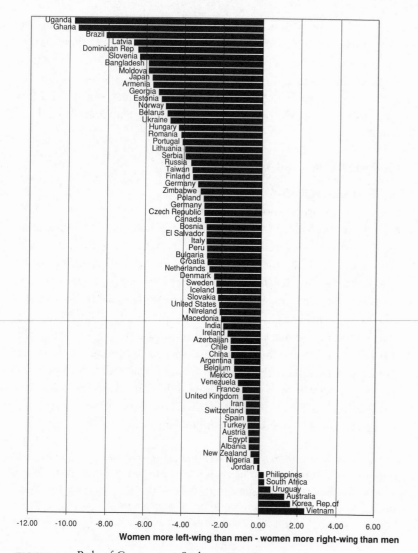

FIGURE 4.1. Role of Government Scale, 1990–2001.

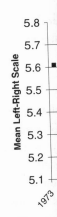

FIGURE 4
shows th
tries incl
Belgium
Union.

at least, the evidence supports the
ingly more favorable to an active r
American public opinion have fou

Ideological Values

But have the broad ideological pos
The longest cross-national series
positions is the Eurobarometer s
European Union countries from t
of the member countries have aff
this does not provide comparisons
the series does provide the best cr
trends in how women and men have
ing the last thirty years. The Euroba
themselves on a ten-point scale ran
This measure of political ideology is
national research, since there is evi
with the idea of a left-right scale
multiparty contexts, at least in We
component of party identification.
shown in Figure 4.2, confirm that t
remained relatively stable since the
fluctuations around the mean: in 1
selves at 5.25 on the left-right scale
in 1999. In the early 1970s, Europe
ologically to the right of men, but
mid-1980s, and by the mid-1990s
men. In 1973, women on average p
to the right of men); thirty years lat
(slightly to the left of men). Moreov
a broader comparison; similar trend
the eleven nations included in every
(Britain, West Germany, Italy, Spain
Africa, Hungary, Sweden, Argentina,
the women in these countries place
on this ideological scale; in the early
difference; and by the mid-1990s, th
had moved to the left of men.

Elector
Ideolog
compe
issues
in man
dence
postin
availa
Respo
for wh
along
based
tries a
ison c
each
group
Table
(the N
to the
chang

industrializing nations such as Latvia and Brazil, and in some postindustrial nations such as Japan and Norway. In some countries, however,
the gender gap is minimal, and there are even a few nations where
women are more conservative than men in their views of the role
of government, such as Vietnam and South Korea. On this indicator,

TABLE 4.2. *Trends in the voting gap in the 1980s and 1990s*

	1981 Gap	1990 Gap	1995 Gap
The Netherlands	.08	.51 **	
Belgium	−.39 **	−.08	
France	−.39 *	−.09	
Canada	.01	.23	
Britain	−.25	−.03	
West Germany	−.06 *	.16 *	.05
Ireland	−.28	−.20	
United States	.14	.15 **	.35 **
Spain	−.08	−.21 *	−.28 **
Denmark	.84 **	.69 **	
Italy	.39 **	.05	

Note: The difference between the mean position of women and men on the ten-point voting scale. A negative figure represents women more conservative than men; a positive figure represents women more left-leaning than men. Sig. ** p. = 01, * p. = 05.
Source: WVS/EVS, 1981–95.

conservative in 1981, this tendency weakens over time, although it does not disappear entirely, except in Spain. The modern gender gap, with women being more left-leaning than men, is evident in every wave in the United States; it consolidates over time in the Netherlands; and it emerges by the 1990s in Canada and West Germany.[25]

Cohort Analysis of Ideological Change

Unfortunately, direct cross-national evidence that could be used to examine voting behavior and ideological trends over many decades in a wider range of societies is unavailable. As in previous chapters, however, we can utilize indirect evidence available through cohort analysis to compare the size and direction of the ideological gap among older and younger generations in over seventy nations included in the pooled WVS/EVS, 1981–2000. Differences between younger and older age groups may be the result of life-cycle effects; social and political values may change as people enter the workforce, marry and have children, or enter retirement. These effects cannot be ruled out on the basis of cross-sectional survey evidence. Cohort effects emerge when formative experiences during childhood, adolescence, and early adulthood leave an enduring imprint on basic social values and core political attitudes.

Consequently, societies experiencing rapid societal modernization and human development should display contrasts between the older generations – those who grew up during World War II and earlier – and succeeding cohorts. In the WVS/EVS surveys, as in the Eurobarometer surveys, political ideology is measured by asking people to place themselves on a ten-point scale ranging from left (1) to right (10). This measure allows consistent comparison within a country at different periods of time, avoids the problems of coding voting preferences on a left-right scale for parties experiencing rapid change, such as during the democratic transition in Central and Eastern Europe, and avoids limitations on the reliability of expert judgments. We calculated an "ideological gap" by finding the difference in the mean self-placement of women and men on these scales; for example, if women place themselves at 5.5 and men at 6.8, the resulting ideological gap is +1.3. For consistency in the analysis, a negative figure indicates that women in a given country see themselves as more conservative than men (the traditional gender gap), while a positive figure indicates that women place themselves further left than men (the modern gender gap). Again, ANOVA is employed to test the statistical significance of the differences in the group means within each society.

Figure 4.3 provides evidence suggesting that the gender gap in political ideology is consistently linked with the process of modernization: different patterns of cohort change emerge in different types of society. In postindustrial nations, the pre-war cohorts display the traditional gender gap, with women consistently placing themselves to the right of men. The ideological gap closes in the middle cohorts, and then reverses polarity among the postwar cohorts, so that younger women consistently place themselves to the left of younger men. The consistency of the slope from older to younger female cohorts suggests a gradual shift among women, who have steadily and persistently moved from right to left. By contrast, there is a fainter pattern in these societies among men, who have remained relatively stable across successive cohorts. Industrialized societies at lower levels of development show a more stable pattern among cohorts, although even here, in the older cohorts women place themselves slightly to the right of the men, while younger women place themselves slightly to the left of younger men. The preindustrial societies show no evidence of cohort change – but, contrary to expectations, women are consistently slightly to the left of

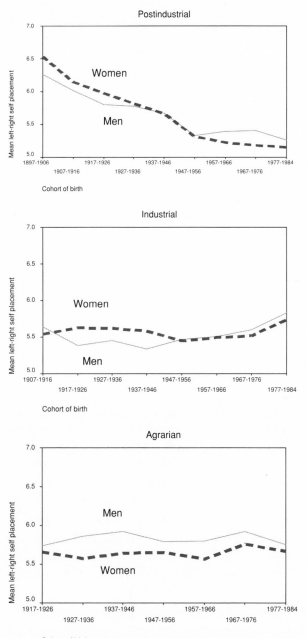

FIGURE 4.3. Ideological left-right self-placement by gender and type of society.

men. This suggests that theories of electoral competition that have been developed to explain partisan loyalties in the context of programmatic parties in Western Europe may not apply in developing nations, where parties are based more on personalistic appeals, leadership factions, and ethnic loyalties.

The pattern of longitudinal ideological trends over thirty years in the Eurobarometer surveys, the patterns of voting behavior in the World Values Surveys / European Values Surveys beginning in the early 1980s, and indirect evidence from cohort analysis all point to the conclusion that the modernization process tends to bring realignment to the left among women, with the greatest evidence of ideological change being evident in the richest nations, where women have experienced the greatest transformation in their lifestyles and sex roles. No comparable realignment seems to have occurred in poorer societies.

Explaining Gender Realignment

To understand support for left-leaning values, and to examine the reasons for gender realignment in postindustrial nations, the roles of both structural and cultural factors need to be considered.

Structural Explanations

Structural accounts explain gender differences in electoral behavior, public opinion, and left-right ideology by women's and men's lifestyles and roles in the workforce, home, and family. In Lipset and Rokkan's classic theory, social class, region, and religion were viewed as the most important political cleavages in many West European countries, because they reflected broadly based and long-standing social and economic divisions within society at the time when the Western democracies were emerging.[26] Contemporary party systems resulted from complex historical processes, notably the national and industrial revolutions experienced by societies from the seventeenth century onwards. In Europe, the cleavage between church and state produced religious support for Christian Democrat parties; the cleavage between landowners and industrialists helped to create agrarian parties; and the cleavage between employers and workers generated the parties of the left. Thus groups based on social class, religion, language, ethnicity, and region became the primary building blocks for the political system. Parties mobilized coalitions of social groups and appealed to their interests. By contrast, gender was usually regarded as secondary, since women's interests were seen as divided by crosscutting cleavages such as class, ethnicity, and generation. The varying pattern of social cleavages across Europe in the nineteenth and early twentieth centuries established the essential framework for contemporary party systems. After the systems were established, Lipset and Rokkan suggest, they "froze" as parties strengthened links with their supporters and integrated new social cleavages. In most countries, women won the franchise after the modern party system was established, and they were therefore absorbed into the existing framework.

The gender gap can be explained within this general theoretical framework in two alternative ways. For dealignment theorists, the development of the modern gender gap is seen as part of a broader loosening of the traditional ties between social groups and parties, particularly the weakening of class alignments.[27] The process of secularization that we have already examined can be expected to play a major role in cultural and political change. In the past, women tended to be more religious; Lipset argues that this, and particularly women's Catholicism, helped to explain greater female support for Christian Democrat parties during the postwar era.[28] As already observed, trends in secularization have gradually weakened religiosity in affluent nations, eroding church-party linkages, although there is far greater religiosity in poorer preindustrial societies. Since the early 1970s, party fragmentation has grown in many established democracies, symbolized by the sudden rise of new regional, xenophobic, and Green parties in countries such as Italy, Canada, France, and Germany. New cleavages in society, produced by the rise of new value priorities, have changed the priorities of the policy agenda, with a decline in the old left-right politics of redistribution and rising emphasis on issues involving the environment, women's rights, and the quality of life.[29] The old cleavages of class and religion have declined in importance, opening the way for the politics of gender, region, and ethnicity to become increasingly salient.

A related explanation argues that structural change in postindustrial nations has produced a divergence in the socioeconomic position of women and men, so that gender can be seen as a basic social cleavage reflecting distinctive political interests. In this view, women's new roles within the family, the labor market, the welfare state, and the community may be expected to lead to different patterns of political participation, partisan loyalties, and political priorities on such issues as child care, family support, public transport, the environment and technology, reproductive rights, welfare, education, and defense. If this process has affected the gender gap in voting behavior, considerable differences in the size of the voting gap could be expected depending on levels of female education, income, age, occupation, and marital status. But findings from previous studies in the United States are divided concerning this explanation. Miller concluded that the socioeconomic experiences of American women and men are insufficient to explain gender differences in the vote, since the gender gap persisted even after controlling for many demographic and social characteristics.[30] But in another study, Susan Carroll noted that the gender gap was strongest among two groups: on the one hand, professional, college-educated, and fairly affluent groups, and on the other hand, the less well-off and unmarried groups.[31] The common factor linking women in these two groups, Carroll suggested, is economic and psychological autonomy from men. A continuing pattern of gender differences by high- and low-income group has been confirmed by more recent American studies.[32] Women's increasing entry into higher education can also be expected to influence their political values and priorities, as many studies of public opinion have reported that education is consistently associated with more liberal attitudes on a wide range of issues, including feminist attitudes.[33] In a related argument, Klein suggests that the entry of more women into the paid labor force in postindustrial nations may have altered their objective economic interests, which may in turn encourage their support for parties of the left.[34] Klein argues that women's work experiences fundamentally alter their roles and expectations, while the social context facilitates a social network with different values. As more and more women enter the paid labor force, they gain direct experience with pervasive patterns of horizontal and vertical occupational segregation.[35] Working women are often overrepresented in low-paid jobs, experiencing pay disparities, lower socioeconomic status, and higher levels of female poverty.[36] Moreover, mobilizing agencies have responded to the feminization of the workforce; in recent decades, trade unions have made increasing efforts to expand their membership base by recruiting working gap in party support.[43] If this is the case, we would expect to find the modern gender gap in postindustrial societies to be stronger among feminist women.

Moreover, there may be broader attitudinal differences between men and women that give rise to gender differences in electoral behavior and partisan support. Studies of public opinion in the United States and Western Europe have found that women often display relatively strong support for government spending on the welfare state, public services, and environmental protection, as well as opting for pacifism in the deployment of military force.[44] These latent gender differences in public opinion can be expected to become manifest in electoral preferences when these issues become salient and divide the major parties. The predominant ethos in Conservative and Christian Democratic parties of the right usually favors traditional roles for women in the home and family, equal opportunities rather than affirmative action to remove problems of sex discrimination in the marketplace, a minimal role for the state in social protection policies, and a stronger role for defense and security services. By contrast, reflecting their core beliefs and overall philosophy, parties of the left have been committed to maintaining a comprehensive welfare state and a strong social safety net for public services such as health, pensions, education, transportation, and child care, as well as pacifism in foreign policy. Women are often the prime beneficiaries of government services such as pensions and child care, as well as constituting many of the employees in professional, administrative, and service work in the health care and educational sectors. Although some Labour, Socialist, and Communist parties retain traditional orientations toward the division of sex roles, these parties usually promote more egalitarian policies toward women, such as the adoption of gender quotas in party posts and candidate recruitment for elected office.[45]

Analysis and Results

Before analyzing the relative impact of structural and cultural explanations, we will first examine the mean conservative ideology scale among women and men in postindustrial societies, using the 1995–2002 World Values Surveys / European Values Surveys. Table 4.3 shows that the gender differences across most categories are modest, with most people women,[37] a process that can also be expected to move this group towards the left.

Lastly, marital status and the presence of dependent children have often been regarded as particularly important structural factors explaining the gender gap in America.[38] Women who are divorced or do not marry have different lifestyles and interests from those who are married or cohabiting, and these differences can be expected to influence their perceptions of women's roles in the family and society and their attitudes toward broader issues such as family policy. In this view, therefore, the electoral behavior and political values of women and men should be predicted by the standard social and demographic background variables available in surveys, including religiosity, education, participation in the labor force, income and socioeconomic status, trade union membership, marital status, and children.[39]

Cultural Explanations

Structural factors can be viewed as interacting with, and causing, shifts in cultural attitudes and values that may subsequently exert an independent effect upon voting choice. We have already demonstrated the contrasts in beliefs about egalitarian versus traditional sex roles; and the Gender Equality Scale used in Chapter 2 can be expected to predict broader political and ideological differences as well. Postmodernization theory suggests that the growth of postmaterialist values among the younger generation in postindustrial societies has led to a gradual erosion of class-based politics, opening the way for greater priority being given to the values of freedom, self-expression, and gender equality.[40] This pervasive cultural shift has increased the salience of issues such as reproductive choice, sexual harassment in the workplace, and equal opportunities, although a time lag can be expected between the emergence of new issues on the policy agenda and the response of the party system.[41] If the modernization process has influenced gender realignment, support for postmaterialist values should be closely associated with female support for parties of the left. In addition, Conover has argued that the electoral gap in America has been strongly influenced by feminism, the women's movement, and mobilization around issues of gender equality.[42] In this view, the growth of feminist identity and consciousness has been the catalyst producing the modern gender

TABLE 4.3. *The Left-Right Ideology Scale by gender in postindustrial societies,*
1995–2001

	Women	Men	Diff
Education			
High	5.25	5.43	0.18
Moderate	5.48	5.56	0.08
Low	5.60	5.46	−0.14
Age group			
Under 30	5.12	5.26	0.14
30–59	5.37	5.39	0.02
60+	5.82	5.72	−0.10
R's occupational class			
Manager/professional	5.52	5.77	0.25
Lower-middle	5.43	5.31	−0.12
Skilled working	5.33	5.20	−0.13
Unskilled working	5.20	5.16	−0.04
Work status			
Paid work	5.42	5.54	0.12
Looking after home	5.53	..	
Marital status			
Cohabiting	5.04	5.29	0.25
Single	5.13	5.21	0.08
Separated	5.20	5.27	0.07
Divorced	5.26	5.17	−0.09
Widowed	5.26	5.61	0.35
Married	5.51	5.56	0.05
Children			
No children	5.16	5.21	0.05
At least one child	5.44	5.47	0.03
Religiosity			
Attend service every week	4.99	5.02	0.03
Never attend	5.91	6.08	0.17
Gender equality			
Traditionalist	5.90	5.97	0.07
Egalitarian	5.49	5.51	0.03
Religion			
Catholic	5.68	5.67	−0.01
Protestant	5.63	5.79	0.16
Orthodox	5.38	5.4	0.02
Jewish	5.74	5.51	−0.23
Muslim	5.67	6.08	0.41
All	5.41	5.44	

Note: The mean position of women and men on the ten-point Left-Right Ideology Scale,
coded from left (low) to right (high). In the "difference" column, a negative figure represents women more conservative than men; a positive figure represents women more
left-leaning than men.

Source: Pooled WVS/EVS, 1995–2001.

clustered in the center of the ten-point scale. Nevertheless, some gender differences are evident; women are slightly more conservative than men among the less educated, the oldest (60+) generation, those looking after the home rather than in the workforce, the lower-middle or working classes, the divorced, and those of Catholic or Jewish faith. By contrast, men are slightly more conservative than women across all other categories, with this pattern clearest among Muslims, those with a university education, and the under thirty age group. If we extrapolate from these preliminary findings to the broader social trends that we have already observed, it suggests that more left-leaning women are found among the younger generation of well-educated working women, a group that has expanded in recent decades. Not all of the results point in a consistent direction, but if these patterns persist, it suggests that, owing to trends in educational and employment opportunities and the long-term process of generational turnover, women will probably gradually drift further to the left of men in the future.

Nevertheless, these preliminary findings could be spurious, and we have not yet explored the impact of cultural values. For a more comprehensive multivariate analysis, we will use ordinary least-squares regression models with the ten-point left-right ideological scale as the dependent variable, again using the pooled 1995–2000 WVS/EVS across all nations. Pooling the data assumes that ideological positions should be relatively stable, so that there will be minimal change over the last two waves of the surveys. There may be some short-term fluctuations in particular countries – for example, those caused by a change of party government – but these effects would tend to cancel out across many societies. A negative coefficient in the models indicates that women are more conservative than men; a positive coefficient indicates that women place themselves to the left of men. In Model 1, we explore the impact of gender on the left-right ideology scale without any controls. This indicates the direction and significance of the direct effect of gender on political ideology. Model 2 then adds structural controls, including age, education, religiosity, class, labor force participation, marital status, and trade union membership, in that order, for the reasons already discussed. (See Appendix B for full details of the items and coding.) Model 3 adds cultural factors, measured by the Gender Equality Scale already used in Chapter 3, support for postmaterialist values, and a scaled battery of two items measuring attitudes toward the role of government. Our analysis is designed to determine whether gender remains a significant predictor of political ideology after controlling for these factors. The results of the full models are given in detail in Table 4.4 for the pooled sample in all societies; Table 4.5 compares the results of the full model for postindustrial, industrialized, and preindustrial societies.

Model 1 in Table 4.4 indicates that gender does predict ideology, with women leaning left, confirming the existence of the modern gender gap. Differences between men and women are modest in size but statistically significant. Model 2 shows that gender remains important even after controlling for social structure – in fact, the gender coefficient becomes stronger. As already observed, the effects of gender interact with age. The results of the model suggest that the modern gender gap cannot be explained, as some previous research suggests,[46] as simply the result of differences between women and men in religiosity, class, age, marital status, or participation in the labor force. In postindustrial societies, the pattern of the ideological gender gap by age group is an important indicator of generational change: among the youngest group, women are more left-leaning than men, while among those over sixty-five the gender gap reversed, with women more conservative. In view of the long-term process of population replacement, this pattern may have important future consequences, moving women gradually further left. The other social variables behave in the expected manner, with stronger conservative values being evident among the older generation, the religious, and the middle class; by contrast, trade union membership, employment, and education were associated with more left-leaning positions. Lastly, Model 3 adds the attitudinal variables, which reduce the effect of gender, which nevertheless remains significant. In the final model, support for postmaterialist values, the Gender Equality Scale, and the Role of Government Scale are among the strongest predictors of left-right ideology, along with religiosity, although the structural variables also remain significant, with the exception of age. This final model suggests that the modern gender gap is more strongly influenced by culture than by social structure.[47] In other words, women have moved to the left ideologically primarily because of a broad process of value change; the shift towards more egalitarian attitudes associated with postmaterialism and sex roles are

TABLE 4.4. *The impact of gender on the Left-Right Ideology Scale, 1995–2001*

	Model 1: Gender with No Controls			Model 2: Gender + Social Controls			Model 3: Gender + Social + Cultural Controls		
	B	Beta	Sig.	B	Beta	Sig.	B	Beta	Sig.
Male gender (1)	.110	.024	***	.249	.053	***	.132	.028	***
Social structure									
Age (years)				.002	.017	***	.001	.009	N/s
Education (three categories)				-.063	-.021	***	-.076	-.024	***
Religiosity (100-point scale)				.014	.173	***	.012	.147	***
Middle Class (1/0)				.197	.041	***	.223	.047	***
In paid employment (1/0)				-.271	-.055	***	-.242	-.049	***
Married or cohabiting (1/0)				-.024	-.005	N/s	-.055	-.011	**
Union member (1/0)				-.127	-.023	***	-.121	-.022	***
Cultural values									
Gender Equality Scale							-.012	-.097	***
Postmaterialism							-.117	-.062	***
Role of Government Scale							.009	.087	***
Constant	5.52			4.71			5.45		
R	.024			.189			.235		
Adjusted R².	.001			.036			.055		

Note: The models are based on OLS regression analysis using the pooled WVS/EVS, 1995–2001, in fifty-nine nations. The figures are unstandardized (B) and standardized (Beta) coefficients representing the impact of the independent variables on the left-right ten-point ideology self-placement scale, where high equals most conservative. *Model 1* includes gender without any controls, where a positive coefficient denotes men more conservative than women. *Model 2* includes gender effects with social controls for age, education, religiosity (the 100-point scale used in Chapter 3), and dummy variables for respondent's occupational class (middle = 1), work status (full-time, part-time, or self-employment = 1), marital status (married or cohabiting = 1), and union membership (1). A dummy variable for the presence of children was also tested but dropped as insignificant. *Model 3* includes gender effects with social and attitudinal controls, the latter including the 100-point Gender Equality Scale used in Chapter 2, the twelve-item post-materialism scale, and a 100-point Role of Government Scale. Sig. * .05, ** .01, *** .001. All models were checked by tolerance and VIF statistics to be free of multicollinearity problems. See Appendix B for details of all coding and measurements.

Source: Pooled WVS/EVS, 1995–2001.

TABLE 4.5. *The impact of gender on the Left-Right Ideology Scale by type of society, 1995–2001*

	Agrarian			Industrial			Postindustrial		
	B	Beta	Sig.	B	Beta	Sig.	B	Beta	Sig.
Male Gender (1)	.221	.041	***	.071	.016	*	.092	.024	**
Social structure									
Age (years)	.002	.011		−.002	−.010		.002	.019	
Education (three categories)	−.048	−.014					.058	.024	**
Religiosity (100-point scale)	.015	.138	***	.013	.160	***	.009	.141	***
Middle-class (1/0)	.408	.071	***	.067	.014	*	.282	.074	***
In paid employment (1/0)	−.665	−.119	***	−.080	−.017	*	.004	.001	
Married or cohabiting (1/0)	−.170	−.031	***	−.026	−.005		.092	.023	**
Union member (1/0)	−.201	−.031	***	−.145	−.026	***	−.068	−.016	
Cultural values									
Gender Equality Scale	−.021	−.138	***	−.008	−.066	***	−.013	−.109	***
Postmaterialism	−.072	−.032	***	−.090	−.048	***	−.274	−.173	***
Role of Government Scale	.004	.034	***	.010	.092	***	.017	.164	***
Constant	6.09			5.24			5.11		
R	.251			.215			.352		
Adjusted R^2	.062			.046			.123		

Note: See Table 4.4 for details.
Source: Pooled WVS/EVS, 1995–2001.

important components of this process, although structural changes also contribute to it.

Does this result apply to both rich and poor nations? To address this question, Table 4.5 analyzes the final regression model across three types of society. Similar patterns for the ideological gender gap are found across all three models. Gender is significantly related to ideological position, with women more left-leaning than men in all types of society, even after controlling for gender differences in social structure and in political attitudes. The strongest model, explaining the most variance in the left-right ideological scale, is the one analyzing the postindustrial nations. There are many common structural factors, with religiosity and a middle-class occupational status being consistently associated with more conservative values. But the cultural variables prove to be the most significant and consistent predictors of positions on the ideological scale across all types of society; people who adhere to the values of more egalitarian sex roles and support for postmaterialism are more left-leaning, while those who prefer a minimal role for government are more conservative in their ideological position, in rich and poor nations alike.

Conclusions and Discussion

When women were first enfranchised it was anticipated by many contemporary observers that they would vote as a bloc, thereby transforming party politics. Although this did not happen, even modest gender differences in the electorate have often proved to be significant, and sometimes decisive, for political outcomes. The modern gender gap is now an established feature of the American political landscape, although, despite the extensive body of research on the topic, the reasons for this phenomenon are still not generally understood. Much of the previous literature has attempted to explain the American gender gap on the basis of factors specific to U.S. politics, such as party polarization over issues such as the ERA or the highly polarized politics of abortion and welfare reform.[48] If, in fact, the root cause of this phenomenon reflects broader structural and cultural trends common to postindustrial societies, as we suggest, we would expect to find similar patterns of gender realignment emerging in other postindustrial societies. Commenting on the comparative evidence from the early 1970s, Inglehart argued that gender realignment in advanced industrialized societies was likely to occur in the future:

> We might conclude that sex differences in politics tend to diminish as a society reaches an advanced industrial phase. Or, going beyond our data, one could interpret the cross-national pattern as reflecting a continuous shift to the Left on the part of women: in the past they were more conservative than men: in Post-Industrial society, they may be more likely to vote for the Left. The relative conservatism of women is probably disappearing.[49]

Norris's research based on the 1983 Eurobarometer expressed cautious views about the existing pattern of gender differences in Europe at the time, but also speculated that the conditions might prove ripe for change:

We can conclude that there was no voting gap in European countries in recent years; overall women and men were very similar in their electoral choices and ideological positions. There is a potential gender gap, however, as women and men disagree significantly on a range of issues. These policy differences have not yet translated into voting differences, but they could, given certain circumstances.[50]

By the 1990s, these predictions seem to have been confirmed. The theory developed in this book argues that common developments transforming the lifestyles and values of women and men in postindustrial societies have altered political values and electoral preferences. This analysis points to four main findings.

1. In most nations today, women hold more left-leaning values than men in their attitudes toward the appropriate role of the state versus the market, favoring active government intervention in social protection and public ownership.

2. Although an extensive body of evidence indicates that from the 1950s to the 1980s, women tended to be more conservative than men in their ideology and voting behavior, this pattern has now changed, with women becoming more left-leaning than men in many societies.

3. In explaining this phenomenon, we have demonstrated that the modern gender gap persists in many nations even after introducing a battery of social controls, but that the size of the gap diminishes substantially when we take cultural values into account. This suggests that the modern gender gap reflects differences in the value orientations of women and men, especially in their attitudes towards postmaterialism, the role of government, and gender equality, more than differences in their lifestyles and social backgrounds.

4. Lastly, analysis of generational differences points to intergenerational value change in postindustrial societies. The *modern* gender gap in ideology is strongest among the younger age groups, while the *traditional* gender gap persists among the elderly. If this finding reflects a generational change, as seems likely, rather than a life-cycle effect, it implies that in the long term, as younger

voters gradually replace older generations, the shift toward left-leaning values among women should become stronger in affluent nations.

These results have important implications for understanding the emergence of the modern gender gap in the United States. The evidence indicates that the realignment in the United States is not sui generis, but instead represents an enduring gender cleavage that is now becoming increasingly evident in other postindustrial societies as a result of long-term value changes. The gender gap in the United States has served to increase media attention and public debate about gender issues, to heighten party competition to gain the "women's vote," and to increase incentives for parties to nominate women for public office. The extent to which these developments will occur in other political systems remains to be seen. In order to gain electoral clout, women as a group need to participate at least as much as men, and to show a distinctive political profile. If they do, then these ideological differences promise to have significant consequences for the future power of women in representative democracies. The following chapter examines whether women are becoming increasingly active in public life, particularly through electoral turnout, civic engagement, and participation in new social movements.

5

Political Activism

The earliest studies of political behavior in Western Europe and North America established gender as one of the standard variables routinely used to explain levels of electoral turnout, party membership, and protest activism, alongside the most powerful predictors of age and education.[1] Based on a seven-nation comparative study of different dimensions of political participation conducted during the 1970s, ranging from voting turnout to party membership, contact activity, and community organizing, Verba, Nie, and Kim concluded: "In all societies for which we have data, sex is related to political activity; men are more active than women."[2] During the same era, Barnes and colleagues (1979) found that women were also less engaged in unconventional forms of participation, such as strikes and demonstrations.[3] The literature suggested that the well-established gender gap in many common forms of political participation remained evident during the 1980s and early 1990s in many countries around the world – even in the United States and Western Europe, where women have been enfranchised with full citizenship rights for decades.[4] Nevertheless, given all the other substantial changes in women's and men's lives that have already been documented, we would expect to find evidence that some of these gender differences have gradually diminished or even disappeared over time, with women becoming more active, especially among the younger generations in affluent modern societies.

To examine the broader picture, this chapter starts by comparing patterns of *traditional political activism* via elections and parties; *civic activism* through voluntary organizations, new social movements and community associations; and *protest politics*, exemplified by demonstrations, petitions, strikes, and boycotts. We find that, despite the rising tide in gender equality transforming many other aspects of men's and women's lives, in the public sphere women usually remain less politically active in most nations, contrary to expectations. The gender gap is usually modest, but also consistent and ubiquitous across many major dimensions of civic life, even in postindustrial societies. Part II analyzes the general reasons accounting for this puzzling situation. We compare three explanations that have commonly been offered to explain why people participate in public life.[5] *Structural* accounts stress the way in which social cleavages, such as gender, age, and class, are closely related to the unequal distribution of civic resources, such as time, money, knowledge, and skills. *Cultural* explanations emphasize the attitudes and values that people bring to the electoral process, including their political interest and ideological beliefs. *Agency* accounts stress the role of mobilizing organizations, such as get-out-the-vote drives and social networks generated by parties, trade unions, voluntary organizations, and community associations. In short, these explanations suggest that women don't participate as much as men because they can't, because they won't, or because nobody asked them. The study demonstrates that the gender gap in civic and protest activism is largest among certain social groups – namely, the oldest generation, those not in paid work, the less educated, and those holding traditional views of gender equality – suggesting that long-term social trends such as wider educational opportunities and greater female labor force participation, which are transforming women's lifestyles and values, can be expected gradually to close the activism gap in future decades; but there is a lagged effect between cultural change and political behavior in the public sphere. The conclusion summarizes the findings and reflects upon their consequences for women's voice in public affairs.

Theories of Political Activism

The evidence that women have commonly participated less than men in conventional state-oriented forms of political expression, organization, and mobilization is well established in the previous literature on electoral behavior. Why might we expect this pattern to be starting to shift today, especially in postindustrial societies? As in previous chapters, our theory assumes that structural developments lead to, and interact with, cultural shifts that, under certain circumstances, impact political behavior. The long-term process of value transformation is therefore generally predictable, even if the pace of change within each country is influenced by situation-specific factors. Societal levels of political activism are shaped by the process of modernization, including rising levels of human capital (such as literacy and education). But patterns of political activism within any nation are also dependent on particular institutional contexts and political systems, including the existence of democratic rights and civil liberties, the structure and organization of mass political parties, and the opportunities for political expression, organization, and mobilization within the society. Societal modernization affects the whole population, but it has a particularly important impact on women, reducing the factors that have discouraged them from involvement in the public sphere. Agrarian societies are characterized by sharply differentiated gender roles that discourage women from activity in the paid work force. Virtually all preindustrial societies emphasize traditional sex roles: childbearing and child rearing are regarded as the central goal for women; activities outside the home remain predominately male. Religiosity reinforces traditional sex roles. By contrast, we have shown how gender roles converge in postindustrial societies as a result of the culture shift, the transformation of the paid labor force, education, and the characteristics of modern families. This expansion of equal opportunities occurred during the twentieth century in affluent nations, producing contrasting experiences for the younger generation of women compared to their mothers and grandmothers. As women's lives alter in postindustrial societies, we hypothesize that the process will gradually shape broader norms of political behavior, although there tends to be a substantial time lag before societal changes alter entrenched positions of political power, as reflected in the number of women in elected and appointed office. The expansion of female education and labor force participation should influence political activism, since education has been found to increase cognitive skills, confidence, and practical knowledge that help people make sense of politics, while paid employment allows access to social and organizational networks outside the home.[6]

Although there is limited direct evidence allowing us to compare trends over time in men's and women's activism, these arguments generate certain testable propositions that can be examined with the available survey data.

1. First, if we *compare societies*, the transformation of sex roles in the paid labor force, education, and the family has gone much further in postindustrial than in agrarian nations, as has the process of value change. This suggests that gender differences in activism should also have narrowed most in postindustrial nations, and that the differences remain largest in agrarian societies.

2. If we compare *generations* within postindustrial societies, as indirect evidence of the process of longitudinal change, we would also expect to find important differences in activism by cohorts, given the way that changes in lifestyles and cultural trends have transformed the lives of older and younger groups of women in these nations.

3. Lastly, if we compare *groups within societies*, political activism among women and men would be expected to vary according to *structure* (i.e., participation in the paid labor force, class, education, marital status, union membership, and religiosity), as well as according to *culture* (including attitudes toward gender equality, left-right ideological values, political interest, and postmaterialist values) and *agency* (including the role of social and associational networks).

Dimensions of Political Activism

As the literature has argued, political activism is a multidimensional phenomena, with alternative modes associated with differing costs and benefits.[7] Patterns of political activism are classified in this study into three common dimensions: traditional, civic, and protest activism.

Traditional Political Activism

Voting participation exemplifies traditional state-oriented forms of political activism, representing the simplest and most common form of political expression. As others have argued, however, for these very reasons voting is not typical of other forms of civic engagement. In established democracies, casting a ballot in regular parliamentary elections every few years presents citizens with minimal demands on their time and energies, such as following the campaign in the mass media, and casting a ballot. Although relatively "low-cost," voting participation is also often "low-incentive," since elections remain relatively blunt and insensitive instruments for rewarding or punishing incumbents, for influencing prospective policy outcomes, or for determining collective benefits. The early literature on electoral studies in the 1960s and 1970s commonly reported that in the United States and Western Europe, women were less likely to vote.[8] In more recent decades, however, this orthodoxy has come under challenge; studies suggest that since the early 1980s, traditional gender differences in voting participation may have diminished, and even reversed, in many advanced industrialized countries.[9] In the United States, for example, among the eligible adult population the proportion of citizens who vote has been higher among women than men in every presidential election since 1980.[10] Similar trends are evident in Britain, where the gender gap in turnout reversed in 1979; by the 1997 election, an estimated 17.7 million women voted compared to around 15.8 million men.[11] Moreover, some initial evidence suggests that by the mid-1990s, the gender gap in voting participation may have closed in many other countries, including a wide range of established and newer democracies.[12] This pattern suggests that long-term secular trends, fueled by generational change, may have removed many factors that had inhibited women's voting participation in the past. This phenomenon, combined with the gender gap in party preferences documented in Chapter 4, can boost women's influence at the ballot box. Yet at the same time, the closing of gender differences in voting turnout should not be taken as evidence that the gender gap in political participation has closed across the board: analysis of the most extensive survey of political participation in America shows that during the mid-1990s women continued to be less engaged than men in many other forms of activism, such as campaign contributions, affiliation with political organizations, contacting public officials, and organizing to solve community problems.[13]

Party membership can also be regarded as a traditional form of political activism, because in established democracies parties have long served as one of the central mechanisms linking citizens and the state. Party members can serve many functions, depending on their role in the organizational structure, including carrying out the hum-drum local party work: attending branch and regional meetings, donating money, signing petitions, passing motions, acting as local officers and campaign organizers, displaying window posters and yard signs, helping with door-to-door canvassing and leafleting, training and selecting candidates for office, attending the national party convention, and assisting with community fund-raising events – in short, making tea and licking envelopes. Members help to maintain the ongoing links between party leaders in government and their local supporters during the interelectoral period, as well as during campaigns. Passive party affiliation may make relatively few demands, beyond paying dues and supporting the ticket at elections, but playing an active role in party organizations typically requires far more time and effort than voting. The literature comparing membership in political parties in Western democracies, based on analysis of official party records and survey data, has established that men are more likely to join political parties, as well as to be active as party workers and officeholders.[14] Nevertheless, this pattern varies by type of party organization and also by party ideology, with the Greens and parties of the left traditionally slightly more egalitarian toward women than parties of the far right. Recognizing this problem, the general challenge of declining mass membership, and the need to attract women voters, many Western European parties have developed affirmative action or positive discrimination policies, such as the use of gender quotas designed to increase women's representation within party organizations, and have supported separate party organizations for women.[15]

Union membership is also commonly regarded as an important traditional channel for the expression of economic and political demands, especially for mobilizing and organizing the working class. Organized labor exemplifies traditional mobilizing agencies, which are characterized by the older form of Weberian bureaucratic organization with formal rules and regulations, a small cadre of full-time paid officials, hierarchical mass-branch structures, broad-based rather than single-issue concerns, and clear boundaries demarcating the paid-up card-carrying membership. The experience of holding office in a trade union, or voluntary work linked to such associations, can provide practical training in organizational and leadership skills such as running elections, chairing meetings, producing newsletters, and public speaking, all of which can be useful in the pursuit of elected office in local or regional government. Trade union membership can be regarded as valuable both as a direct form of activism and as an indirect channel, since membership is closely associated with electoral turnout.[16] Unions have traditionally drawn primarily upon a male membership in manufacturing industry, but in recent decades, faced with a shrinking industrial base, many have attempted to widen and diversify by attracting working women. Unions have sought to develop new services and support for their members – for example, stressing the importance of workplace childcare facilities, flex-time and maternity leave policies, financial services, credit card and insurance schemes, and discounted membership fees for young people.[17] As a result of these developments, unions in some countries have been fairly successful in stemming their membership losses, widening their traditional recruitment base, and creating new political alliances with grassroots community organizations and NGOs sharing similar objectives.

Lastly, we can compare two indicators that have been strongly related to the propensity to be active in the public sphere: (1) levels of *political interest*, where there is evidence of a long-standing gender gap,[18] and (2) the frequency of *political discussion* with friends, colleagues, and family, which is the basis for deliberative democracy. Political communication, such as trying to persuade others how to vote during campaigns, debating controversial issues, or simply expressing opinions about political leaders or the government's record, is the least demanding and most ubiquitous form of civic engagement. These indicators are also well suited to comparative cross-national research, since they are less likely to be influenced by the institutional context than alternative measures, such as electoral turnout, party membership, and associational activism. Contrary to assumptions that the public is becoming more apathetic, both political interest and discussion have increased in many nations.[19]

Table 5.1 shows the distribution of women and men in each type of society in the 2000 wave of the World Values Survey/European Values Survey, without any controls, according to five indicators: the propensity to be politically interested, to discuss politics, to vote, to join a political party, and to belong to a trade union. The results confirm that at the end of the twentieth century, there were modest but consistent gender gaps across all of these indicators of traditional political

TABLE 5.1. *Levels of traditional activism by gender and type of society, 2001*

	Politics Interest	Discussion	Turnout	Party Member	Union Member
	% Politics "Very" Important	% Frequently	% Who Vote	% "Belong to Party"	% "Belong to Union"
Postindustrial					
Women	7	12	74	4.9	14.8
Men	10	19	80	8.2	20.5
Diff.	−3	−7	−6	−3.3	−5.7
Industrial					
Women	11	12	73	2.6	10.2
Men	16	19	77	5.6	11.9
Diff.	−5	−7	−4	−3.0	−1.7
Agrarian					
Women	18	10	89	6.9	6.1
Men	31	23	93	11.3	8.2
Diff.	−13	−13	−4	−4.4	−2.1
Total					
Women	12	9	77	4.3	11.0
Men	19	14	82	7.9	14.0
Diff.	−5	−5	−5	−3.6	−3.0

Note: Indicators of traditional activism in the 2000 wave. See Appendix B for details of all items. A negative coefficient denotes that women are less active than men; a positive coefficient indicates that women are more active than men.
Source: WVS/EVS, 2001, including fifty-one societies (nineteen postindustrial, twenty-two industrial, and ten agrarian societies).

activism. Overall, men proved to be more politically interested (by a margin of 7%), more willing to discuss politics frequently (+5%), to vote (+5%), to be party members (+4%), and to join trade unions (+3%). The similarity of the results using different measures is striking and suggests that the gender gap is unlikely to be the product of particular institutional contexts (such as the cost of fee-paying party membership, the length of female suffrage, or the structure of the electoral system), but rather relates to more general aspects of men's and women's lives and values.

We anticipated that the widening of educational opportunities and increased participation in the paid workforce, which have altered women's lives profoundly in modern societies, should gradually close the participation gap. There is some support for this proposition, but it is limited. The gender gaps in political interest and political discussion – the two least demanding forms of traditional activism – do, as expected, prove largest in agrarian societies, where about one in ten women say that they frequently talk about politics, compared to almost one-quarter of the men. These gaps almost close in postindustrial nations. Nevertheless, contrary to expectations, there is no indication that the other gender differences are consistently smallest in postindustrial nations, whether measured by voting turnout, party membership, or union membership. For example, in postindustrial societies 80 percent of men report voting compared to 74 percent of women, and there are similar gender disparities in the other types of societies.

Further, when the pattern of voting participation is broken down in more detail by birth cohort as shown in Figure 5.1, there is no support for the proposition that the gender gap has closed most among the younger generations. Instead, women prove to be slightly less likely than men to cast a ballot among both pre-war and postwar cohorts within each type of society. In poorer agrarian countries, societal development has gradually increased human capital (especially literacy, education, and access to the mass media) and thereby boosted electoral participation among the younger generation. Nevertheless, the impact of these developments has affected women and men alike, rather than closing the gender gap among the youngest cohorts. Although the rising tide has affected many other cultural values and patterns of behavior, as previous chapters suggest, so far it appears to have had only minimal impact on altering women's engagement in these conventional,

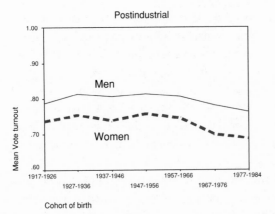

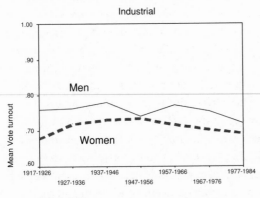

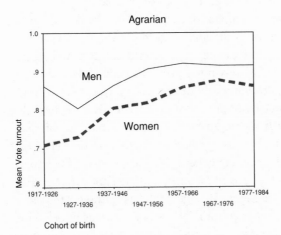

FIGURE 5.1. Voting participation by gender, cohort and type of society, 2001.

elite-directed forms of political mobilization and expression. Clearly, if parties and unions have made efforts to expand their membership among women, these initiatives have not yet closed the gender gap.

Civic Activism

Yet comparisons need to go beyond the bureaucratized, elite-directed forms of political participation that were the primary focus of attention in earlier decades. The late twentieth century experienced a transformation in the agencies of political activism (collective organizations), the repertoires (the actions commonly used for political expression), and the targets (the political actors that participants seek to influence).[20] Civic activism within voluntary organizations, community associations, and new social movements represents a distinct dimension of political involvement. Recent decades have witnessed the rise of more amorphous ad hoc forms of civic engagement, exemplified by the second-wave women's movement and other countercultural movements concerned with the environment, nuclear power, anti-globalization, trade and debt relief, as well as with peace, human rights, and conflict resolution.[21] Transnational policy networks, symbolized by the events at Seattle, Gothenberg, and Genoa, represent the development of a global civil society networking these groups into coalitional alliances.[22] Theories of new social movements suggest that these organizations differ from traditional mobilizing agencies, such as parties and trade unions, in a number of important regards: they are characterized by relatively loose networks and flat, decentralized structures; their modes of belonging are based on shared issue concerns and identity politics rather than on formal fee-paying membership; and they employ mixed action repertoires to achieve their goals.[23] New social movements are strongest in postindustrial nations; but in many agrarian societies networks of community groups, myriad NGOs, and grassroots voluntary associations have developed within local communities to address basic issues of livelihood, such as access to clean water, the distribution of agricultural aid, health care, and schools.[24] If studies focus exclusively on card-carrying membership and electoral politics, this could exclude many more amorphous forms of political engagement that have become increasingly common today. Women may be more active in these alternative channels than via traditional modes of political expression; a rich body of literature has sought to understand the multiplicity of women's movements and women's political behavior in community organizations, NGOs, women's rights activist groups, feminist movements, and radical struggles within many different countries, emphasizing the importance of specific locations and contexts.[25] Studies have also examined support for feminist attitudes and values in Western Europe.[26] So far, however, few studies based on systematic survey evidence have compared cross-national indicators of women's active involvement in women's groups and new social movements in a wide range of societies.

Social capital theories have also stimulated further interest in the study of voluntary associations and community groups. The core claims of Putnam's theory of social capital is that typical face-to-face deliberative activities and horizontal collaboration in voluntary associations far removed from the political sphere – such as sports clubs, agricultural cooperatives, and philanthropic groups – promote interpersonal trust, fostering the capacity to work together and creating the bonds of social life that are the basis for civil society and democracy.[27] Organized groups not only achieve certain instrumental goals, it is argued, but also, in the process of doing so, create the conditions for further collaboration, or social capital. In contrast to voting, far more time, energy, and initiative is needed to work within voluntary organizations and community associations – attending local meetings, organizing community groups, editing newsletters, and so on. If this is the case, then it is important to examine gender differences in these organizations.

Previous studies have often treated social capital as gender-neutral, but comparison of belonging to a wide range of different types of social and political organizations, shown in Table 5.2, reveals how far membership is differentiated by sex. Some groups are predominately male, including political parties, sports clubs, the peace movement, professional associations, unions, and community associations. By contrast, there are other voluntary associations where women predominate, especially those related to the traditional role of women as caregivers, such as those concerned with education and the arts, religious and church organizations, and associations providing social welfare services for the elderly or handicapped, as well as women's groups. The comparison provides no support for the popular assumption that more women than men are engaged in new social movements,

TABLE 5.2. *Gender ratio in civic associations, 2001*

	% Women	% Men	Gap
Political parties or groups	38	62	−24
Sports or recreation	38	62	−24
Peace movement	42	58	−16
Professional associations	43	57	−14
Labor unions	47	53	−6
Local community action groups	48	52	−4
Youth work (e.g., scouts, guides, youth clubs, etc.)	49	51	−2
Conservation, environmental, or animal rights	50	50	0
Third world development or human rights	52	48	+4
Education, arts, music, or cultural activities	53	47	+6
Religious or church organizations	56	44	+12
Voluntary organizations concerned with health	56	44	+12
Social welfare for the elderly, handicapped, or deprived	58	42	+16
Women's groups	87	13	+72
All	53	47	+6

Note: Q: "*Please look carefully at the following list of voluntary organizations and activities and say which, if any, do you belong to?*" The table lists the percentage of women and men in the membership of each type of group, with the gender gap representing the difference between women and men. See Appendix B for details of all items. A negative coefficient denotes that women are less likely to belong than men; a positive coefficient indicates that women are more likely to belong than men.
Source: WVS/EVS, 2001.

such as those working for peace, protection of the environment, and improved community housing and health; instead, the gender ratio within each type of group varies according to the type of issue concern. The extent of sex segregation in associations means that it is particularly important to include a wide range of groups in any reliable comparison of civic engagement, along with alternative measures distinguishing self-reported "belonging" from "activism." Two alternative scales were constructed to gauge membership and activism within civic associations. To measure membership in multiple overlapping social networks, *Vol-Org* summarizes, the mean number of different types of organizations that people joined, based on the full range of fourteen different types of organizations included in the survey. Since some support is relatively passive, while other work is highly demanding of time and energy, as an alternative indicator *Vol-Act* summarizes how much

TABLE 5.3. *Civic activism by gender and type of society, 2001*

	Belong to How Many Civic Organizations (Mean Vol-Org)	Active in How Many Civic Organizations (Mean Vol-Act)
Postindustrial		
Women	1.46	.94
Men	1.50	.90
Diff.	−.04	+.04
Industrial		
Women	.71	1.04
Men	.86	1.07
Diff.	−.15	−.03
Agrarian		
Women	1.26	1.61
Men	1.50	1.74
Diff.	−.24	−.13
Total		
Women	1.10	1.13
Men	1.24	1.17
Diff.	−.14	−.04

Note: Q: Belong: *"Please look carefully at the following list of voluntary organizations and activities and say which, if any, do you belong to?"* Active: (if belong) *"And for which, if any, are you currently doing unpaid voluntary work?"* The civic activism scale includes belonging to the fourteen organizations listed in Table 5.1. See Appendix B for details of all items. A negative coefficient denotes that women are less active than men; a positive coefficient indicates that women are more active than men.
Source: WVS/EVS, 2001.

unpaid voluntary work people said that they currently did for any of the different types of organizations on the list.

Table 5.3 presents the scores on each of these scales among women and men, broken down by each type of society, based on the 2001 wave of the survey.[28] The results demonstrate that in agrarian societies men are not simply more likely to join parties and unions; rather, this pattern is part of a persistent gender difference evident across a wide variety of civic associations, community organizations, and new social movements. Men belonged to more civic associations (Vol-Org), with a modest but consistent gender gap found across all types of society, but the size of the gap was far smaller in postindustrial than in industrial and agrarian societies. Moreover, the comparison of unpaid voluntary work (Vol-Act) shows that men are more active in these organizations in agrarian societies, but that the gender gap actually reverses in postindustrial societies, with women being slightly more active in these organizations than men. The patterns suggest that, overall, men continue to predominate as members and activists in less prosperous developing societies, but that the gender gap in civic activism has diminished substantially, or even reversed itself, in more affluent nations.

The contrasts among types of society are revealed even more sharply when membership in civic organizations is analyzed by birth cohort. Figure 5.2 shows the patterns in how many organizations people join (Vol-Org). In postindustrial nations, men prove more active among the pre-war group, but a closure or even reversal of this pattern is evident among the postwar generation. In industrialized nations, by contrast, there are more stable trends, with women consistently less likely than men to belong to many civic organizations. Lastly, agrarian societies show the strongest traditional gender gap, with men far more likely than women to belong to these associations across all cohorts.

Protest Activism

The last distinct form of participation concerns protest activism. The era since the early 1970s has witnessed a substantial rise in activities such as demonstrations, boycotts, and petitioning in postindustrial societies.[29] The popularity of these activities elsewhere can be demonstrated by the massive protests organized around events such as the meetings of various international bodies, including the World Trade Organization and the World Bank, and peace demonstrations protesting American actions in Afghanistan. During the early 1970s, Barnes and colleagues (1979) demonstrated that women were less likely to protest in many European countries, as well as being less engaged through conventional channels such as campaign rallies.[30] Yet this pattern needs to be reexamined, since in recent decades some studies have detected a "normalization" of the population engaged in political protest.[31] Previous work focused on "protest potential," or the propensity to express dissent.[32] Yet this can be problematic: surveys are usually better at tapping attitudes and values than at measuring actual behavior, and they are generally more reliable at reporting routine and repetitive actions ("How often do you attend church?") as opposed to occasional acts. Unfortunately, answers to hypothetical questions

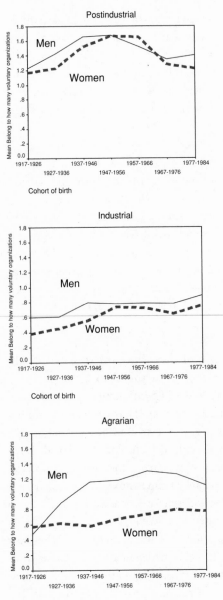

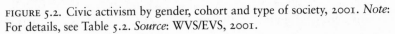

FIGURE 5.2. Civic activism by gender, cohort and type of society, 2001. *Note*: For details, see Table 5.2. *Source*: WVS/EVS, 2001.

TABLE 5.4. *Protest activism by gender and type of society, 2001*

	% Have Engaged in at Least One Protest Act	Protest Activism Scale
Postindustrial		
Women	62.3	.98
Men	65.6	1.17
Diff.	−3.3	−0.19
Industrial		
Women	29.7	.43
Men	34.4	.54
Diff.	−4.7	−0.11
Agrarian		
Women	24.8	.39
Men	32.6	.58
Diff.	−7.8	−0.19
Total		
Women	40.2	.62
Men	48.8	.77
Diff.	−8.6	−0.15

Note: Protest activism: "*Now I'd like you to look at this card. I'm going to read out some different forms of political action that people can take, and I'd like you to tell me, for each one, whether you have actually done any of these things, whether you might do it, or would never, under any circumstances, do it.*" Signing a petition, joining in boycotts, attending lawful demonstrations, joining unofficial strikes, and occupying buildings or factories. (%"*Have actually done.*") See Appendix B for details of all items. A negative coefficient denotes that women are less active than men; a positive coefficient indicates that women are more active than men.
Source: WVS/EVS, 2001.

("Might you ever demonstrate or join in boycotts?") may well prove poor predictors of actual behavior. These items may prompt answers that are regarded as socially acceptable, or just tap a more general orientation toward the political system (such as approval of freedom of association or tolerance of dissent).[33] Given these limitations, this study focuses on those things that people say they actually *have* done, taken as the most accurate and reliable indicator of protest activism, and excludes things that people say they *might* do, or protest potential.

Table 5.4 reveals that the gender gap detected by studies in the mid-1970s persists today, with women continuing to be slightly less active in protest politics in a consistent pattern, so that overall about 49% of men report having engaged in at least one protest act, compared to

40% of women. Nevertheless, two important qualifications need to be made to this generalization. First, the gender gap in protest activism is again greater in agrarian (8%) than in industrialized (5%) or postindustrial nations (3%). As observed with indicators of associational activism, this suggests that societal modernization not only expands the general propensity to engage in protest politics, which is far more common in affluent nations, but also tends to close the gender gap in this form of political expression and mobilization. Equally importantly, if we break down the pattern by birth cohort, as shown in Figure 5.3, it is apparent that the difference between men and women in each type of society is smallest among the youngest generation. The gradual closing of the gender gap is steady in successive postwar cohorts in more affluent nations, but it is also evident among the youngest groups elsewhere.

To summarize the results, one might expect that by the end of the twentieth century the rising tide would have shrunk the gender gap in political activism, particularly in postindustrial societies, so that women and men would be participating in public affairs at roughly equal levels. Instead, we find that, despite the major changes in lifestyles, in the workforce, and in the home and family discussed earlier, women continue to be less engaged than men in many common modes of political life. The gender gap here is usually modest, but it is also consistent; men continue to predominate in traditional forms of activism, as members in voluntary organizations, community associations, and new social movements, and in the common forms of protest politics. Nevertheless, an important qualification needs to be made to this observation – namely, that there is evidence that gender differences are greatest in poorer developing societies, and moreover that there is some closure on some indicators among the youngest generation.

Explaining Political Activism

Alternative structural, cultural, and agency factors may help to explain the residual gender differences. Structural explanations focus on the fact that within particular nations, there are usually substantial gaps in participation between rich and poor, young and old, as well as between college graduates and high school dropouts. At the individual

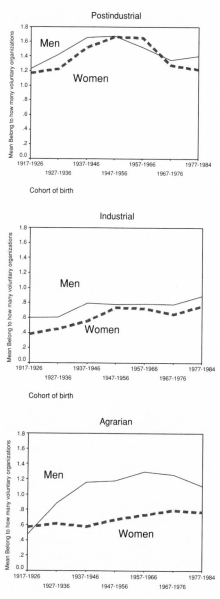

FIGURE 5.3. Protest politics by gender, cohort and type of society, 2001. *Note*: For details, see Table 5.4. *Source*: WVS/EVS, 2001.

level, structural accounts focus on the *resources* facilitating political action – such as time, money, skills, and knowledge – which are unequally distributed among groups throughout the population.[34] It is well established that education is one of the best predictors of participation, providing cognitive skills and civic awareness that allow citizens to make sense of the political world.[35] People with higher socioeconomic status – those possessing the advantages of more education, income, and more secure careers – are usually more active in politics. "At home, in school, on the job, and in voluntary associations and religious institutions, individuals acquire resources, receive requests for activity, and develop the political orientations that foster participation."[36] Organizing, chairing, and attending group meetings, contacting elected officials, editing newsletters, drafting press releases, and raising campaign funds – let alone running for elected office – all require certain skills, time, and energy. Moreover, since resources are unevenly distributed throughout societies, these factors help to explain differences in political participation related to gender, as well as those commonly found by race/ethnicity, age, and social class.

Cultural explanations argue that in addition to skills and resources, civic engagement also requires motivation and interest to become active in public affairs. These attitudes may be affective, (for example, if people vote out of a sense of duty) or instrumental (if they are driven by the anticipated benefits of the activity). Political interest, including beliefs in the importance of politics and the propensity to discuss public affairs, is one of the most common predictors of participation found in many studies. As we have seen, women continue to express slightly less interest in politics; in the 2001 wave of the survey, 14% of men said that they thought politics was "very important," compared to only 9% of women. In explaining why women are less engaged, however, we would also expect that beliefs about gender equality might impact activism, with the most traditional views of the appropriate role of women associated with lower levels of female activism. In addition, political ideologies could play a role here, since we would anticipate that people on the left would be more in favor of activities such as protest politics than those on the right. We would also expect that postmaterialist values might be positively related to more participatory citizenship, especially in terms of civic activism within community groups and new social movements, as well as to protest politics, since these values are closely associated with beliefs in self-expression and democratic participation.

Lastly, agency explanations suggest that the social networks and group norms that are derived from membership in groups and associations help to draw people into political life, providing encouragement to become more active. Rosenstone and Hansen exemplify this approach in the United States: "We trace patterns of political participation – who participates and when they participate – to the strategic choices of politicians, political parties, interest groups, and activists. People participate in politics not so much because of who they are but because of the political choices and incentives they are offered."[37] As such, membership in trade unions and in parties can be regarded as primary forms of activism, but each also functions as a secondary influence that could encourage other forms of participation, such as political discussion, electoral turnout, and campaign work. In the same way, community groups, voluntary associations, and social networks can help to draw neighbors, friends, and workers into the political process.[38] In this regard, women may be less engaged in electoral, campaign, and protest politics because they are more isolated from these associational and social networks. When asked about contact with different groups in the 2000 wave of the WVS/EVS, men were more likely than women to report that they spent time every week with friends (57% to 51%), with colleagues at work (29% to 19%), and with people at sports clubs and voluntary organizations (21% to 14%).

In order to examine these explanations, Table 5.5 analyzes the distribution of women and men in each of the major social groups in terms of civic activism and protest politics in postindustrial societies. The results confirm that there is a similar gender gap (4%) in both indicators of activism. But the gender gap in civic activism is greatest among certain groups, namely, the oldest sixties-plus generation, the unskilled working class, those not in paid work, those who are married or living as married, and traditionalists in terms of their beliefs about gender equality. Similar, although not identical, patterns are evident in predictors of the gender gap in protest politics. Yet interaction effects could confound these initial observations – for example, if age, work status, and education were interrelated – so multivariate analysis is needed to confirm these patterns. As in previous chapters, the regression models

TABLE 5.5. *Civic and protest activism by gender in postindustrial societies, 2001*

	% Belong to at Least One Civic Organization			% Have Done at Least One Protest Act		
	Women	Men	Diff.	Women	Men	Diff.
Education						
High	50	55	−5	69	69	0
Moderate	53	55	−2	67	69	−2
Low	39	43	−4	43	52	−9
Age group						
Under 30	48	52	−4	65	63	+2
30–59 years old	50	54	−4	68	70	−2
60+	41	49	−8	48	58	−10
Occupational class						
Managerial/professional	61	63	−2	74	71	+3
Lower-middle	54	56	−2	68	69	−1
Skilled working	44	49	−5	60	61	−1
Unskilled working	43	50	−7	52	54	−2
Work status						
In paid work	51	54	−3	66	66	0
Not in paid work	42	48	−6	56	64	−8
Marital status						
Married or cohabiting	47	54	−7	62	66	−4
Not	48	52	−4	63	66	−3
Children						
No children	51	54	−3	64	65	−1
At least one child	47	52	−5	62	66	−4
Religiosity						
Attend service every week	59	54	−5	58	65	−7
Never attend	38	47	−9	68	68	0
Gender equality						
Traditionalist	40	47	−7	58	57	+1
Egalitarian	55	57	−2	69	70	−1
Religion						
Catholic	48	55	−7	56	60	−4
Protestant	49	53	−4	68	69	−1
All	48	52	−4	62	66	−4

Note: The proportion of women and men who belong to at least one of the fourteen types of civic organizations or who have engaged in at least one of the five types of protest acts. In the "difference" column, a negative figure represents women less active than men; a positive figure represents women more active than men.

Source: WVS/EVS, 2001.

in Table 5.6 first enter the impact of gender on protest activism without any controls, using the pooled WVS/EVS 2001 for all societies. Model 2 then examines the impact of gender after controlling for the social structural factors most commonly associated with protest politics (including levels of human and political development, age, education, religiosity, class, work status, marital status, and union membership). Model 3 repeats the procedure with controls for cultural values and beliefs (including the scales for gender equality, postmaterialism, left-right ideology, and political interest).

The results in Table 5.6 show that in the first model without any prior controls, as already noted, gender has a modest but significant effect on protest activism: men remain more likely to protest than women. Once structural controls are introduced, however – particularly the impact of levels of democratization, education, class, age, union membership, and religiosity – then the effect of gender on protest activism becomes insignificant. That is to say, protest activism can be attributed to many basic social characteristics reflecting ways in which women's and men's lives and backgrounds continue to differ, such as access to educational opportunities (which makes people more likely to engage in protest) and level of religiosity (which makes people less likely to protest). Once these social differences are controlled, then women are as likely to protest as men.

Conclusions

The previous literature has argued that significant differences in political activism exist between women and men, even in postindustrial nations such as the United States and in Western Europe. Given the overwhelming consensus in the literature on women and politics, we expected that these gender gaps might persist, but we also expected that the gaps would have diminished most in countries where women have experienced the greatest changes in educational and employment opportunities. Building on previous chapters, we hypothesized that the process of societal modernization would influence the political activism of women and men, just as it has transformed social and political values. The results of the analysis suggests three main conclusions:

1. Across most forms of political activism, the survey evidence indicates that a modest but consistent gender gap persists across all

TABLE 5.6. *The impact of gender on protest activism, all societies, 2001*

	Model 1: Gender with No Controls			Model 2: Gender + Social Controls			Model 3: Gender + Social + Cultural Controls		
	B	Beta	Sig.	B	Beta	Sig.	B	Beta	Sig.
Gender (male = 1)	.079	.037	***	.027	.012		.012	.006	
Social structure									
Level of development (HDI 1998)				.238	.04	**	.151	.03	***
Level of democratization (FH 2000)				.185	.22	***	.174	.21	***
Age (years)				.004	.05	***	.002	.04	***
Education (three categories)				.253	.19	***	.170	.13	***
Religiosity (100-point scale)				−.003	−.08	***	−.003	−.06	***
Middle Class (1/0)				.059	.06	***	.030	.03	***
In paid employment (1/0)				.024	.01		.018	.01	
Married or cohabiting (1/0)				.032	.02		.031	.01	
Union member (1/0)				.527	.15	***	.467	.13	***

Cultural values

	Model 1		Model 2		Model 3	
	B	Beta	B	Beta	B	Beta
Gender equality (100-pt scale)					.004	.07 ***
Postmaterialism (twelve-item scale)					.092	.11 ***
Left-Right Ideology Scale					.000	.01
Political interest scale					.109	.22 ***
Constant	.809		868		1.850	
R	.037		.423		.492	
Adjusted R².	.001		.178		.240	

Note: The models are based on OLS regression analysis. The figures are unstandardized (B) and standardized (Beta) coefficients representing the impact of the independent variables on the activism scales, where high equals most active. *Model 1* includes gender without any controls, where a positive coefficient denotes that men are more right-wing than women. *Model 2* includes gender effects with social controls for level of human development (HDI 1998), level of democratization (Freedom House 2000), age, education, religiosity (the 100-point scale used in Chapter 3), and dummy variables for respondent's occupational class (middle = high), work status (full-time, part-time, or self-employment = 1), marital status (married or cohabiting = 1), and union membership (1). A dummy variable for the presence of children was also tested but dropped as insignificant. *Model 3* includes gender effects with social and attitudinal controls, the latter including the 100-point Gender Equality Scale used in Chapter 2, the twelve-item postmaterialism scale, and a ten-point Left-Right Ideology scale. Sig. *.05 **.01 ***.001. All models were checked by tolerance and VIF statistics to be free of multicollinearity problems. See Appendix B for details of all coding and measurements.

Source: Pooled WVS/EVS, 2001.

societies, with women being less active than men. This is manifest in comparing traditional forms of activism (political interest and discussion, voting turnout, party and union membership); membership and activism across a range of fourteen different types of voluntary organizations, community associations, and new social movements; and forms of protest activism, such as demonstrations and boycotts.

2. Nevertheless, the gender gap in who belongs to civic associations varies substantially by the type of organization. Men tend to dominate some organizations, such as sports clubs and professional associations, while women predominate as members of religious, health-related, and social welfare groups. There was no support for the proposition that women are more likely than men to belong to new social movements, such as those concerned with peace or the environment.

3. In addition, the size of the activism gap varies in a predictable pattern by type of society. Agrarian societies tend to display the largest gender gap in political interest and discussion, membership and activism in voluntary organizations, and protesting. Nevertheless, even in postindustrial societies the traditional gender gap generally persists; patterns have rarely reversed, so that changes in political behavior in the public sphere seem to have lagged behind cultural shifts.

Yet the evidence suggests that these lags will diminish in the future. Although women generally remain less engaged than men, the gender gap in civic and protest activism is greatest among certain social groups that are diminishing in size – namely, the oldest cohorts of women, those not in paid work, the less educated, and those holding traditional views of gender equality – suggesting that long-term social trends, such as secularization and female labor-force participation, that are transforming women's lifestyles and values may close the gap in future decades. The demographic process of generational turnover, in particular, will probably influence the pace of long-term change. How far this development will eventually overcome the well-established democratic deficit in women as political leaders is the subject of the next chapter.

6

Women as Political Leaders

One fundamental problem facing democracies is the continued lack of gender equality in political leadership. The basic facts are not in dispute: today, worldwide, women represent only one in seven parliamentarians, one in ten cabinet ministers, and, at the apex of power, one in twenty heads of state or government. Multiple factors have contributed to this situation, including structural and institutional barriers. But what is the role of political culture in this process? Do attitudes towards women as political leaders function as a significant barrier to their empowerment, and, in particular, how important is culture in comparison to structural and institutional factors?

Our thesis is that (a) contemporary attitudes toward women's leadership are more egalitarian in postindustrial than in post-Communist or developing societies; (b) traditional attitudes toward gender equality remain a major obstacle to the election of women to parliament; (c) culture continues to prove a significant influence on the proportion of women in elected office, even controlling for social structural and political institutions; but that (d) there is evidence that, as a result of modernization, these cultural barriers have been fading somewhat among the younger generation in postindustrial societies. After we set out the theoretical framework and core argument, our analysis testing these propositions will draw on evidence from the World Values Surveys / European Values Surveys for 1995–2001. The conclusion considers the implications of the analysis for strategies to advance women's voice and power.

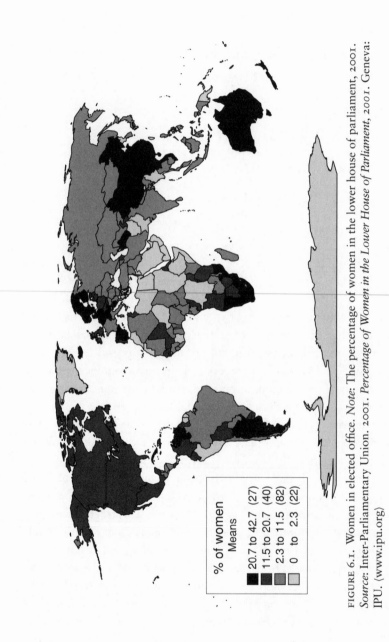

FIGURE 6.1. Women in elected office. *Note:* The percentage of women in the lower house of parliament, 2001. *Source:* Inter-Parliamentary Union. 2001. *Percentage of Women in the Lower House of Parliament, 2001.* Geneva: IPU. (www.ipu.org)

% of women
Means
20.7 to 42.7 (27)
11.5 to 20.7 (40)
2.3 to 11.5 (82)
0 to 2.3 (22)

ortional representation (PR) and the adoption of gender quotas in
uitment processes by political parties. This approach has become
easingly popular; indeed, it is probably accepted as the mainstream
pective in the literature today. Institutional accounts suggest that
rules of the game are the prime driver that can help to explain sys-
atic differences in women's representation across relatively similar
s of society, as well as being the most important factor that can
r women's political activism through public policy reforms.[8]

mong institutional factors, the *level of democratization* provides the
st general context. In general, the transition and consolidation of
ocratic societies can be expected to promote widespread political
civil liberties, including women's rights to vote and to stand for
ted office, as well as strengthening parties and institutionalizing
channels of political recruitment into parliament and government.
monitor democratization, we can include the standard measure us-
the Freedom House seven-point scale of political rights and civil
rties. Yet the role of democracy in promoting the involvement of
stantial numbers of women in public life remains under dispute,
e Reynolds found no significant relationship between levels of de-
cratization and women's parliamentary representation worldwide.[9]
here is a weak relationship, this may be due to the continued use of
rmative action strategies for women's representation in Communist
ems such as Cuba and China, as well as the decline in the pro-
tion of women in parliaments in Central and Eastern Europe
er such quotas were abandoned in the transition to democratic
ctions.

Ever since Duverger, the type of *electoral system* has been regarded as
important facilitating condition; many studies have demonstrated
t far more women are commonly elected under proportional party
s than via majoritarian single-member constituencies.[10] The level
party competition, in terms of the number and ideological polariza-
n of parties, is another factor that may influence opportunities for
didacy; this factor includes whether the country has a predominant
e-party system, such as in Japan; a two-party system, exemplified by
United States; a moderate multiparty system, such as in Germany;
a polarized multiparty system, such as in the Ukraine, Ecuador, and
ael.[11] Greater party competition may increase the access points for
ale candidacies, although this in itself does not necessarily lead to

Explaining the Barriers to Women in Public Life

The paucity of women in elected office is well established, despite
greater moves toward gender equality in many other spheres. The special session of the United Nations General Assembly on "Women 2000:
Gender Equality, Development and Peace" followed a long series of international conferences calling for the empowerment of women. The
session focused on full recognition of women's rights and fundamental freedoms and demands for progress toward gender equality in education and health care, in work and the family, and in the public
sphere.[1] Women have mobilized at the grassroots, national, and global
levels to press government agencies and nonprofit organizations to in-
corporate these agendas into national programs for action. The UN
report *The World's Women 2000*, which reviewed how far these goals
and objectives had been met, concluded that substantive advances for
women have occurred in the areas of access to education, health care,
and reproductive services, as well as in human rights – for example,
the greater recognition of the issues of domestic violence and sexual
trafficking.[2]

At the same time, progress has perhaps proved most difficult in the
inclusion of women's voices in politics and government. Out of 191
nations worldwide, only 9 currently have a woman elected head of
state or government. Despite some well-known world leaders, such
as Margaret Thatcher, Gro Harlem Bruntland, and Golda Meir, only
thirty-nine states have *ever* elected a woman president or prime
minister. According to the UN report, women today represent less than
one-tenth of the world's cabinet ministers and one-fifth of all submin-
isterial positions. The Inter-Parliamentary Union estimates that there
were about 5,500 women in parliament worldwide in spring 2002, representing 14.3% of all members, up from 9% in 1987.[3] If growth at
this level is maintained (0.36% per annum), a simple linear projection
predicts that women parliamentarians will achieve parity with men at
the turn of the twenty-second century.

Despite this overall slow progress, women elected representatives have moved ahead much faster in some places than in others
(see Figure 6.1). It is well known that women parliamentarians do best
in the Nordic nations, where they comprise on average 38.8% of MPs
in the lower house. Sweden leads the world; half of all ministers in

Goran Persson's cabinet and 149 members of the Riksdag (43%) are women, up from 10% in 1950. The proportion of women members of parliament elsewhere is lower, including in the Americas (15.7%), Asia (14.3%), Europe excluding the Nordic states (14.0%), sub-Saharan Africa (12.5%), and the Pacific region (11.8%). The worst record for women's representation is the Arab region, where women represent less than 5% of elected representatives; women continue to be barred by law from standing for parliament in Kuwait, Quatar, Saudi Arabia, Oman, and the United Arab Emirates. Therefore – despite many official declarations of intent made by governments, NGOs, and international agencies pledged to establish conditions of gender equality in the public sphere – in practice, major barriers continue to restrict women's advancement in public life.

The literature suggests that a variety of factors contribute to this phenomenon, including the role of *structural barriers*, such as levels of socioeconomic development and the proportion of women in professional and managerial occupations; the importance of *political institutions*, such as the use of proportional representation electoral systems and gender quotas in party recruitment; and the impact of *political culture*, including the predominance of traditional attitudes toward women in decision-making roles.[4]

Structural Barriers

Early sociological accounts commonly regarded the social system – including the occupational, educational, and socioeconomic status of women – as playing a critical role in determining the eligibility pool for elected office. In developing societies, where they are generally disadvantaged due to poor child care, low literacy, inadequate health care, and poverty, women may find it difficult to break into elective office. Reynolds found that levels of socioeconomic development were significantly related to the proportion of women parliamentarians worldwide.[5] Comparative studies of established democracies have emphasized the importance of the pool of women in the professional, administrative, and managerial occupations that commonly lead to political careers.[6] Fields such as law and journalism commonly provide the flexibility, financial resources, experience, and social networks that facilitate running for elected office. In recent decades in many postindustrial societies women have forged ahead in management and the

professions in the private and public sectors, an
enrollment in higher education.

Yet there are many reasons why structural ex
account for the barriers facing women seeking el
counts fail to explain major disparities in the pr
national parliaments across relatively similar typ
the contrasts between Canada (were women are
tarians) and the neighboring United States (12.9
between Italy (11.1%) and the Netherlands (36
Africa (29.8%) and Niger (1.2%). A ranked cc
portion of women elected to the lower houses
most recent elections worldwide confirms that h
nomic development are not necessary conditions
for example, female representation is far great
poorer societies, such as Mozambique (rankin
South Africa (tenth), and Venezuela (eleventh),
most affluent, such as the United States (fiftieth)
and Japan (ninety-fourth). In many postindustria
transformation in women's and men's lifestyles,
continued to elude women. This pattern is exer
States, where almost a third of all lawyers (29
figure that is increasing as the proportion of wo
law school has shot up eightfold, from 5.4% in 1
Law remains the most common training ground
in America; yet despite the rising numbers of
9 out of 100 U.S. senators are female. This su
provements in women's educational and profes
facilitating conditions for women's empowermen
may be insufficient by themselves for women t
and that something more that the eligibility poo
relationship between socioeconomic developmer
women parliamentarians can be examined furthe
of *Gender-related Development*, which combines i
literacy, longevity, education, and real GDP per

Institutional Barriers

One alternative explanation is provided by *insti*
phasizing the importance of the political system

more women being elected. We can test whether the proportion of women in parliaments is significantly related to the *level of democratization*, the type of *electoral system* (classified simply as majoritarian, mixed, or proportional), and the *level of party competition* (measured by the number of parliamentary parties). Institutional accounts may therefore provide many important insights into why women leaders have moved ahead further and faster in some countries than in others. Yet puzzles remain about why apparently similar institutional reforms may turn out to have unanticipated consequences, even among relatively similar political and social systems. Why should national-list PR have a very different impact on women's election in, say, Israel than in the Netherlands? Why should the use of gender quotas for candidacies seem to work better in, say, Argentina than in Ecuador? Rather like the failure of Westminster-style parliaments in many African states during the 1960s, transplanted institutions do not necessarily flourish in alien environments.

Cultural Barriers
Structural and institutional explanations therefore need to be supplemented by accounts emphasizing the importance of political culture. Ever since the seminal study on women and politics conducted during the mid-1950s by Duverger,[12] it has often been assumed that traditional attitudes toward gender equality influence women's advancement in elected office, although, despite the conventional wisdom, little systematic cross-national evidence has been available to verify this proposition. Theories of socialization have emphasized the importance of the division of sex roles within a country – especially egalitarian versus traditional attitudes toward women in the private and public spheres. Studies of the process of political recruitment in established democracies such as Britain, Finland, and the Netherlands have found that these attitudes influence both whether women are prepared to come forward as candidates for office (the *supply* side of the equation) and the criteria used by gatekeepers – such as party members and leaders, the news media, financial supporters, and the electorate – when evaluating suitable candidates (the *demand* side).[13] In cultures with traditional values concerning the role of women in the home and family, many women may be reluctant to run and, if they do seek office, may fail to attract sufficient support to win. A recent study by the Inter-parliamentary Union found

that female politicians in many countries mentioned hostile attitudes toward women's political participation as one of the most important barriers to running for parliament.[14] Cultural explanations provide a plausible reason why women have made such striking advances in parliaments in the Nordic region compared to other similar European societies such as Switzerland, Italy, and Belgium – all of which are affluent postindustrial welfare states and established parliamentary democracies with proportional representation electoral systems. Karvonen and Selle suggest that in Scandinavia a long tradition of government intervention to promote social equality may have made the public more receptive to the idea of positive actions, such as gender quotas, designed to achieve equality for women in public life.[15] Abu-Zayd suggests that culture is an important reason why many nations with strict Islamic traditions have often ranked at the bottom of the list in terms of women in parliament, despite some prominent exceptions among Islamic societies in top leadership positions.[16]

Traditional attitudes toward gender equality have often been regarded as an important determinant of women's entry into elected office, yet so far little systematic cross-national evidence has been available to prove this thesis. Most comparative studies have been forced to adopt proxy indicators of culture – such as the historical prevalence of Catholicism within Western European societies, understood as representing more traditional attitudes toward women and the family than those of Protestant religions.[17] An early comparison by Margaret Inglehart found that women's political activism was lower in Catholic than in Protestant countries of Western Europe, and suggested that this was because the Catholic Church was more hierarchical and authoritarian in nature than the Protestant churches.[18] A more recent worldwide comparison of women in politics in 180 nation-states by Reynolds found that the greatest contrasts were between predominantly Christian countries (whether Protestant or Catholic) and all others, including Islamic, Buddhist, Judaic, Confucian, and Hindu countries, all of which had lower proportions of women in legislative and cabinet offices.[19] An alternative approach has compared attitudes in Western Europe toward the women's movement, feminism, and sex-role equality in the home and workplace.[20] This approach provides insights into support for feminism within Western Europe, but it is difficult to know how far we can generalize from these findings, or whether comparable results would be evident across a broader range of societies.

It also remains unclear in the existing literature how far attitudes toward women in office may have been transformed over time in different types of society, particularly among the younger generation. Previous work by the authors has demonstrated that gender differences in electoral behavior have been realigning, with women moving to the left of men in postindustrial societies, especially among the younger generation, although this process is not yet evident in post-Communist or developing societies.[21] Just as the process of modernization has affected mass electoral attitudes and party preferences, so it may have eroded traditional views of the appropriate division of sex roles in the home and family, as well as in the paid labor force and the public sphere.

Given these alternative hypotheses, this study uses survey and aggregate evidence to compare how far political culture is systematically related to the advancement of women in elected office in a wide range of countries. We will focus on four related propositions – namely, that

1. There are substantial differences in attitudes toward women's leadership among postindustrial, post-Communist, and developing societies;
2. Traditional attitudes are a major barrier to the election of women to parliament;
3. Culture continues to be a significant influence on the proportion of women parliamentarians, even with the introduction of prior structural and institutional controls; but that
4. These cultural barriers have been fading most rapidly among the younger generation in postindustrial societies.

Attitudes toward Women's Political Leadership

First, how does the public regard women as political leaders today, and how do attitudes vary systematically across different types of postindustrial, post-Communist, and developing societies? The third wave of the WVS/EVS contains many items measuring attitudes toward sex role equality in the home and family, the labor force, and the public sphere, as well as measuring confidence in the women's movement. The basic indicator measuring support for gender equality in political leadership is the four-point scale asking respondents how far they agree or disagree with the following statement:

"People talk about the changing roles of men and women today. For each of the following statements I read out, can you tell me how much you agree with each? Do you strongly agree, agree, disagree, or disagree strongly? . . . On the whole, men make better political leaders than women do."

The comparison of responses in Figure 6.2, ranking countries from most egalitarian to most traditional, shows that there are substantial cross-national differences in attitudes toward gender equality in politics. Countries that proved most positive towards women's leadership included the Nordic nations (Norway, Sweden, and Finland) as well as many postindustrial societies, such as New Zealand and Australia, the United States and Spain. Countries that proved most traditional included some of the poorer developing societies, such as Egypt, Jordan, Iran, and Nigeria.

In order to explore how far responses to women and men as political leaders reflect deeper cultural values, these attitudes were also compared with a multi-item scale reflecting a much broader range of traditional versus secular-rational values, based on factor analysis developed elsewhere.[22] This scale includes items reflecting belief in the importance of religion and adherence to traditional moral standards on issues such as divorce, euthanasia, and the family. The correlation analysis showed the Scandinavian and West European societies to be consistently the most rational in their moral and ethnical values, as well as the most favorable towards gender equality in politics. By contrast, Nigeria, Jordan, and Egypt emerged as the most traditional on both dimensions, along with Iran and Azerbaijan. Attitudes toward women and men as political leaders are closely linked with a broader ideological dimension on a wide range of ethnical and moral issues, indicating that this measure reflects a deep-rooted set of values.

The Relationship between Cultural Attitudes and Women in Parliament

So far we have shown that systematic cross-national differences in attitudes toward women's political leadership are associated with levels

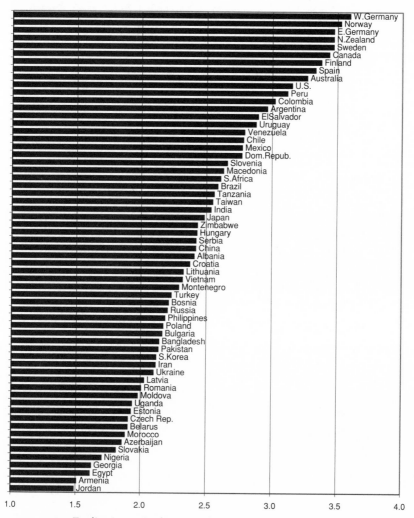

FIGURE 6.2. Egalitarian attitudes toward women in politics. *Note*: "Men make better political leaders than women." (% Disagree). *Source*: Pooled WVS/EVS, 1995–2001.

of socioeconomic development, and moreover that these egalitarian attitudes are related to broader cultural indicators. But do these cultural patterns matter in practice? In particular, do more egalitarian attitudes toward women leaders influence the proportion of women actually elected to office? We have already mentioned the substantial differences worldwide in the proportion of women in lower houses of

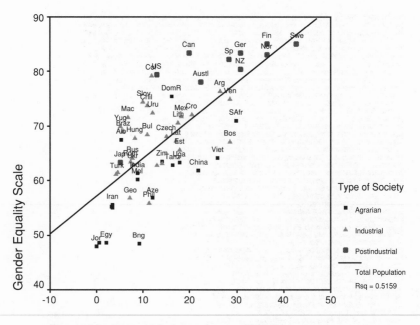

Percentage women in lower house (2000)

FIGURE 6.3. Gender equality and women in elected office. *Note*: For details about the Gender Equality Scale, see Figure 2.1 and Chapter 2. The percentage of women elected to the lower house of parliament, 2000, is from Inter-Parliamentary Union. 2001. *Percentage of Women in the Lower House of Parliament, 2001*. Geneva: IPU. ⟨www.ipu.org⟩ *Source*: Pooled WVS/EVS, 1995–2001.

parliament, ranging from about 39% in Scandinavia to less than 5% in the Arabic-speaking societies. Figure 6.3 shows the simple relationship between egalitarian attitudes toward women leaders and the proportion of women elected to the lower house of the national parliament, following the election closest to the date of the survey in each country, during the mid to late 1990s.

The results demonstrate the strong and significant relationship between attitudes toward women's political leadership and the actual proportion of women in parliament ($R = 0.57$, sig. .01). Countries with egalitarian cultures have more women in power. The scattergram displays a fairly tight regression, with the Scandinavian countries at the forefront on both indicators in the top right-hand corner. In the bottom corner can be found Jordan, Egypt, Pakistan, and many of the

Central Asian post-Communist states, including Georgia, Belarus, and the Ukraine. Yet there are some striking outliers to this general pattern that also deserve attention. Some established democracies, including Australia, Spain, and the United States, fall below the regression line, displaying more egalitarian attitudes than might be expected given the actual proportion of women elected to parliament. In these countries, public opinion seems to run ahead of the opportunities that woman have when pursuing public office. On the other hand, Bosnia Herzegovina, South Africa, and China all have more women parliamentarians than would be expected from their cultural attitudes alone, suggesting that in these societies affirmative action strategies adopted to boost women's leadership, such as the use of gender quotas in South Africa and China, may be ahead of public opinion.

The pattern of causation cannot be determined from any simple correlation, and we cannot rule out reciprocal effects. It could well be that the experience of having many women involved in political life could shift public opinion in a more egalitarian direction, dispelling traditional stereotypes about men making better political leaders than women. Nevertheless, it seems likely that the causal direction flows primarily from political culture toward the success of women in elected office, since more egalitarian attitudes could persuade more women that they should seek opportunities for elected office and could simultaneously influence the electorate's evaluation of candidates. One way that this can be tested further is by examining the relationship between the proportion of women in parliament and the broader scale of traditional versus rational values. That analysis shows that there is a strong and significant correlation between these factors ($r = .408$, $p.004$). Since these broader moral values would not be greatly affected by the presence of women in office, this strongly suggests that culture drives the success of women in elected office, rather than vice versa.

Cultural, Institutional, and Social Barriers to Elected Office

So far we have demonstrated that culture matters, but not *how much* it matters compared to other social and institutional factors associated with gender equality in politics. The relationship could, after all, prove to be spurious if something else is simultaneously driving

TABLE 6.1. *Explaining the proportion of women in parliament*

	Model1: Social			Model 2: Social + Institutional			Model 3: Social + Institutional + Cultural		
	Beta	SE	Sig.	Beta	SE	Sig.	Beta	SE	Sig.
Social									
Human development	15.3	12.4	n.s.	17.9	15.5		−21.2	15.0	
Political development	3.4	1.1	***	2.7	1.4	*	1.9	1.1	
Institutions									
Type of electoral system				−4.7	4.3		.95	3.7	
District magnitude				.01	.01		.01	.01	
Number of parliamentary parties				−.69	.71		.12	.59	
Culture									
Gender Equality Scale							.78	.17	***
Constant	−15.3			−7.9			−31.9		
Adjusted R2	.38			.38			.61		

Note: The models represent standardized beta coefficients derived from OLS regression analysis models, with the proportion of women in the lower house of parliament in fifty-five nations worldwide as the dependent variable. The year of the aggregate data was selected to match the year of the WVS/EVS survey in each country. The variables were entered in the listed order.

Level of gender-related development: UNDP. 1999. *United National Development Report, 1999.* New York: UNDP/Oxford. ⟨http://www.undp.org⟩

Level of democratization: Freedom House. 2000. *Annual Survey of Freedom, Country Ratings 1972–73 to 1999–00.* ⟨http://www.freedomhouse.org⟩

Electoral system: IDEA. 1997. *The International IDEA Handbook of Electoral System Design.* ⟨http://www.idea.int⟩

Number of parliamentary parties: Calculated by counting all parties with more than 3% of the seats in the lower house of parliament with data derived from *Elections Around the World.* (www.agora.stm.it/elections/alllinks.htm)

Egalitarian attitudes: Responses to: "*On the whole, men make better political leaders than women do.*" Four-point reversed scale. WVS/EVS, 1995–99. ⟨http://wvs.irs.umich.edu⟩

Proportion of women in parliament: Inter-Parliamentary Union, 2000. *Women in National Parliaments.* ⟨www.ipu.org⟩ For details of all items, see Appendix B.

Source: Pooled WVS/EVS, 1995–2001.

both egalitarian attitudes and the success of women leaders. Multivariate analysis is required to test whether the main relationship remains significant even with controls. Accordingly, regression models were run to estimate the relative impact of cultural, structural, and institutional factors on women's representation in parliaments worldwide.

The first model in Table 6.1 shows the simple correlations between the independent variables and the proportion of women in the lower house of parliament, without any controls. Subsequent models enter the effect of human development alone, then the additional effect of political institutions, then finally the complete model including all variables. Model 1, without any controls, shows that all of the factors, with the exception of the number of parliamentary parties, proved to be significantly correlated with the proportion of women in elected office. But we cannot determine whether these effects are real or spurious without further analysis. Model 2 shows that the independent effect of the human development index is significant, but Model 3 reveals that this effect is in fact due to the relationship between development and the process of democratization. When the model controls for the level of democratization, the gender-related development index drops out as a significant factor. In Model 3, we find, somewhat surprisingly, that when controls are introduced, neither the type of electoral system nor the number of parties proves to be an important influence on the proportion of women in parliament, in contrast to the results of many other studies. The simple measure of majoritarian versus proportional electoral systems may fail to capture other important variations, such as district magnitude or the level of disproportionality. Lastly, when the measure of egalitarian attitudes toward women leaders was added in Model 3, the results emphasize the importance of culture, which proved to be not only strong but also the only significant factor in the equation, even with the battery of prior controls. If the measure of attitudes had not been derived from a source independent of the actual proportion of women in legislatures, we would be tempted to doubt this relationship, but the final model is clear and dramatic. The relationship between political culture and women's empowerment already observed in Figure 6.1 survives unscathed, despite our best attempts to explain it away with a variety of control variables that are prominent in the literature.

Generational Shifts in Cultural Attitudes

If culture is important, it is important to determine whether traditional views about women's suitability for political office are changing. The question measuring attitudes towards men's and women's leadership was not included in earlier waves of the WVS/EVS, so we are unable to compare trends over time directly, but cohort analysis can be used, analyzing the distribution of attitudes among generations within each type of society. Much evidence based on theories of socialization suggests that people's attitudes are shaped by formative experiences in their early years, and that individuals' basic values are relatively stable by the time they reach adulthood.[23] During the twentieth century, in postindustrial societies the formative experiences of the younger generation of women and men have differed from those of the older generation. Women's and men's sex roles have been affected by a long series of critical developments, ranging from the impact of the extension of suffrage and full citizenship rights to the entry of more women into higher education and the paid labor force, the rise of the second wave women's movement in the mid-sixties, radical shifts in sexual mores and lifestyles, and dramatic changes in families, marriage, and the sexual division of labor and child rearing within the home, as well as the experience of seeing more women as leaders and statesmen in public life. All of these factors can be expected to have altered the norms about the appropriate role of women in the public sphere and the suitability of women for elected office. The historical traditions in post-Communist and developing societies have followed a more complex and distinctive pathway – for example, the different experiences of women in the workforce, the widespread use of quotas in parliaments under the dominance of the Communist party and their subsequent abandonment, and the role of the organized women's movement in Central and Eastern Europe. As a result, we would expect that although some generational shifts in attitudes will be evident, the pace of change will be slower in these countries.

Figures 6.4 and 6.5 confirm these expectations. The traditional belief that men make better leaders than women shows a substantial decline among cohorts in postindustrial societies, with younger postwar generations being far more egalitarian than their parents and grandparents. Yet in post-Communist and developing societies, attitudes among

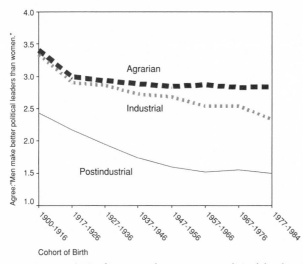

FIGURE 6.4. Attitudes toward women as political leaders by cohort. *Source*: Pooled WVS/EVS, 1995–2001.

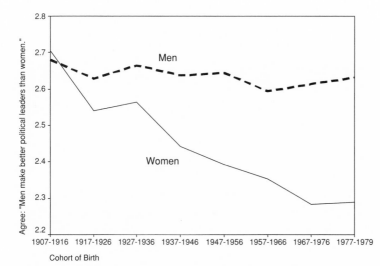

FIGURE 6.5. Attitudes toward women leaders by gender. *Source*: Pooled WVS/EVS, 1995–2001.

younger and older generations are almost identical, with only a modest shift toward less traditional views among the young. Moreover, when we disaggregate the cohort analysis for women and men, the most striking pattern is how far the gender gap on this issue has widened among the younger generation. In the pre-war generation, there was no difference by sex: women were as traditional in their attitudes as men, or even slightly more so. The gap widens steadily by successive cohorts, until by the youngest generation the gap has become considerable. This suggests that through the gradual process of demographic turnover, attitudes toward women in public leadership may become more polarized over time, with women becoming increasingly likely to raise this issue. The process of modernization will proceed in the broader political culture, even if no other strategies or institutional reforms are adopted to hasten the election of more women to office. Nevertheless, there is little evidence that a similar process is transforming public opinion in post-Communist and developing countries, where traditional values are prevalent among younger and older citizens alike.

Conclusions: The Implications for Change

The idea that the values endemic in the broader political culture affect the success of women in elected office has always seemed plausible, but it has rarely, if ever, been proved in a convincing fashion using systematic comparative evidence. People have long suspected that some 'X' factor distinguished the striking advancement of women in parliaments in the Scandinavian north from their European neighbors in the Mediterranean south, as well as from women in Latin America, Asia, sub-Saharan Africa, and the Arab states. Yet capturing the 'X' factor has proved ellusive, using existing aggregate data.

What this study demonstrates is that egalitarian attitudes toward women in office are more widespread in postindustrial societies, reflecting broad patterns of socioeconomic development and cultural modernization. Moreover, these attitudes are not simply interesting in themselves. They seem to have a powerful impact on political reality, since egalitarian values are significantly associated with women being successfully elected to office. Culture matters. Lastly, the more egalitarian attitudes evident among the younger generation in postindustrial societies, especially among younger women, suggests that over time we can expect to see continued progress in female representation in these societies. The empowerment of women remains a complex process, and as the cases of Australia, the United States, and Spain demonstrate, favorable attitudes toward women's leadership, by themselves, are not sufficient to produce breakthroughs, since there remain social structural and institutional barriers, especially in the short term. Nor can we expect an overnight transformation in deep-rooted traditional beliefs about the appropriate division of sex roles prevalent in many developing and post-Communist societies.

Nevertheless, cultural change in postindustrial societies produces a climate of opinion that is potentially more receptive to effective policy reforms designed to boost the number of women in elected office, including the use of positive discrimination or affirmative action strategies such as gender quotas. Many studies suggest that reforms to the regulations governing the formal criteria of eligibility to stand for elected office, set by law and by internal party rules, play a critical role in promoting gender equality. Positive measures include quotas requiring a certain proportion of female candidates, such as those implemented by law at the local level in India and adopted during the 1990s for elections to the national parliaments of ten Latin American nations.[24] The French parity movement achieved passage of legislation in the summer of 2000 guaranteeing equal numbers of male and female candidates on party lists in local, regional, parliamentary, and European elections. Elsewhere, the adoption of quotas for female candidates in internal party rules has proved to be one of the most important and successful means for getting more women into office, especially in bureaucratic mass-branch parties where the rules count.[25] Many parties in northern Europe introduced quotas during the 1970s, followed by Social Democratic parties in Germany, Spain, Portugal, and the UK. The situation is more varied in Eastern Europe, Asia, and Africa, although again parties of the left – such as the MPLA in Angola, the Popular Front in Côte d'Ivoire, and the SWAPO party in Namibia – have been more sympathetic to their introduction.[26] Their impact can be demonstrated in "natural experiments" by comparing changes in the proportion of women MPs in particular parties over successive elections. The introduction of all-women short lists in target seats by the British Labour party, for example, led to a doubling of the proportion of women at Westminster from 1992 to 1997. In all of these cases, if the public is broadly sympathetic to getting more women into public life, then parties may feel more willing to introduce institutional reforms and affirmative action strategies in order to achieve these aims.

Trying to alter deep-seated attitudes toward sex roles in public life may prove a frustrating exercise; such attitudes may be impossible to transform in the short term even with extensive educational and public awareness campaigns. But in the longer term, the secular trends in value change associated with the process of modernization, especially among younger generations of women and men, are likely to facilitate the process of getting more women into power. The combination of cultural shifts in attitudes and institutional reform of recruitment processes holds considerable promise that projections can perhaps be accelerated to create a more optimistic scenario for democracy, so that women achieve political parity well before the dawn of the twenty-second century.

CONCLUSIONS

7

Conclusions

Gender Equality and Cultural Change

Many cures have been proposed for the disparity of opportunity facing women in education and work, in the family, and in public office. During the 1960s, developmental theories held that economic growth alone, by "lifting all boats," could go a long way toward alleviating problems that women face in poorer societies, including those of health and infant mortality, literacy and schooling, subsistence wages and insecurity. In the following decade, the role of the state in this process came to center stage, especially with the emphasis on international agreements, legislative initiatives, public policies, and structural reforms designed to strengthen women's rights and opportunities. We do not wish to understate the impact that these measures can have, as is illustrated by the effect of gender quotas on women's representation in parliaments. Nevertheless, the core thesis of this book is that cultural norms, values, and beliefs also shape the transition to gender equality. These include how far economic growth serves women's needs and priorities, and how far de jure rights, formal conventions, and legal treaties are implemented and translated into effective reforms.

Human development fuels more egalitarian attitudes toward women in virtually any society, although this process, particularly the pace of cultural change, is mediated by particular religious legacies, historical traditions, and institutional structures in each country. Many other factors can accelerate or retard these trends in a given society, including social movements, NGOs, and coalitional networks organized by feminists and by their opponents; intellectual developments conveyed by seminal theorists, the mass media, and academe; and the impact of the policy process, including government leaders, parliaments, and the courts. Globalization has also strengthened international networks of women who work with local and regional grassroots associations. There are pressures and counterpressures in any major social trend, just as ocean tides ebb and flow. Historical accounts of the women's movement or of advances in women's rights have often stressed that certain cultural or ideological shifts are sui generis, depending upon particular contingent factors within each country that act as the catalyst for widespread change in sex roles. Examples include the success of grassroots women's organizations in support of specific initiatives, such as the parity movement in France, equal pay in Europe, and the UN World Conferences; landmark legal initiatives, including passage of equal pay regulations and sex discrimination acts; and dramatic legal cases on issues such as divorce rights and abortion that come before the courts. If contingent factors did have a major impact on beliefs and values about gender equality, then we might expect to find somewhat erratic patterns of cultural change across different countries and types of societies. And indeed, the specific timing of landmark changes, such as the enfranchisement of women, the passage of abortion laws, and substantial gains for women in elected office, are often contingent on nation-specific factors. The contrasts in gender equality between advanced industrialized nations that are in other respects fairly similar, such as Germany and France, or the United States and Canada, show that gains for women are far from automatic and inevitable. In particular, social behavior and public policies can often lag well behind cultural shifts in attitudes toward sex roles. Moreover, in some cases concrete gains for women – for example, the election of women leaders as prime ministers or presidents in traditional societies – can run ahead of public opinion in a particular nation. In the longer term, however, it seems clear that modernization brings systematic, *predictable* changes in attitudes toward gender roles.

The comparison of many different nations around the globe confirms our thesis that the impact of modernization is not strictly linear; instead, it operates in two key phases. To summarize the developments, Table 7.1 shows how a wide range of cultural, economic,

TABLE 7.1. *Indicators of gender equality*

	Type of Society			
	Agrarian	Industrial	Postindustrial	N
Cultural indicators				
Gender Equality Scale	61	68	80	58
Religiosity scale	71	56	53	71
Economic indicators				
Female adult economic activity rate, 1997 (%)	35	35	42	162
Female administrators and managers (% of total)	15	25	26	102
Female professional and technical (% of total)	35	49	47	102
Social indicators				
Contraceptive prevalence rate, 1990–98 (%)	32	60	74	142
Births to mothers under 20, 1991–97 (%)	12	11	4	90
Dependency ratio, 1997 (%)	82	54	50	165
Female primary level education (% age group)	69	94	100	139
Female secondary level education (% age group)	45	77	95	128
Female adult literacy rate, 1997 (%)	56	90	97	123
Gender-related development index, 1997	.54	.79	.91	142
Political indicators				
Year women were first enfranchised	1955	1942	1922	175
Women in the lower house of parliament, 2000 (%)	8.7	11.2	24.5	174
Gender empowerment measure	.34	.46	.66	102

Note: Mean economic, social, political and cultural indicators. See Appendix A for the classification of nations and Appendix B for concepts and measures. N = number of societies.
Source: Economic, social, and political indicators calculated from UNDP. *UNDP Human Development Report 2000*. New York: UNDP/Oxford University Press. Cultural indicators calculated from the World Values Surveys.

social, and political indicators relating to women's lives, derived from official sources and collected by the United Nations Development Program, vary systematically across agrarian, industrial, and postindustrial countries around the world. As Table 7.1 shows, the shift from agrarian toward industrial societies has dramatic consequences. This transition alters the traditional family, as is indicated by the doubling in the contraception prevalence rate (the proportion of married women of childbearing age using contraception) as women gain greater control over childbearing and family size, and the dramatic cuts in the dependency ratio (measured by the population under fifteen and over sixty-five as a proportion of the working-age population). Women make important gains as administrators and managers, and in the professions. This transition also gives women skills to compete in the economic marketplace: female rates of literacy almost double, and the enrollment of girls in primary and secondary education rises sharply. There is a substantial improvement in the UNDP Gender-related Development Index (calculated in the same way as the Human Development Index but adjusted for the disparities between men and women). This stage also alters (but does not transform) the traditional division of sex roles and childcare responsibilities within the home and family. The move from the industrial to the postindustrial phase brings a transition toward greater gender equality in cultural attitudes, as women gain more opportunities in university (tertiary) education and move further up the career ladder in management and the professions. This stage sees substantial progress toward greater (but not yet equal) political influence within elected and appointed bodies – for example, doubling the proportion of women in parliament – and sharp improvements in the UNDP Gender Empowerment Measure (combining economic participation and decision making, political participation and decision making, and power over economic resources). Lastly, as discussed in earlier chapters, cultural attitudes toward sex roles respond to, and interact with, these social trends. The five-item Gender Equality Scale, including items on work, politics, and the family and derived from the World Values Surveys / European Values Surveys, 1995–2001, shows far more egalitarian attitudes for those living in affluent postindustrial societies than for those living in agrarian societies. The religiosity scale, discussed in detail in Chapter 3, shows the reverse pattern; by far the strongest religious faith is found among those living in agrarian societies.

The shifts in attitudes toward sex roles that we have documented do not occur in isolation. Instead, they correspond to broader social and cultural shifts relating to the transition from traditional to secular-rational values (linked to the decline of the traditional family) and from survival to self-expression values (associated with the rise of gender equality). What are the consequences of these developments? Cultural shifts in modern societies are not sufficient by themselves to guarantee women equality across all major dimensions of life; nevertheless, by underpinning structural reforms and women's rights, and by strengthening public support for women's movements and organizations, they can be expected to greatly facilitate this process. Cultural change in attitudes toward the roles of women and men can thus be regarded as a necessary, although not sufficient, condition for the consolidation of gender equality.

Gender Equality and Cultural Change

If beliefs about traditional sex roles and gender equality have changed in response to specific events and developments, then the trends that we have documented could prove to be a transient phenomenon that might be swept away by an antifeminist backlash. But if the rising tide of egalitarian attitudes that we have documented is part of a broader, deep-rooted process of social and cultural change, then it is likely to prove enduring.

How do beliefs about gender equality relate to broader dimensions of social values? Factor analysis of national-level data from the forty-three societies included in the 1990 WVS/EVS found that two main dimensions accounted for over half of the cross-national variance in more than a score of variables tapping basic values across a wide range of domains, ranging from politics to economic life and sexual behavior.[1] (The items included in these scales are listed in Appendix B.) These dimensions of cross-cultural variation are robust; when the 1990–91 factor analysis was replicated with the data from the 1995–98 surveys, the same two dimensions of cross-cultural variation emerged – even though the new analysis was based on twenty-three additional countries not included in the earlier study.[2] Each dimension taps a major axis of cross-cultural variation involving many different basic values.

The first dimension, *traditional/secular-rational*, reflects the contrasting value systems found in religious versus secular societies. Traditional societies emphasize the importance of parent-child ties in traditional families and deference to authority, along with absolute moral standards, and they reject divorce, abortion, euthanasia, and suicide. Traditional societies are highly patriotic and nationalistic. Societies with secular-rational values display the opposite preferences on all of these topics.

The *survival/self-expression* dimension includes a wide range of beliefs and values. A central component involves the polarization between materialist and postmaterialist values. These values reflect an intergenerational shift away from an emphasis on economic and physical security and toward an increasing emphasis on self-expression, subjective well-being, and quality of life concerns. Societies emphasizing survival values have relatively materialist orientations, show relatively low levels of subjective well-being, report relatively poor health, tend to be intolerant toward out-group minorities, rank low on interpersonal trust, and emphasize hard work, rather than imagination or tolerance, as the most important value to teach a child. By contrast, societies emphasizing self-expression values display the opposite preferences on all of these topics.

During the late twentieth century, the shift from survival to self-expression values, and from religious to secular values, has continued throughout advanced industrial societies. The move toward greater equality between women and men is a central component of a much broader dimension of cultural change. Self-expression values tend to be more evident among generations in affluent nations that grew up under conditions in which basic survival and security could be taken for granted. Such conditions include the existence of a welfare state and nonprofit schemes to cope with risks of unemployment and old age; the rule of law and effective policing to minimize the threats of crime and violence; widespread access to physicians and hospitals, mitigating problems of sickness and ill health; and sufficient affluence to allow most people to enjoy a comfortable and relatively safe lifestyle and some private assets and savings, such as home ownership, as a hedge against future uncertainties. In addition, life-threatening natural disasters such as famine, plague, and earthquake have come under increasing control in affluent nations. In these conditions, there should be a declining priority given to basic survival, so that other values come to the fore.

FIGURE 7.1. Cultural map of the world.

Figure 7.1 illustrates where each of the societies examined here, containing most of the world's population, is located today on these two dimensions, providing a cultural map of the world on these scales. We find large and pervasive differences between the worldviews of people in rich and poor societies; their basic values and beliefs differ on scores of key variables, in a coherent pattern. Richer societies tend to rank high on both of these dimensions, while low-income societies rank low. Does this mean that economic development brings predictable changes in prevailing values? The data indicate that it does: time-series evidence shows that with economic development, societies tend to move from the lower left of Figure 7.1 toward the upper right – from the values prevailing in low-income societies toward the values prevailing in high-income societies.[3] The first dimension, traditional or secular-rational values, is strongly linked with the transition from agrarian society to industrial society. The survival/self-expression dimension, on the other hand, is linked with the transition from industrial society to a knowledge economy. Table 7.2, using a wide range of indicators of societal development, shows that the traditional versus secular-rational scale is significantly correlated at the national level with many social indicators, notably the dependency ratio, the Human Development Index, and life expectancy. But economic differences are not the whole story. Religious traditions seem to have an enduring impact on contemporary value systems, as Max Weber, Samuel Huntington, and others have argued.[4] Postindustrial societies prove to be the most secular and postmaterialist, but within this group there are distinctions between the Protestant countries of northern Europe and the historically Roman Catholic nations of Western Europe, reflecting the fact that their publics have relatively similar values on political, religious, and economic questions, as well as similar attitudes toward gender roles, child rearing, and sexual behavior. And the ex-Communist states form another cluster (proving secular but materialistic in orientation). The publics in Latin American countries also share relatively similar values. The most traditional and materialistic publics live in the sub-Saharan African countries (Tanzania, Nigeria, Zimbabwe, and Uganda), proving similar to some of the Islamic North African and Middle Eastern nations (e.g., Egypt and Jordan). Societies that experience substantial economic development tend to move from the lower left toward the upper right of the map. But cultural change is path-dependent. The fact that a society was historically Protestant or Orthodox or Islamic or Confucian gives rise to cultural zones with distinctive value systems that persist even when we control for the effects of economic development. A society's culture reflects its entire historical heritage, including religious traditions, colonial ties, the experience of Communist rule, and its contemporary level of economic development.

Attitudes toward gender equality are central to this much broader and more diffuse process of cultural change. The survival versus self-expression values (which subsumes materialist versus postmaterialist values) are strongly correlated with attitudes toward the role of women, as is demonstrated by Table 7.3. Such questions as whether "a woman has to have children to be fulfilled," whether

TABLE 7.2. *Social indicators and the value scales*

	Traditional versus Secular-Rational	Sig.	Survival versus Self-expression	Sig.	N
Development indicators					
Dependency ratio, % 1997 (UNDP)	.73	***	.21	N/s	62
Doctors per 100,000 pop. 1993 (UNDP)	.68	***	.20	N/s	54
Human Development Index, 1998	.58	***	.62	***	62
Life expectancy, 1998 (UNDP)	.50	***	.53	***	63
Divorces (as % of marriages), 1996 (UNDP)	.45	***	.14	*	37
Per capita GDP, 1998 (in US$ PPP UNDP)	.43	***	.79	***	62
Level of democracy (reversed FH rate 2000)	.40	***	.56	***	65
% Urban population, 2000 (UNDP)	.37	***	.42	***	62
% GNP from services, 1997 (UNDP)	.18	N/s	.46	***	56
% GNP from agriculture, 1997 (UNDP)	-.24	N/s	-.52	***	47
Gender-related indicators					
Gender-related development, 1997 (UNDP)	.57	***	.65	***	59
Gender empowerment measure (GEM) (UNDP)	.49	***	.68	***	47
Sexual Equality Scale (WVS, 1995–2001)	.33	*	.68	***	54
Religious indicators					
Strength of Religiosity Scale (WVS)	-.84	***	-.21		68
Society with Islamic predominant religion	-.29	*	-.19		68
Society with Christian predominant religion	.19		.75	***	68

Note: Correlations between social indicators and societal-level means on the traditional versus rational-secular scale and the survival versus self-expression scale. The traditional values scale is measured by support for the following items: God is very important in respondent's life; it is more important for a child to learn obedience and religious faith than independence and determination; autonomy index; abortion is never justifiable; respondent has strong sense of national pride; respondent favors respect for authority. Support for secular-rational values is measured by the opposite position on all of the above. UNDP. *Development Indicators, 2001*. New York: Oxford University Press/UNDP.
Source: WVS/EVS, 1995–2001.

TABLE 7.3. *The relationship between gender equality and survival values*

	Corr.
Men make better political leaders than women.	.86
A woman has to have children to be fulfilled.	.83
A child needs a home with both a father and a mother in order to grow up happily.	.73
When jobs are scarce, a man has more right to a job than a woman.	.69

Note: The survival values scale is measured by support for the following items: respondent gives priority to economic and physical security over self-expression and quality of life (four-item materialist/postmaterialist values index); respondent describes self as not very happy; homosexuality is never justifiable; respondent has not and would not sign a petition; you have to be very careful about trusting people. Support for self-expression values is measured by the opposite position on all of the above. The original polarities vary; the above statements show how each item relates to this values index.
Source: WVS/EVS, 1990 and 1996.

"when jobs are scarce, men have more right to a job than women," and whether "a university education is more important for a boy than a girl" all show strong correlations with the survival self-expression dimension. But one item taps this dimension particularly well: the question of whether "men make better political leaders than women." Responses to this question are very strongly correlated with the survival/self-expression dimension ($r = .86$) – indeed, they are almost as strongly correlated with it as is the materialist/postmaterialist values battery. This is remarkable, because materialist/postmaterialist values are measured by a multi-item battery that was explicitly designed to gauge intergenerational value change. The question about whether men make better political leaders than women, by contrast, is a single item. It nevertheless taps the survival/self-expression dimension almost as strongly as does the materialist/postmaterialist values battery, and better than any of the other variables included in the WVS/EVS. To put gender equality on the same footing as the other values, we reran the factor analysis used earlier, replicating it in every detail but one: we added the question, "Do men make better political leaders than women?" The resulting analysis produced essentially the same factor structure as that reported earlier, with one difference: the question about gender roles displayed the highest loading on the survival/self-expression dimension (a loading of .91, slightly *higher* than that of the materialist/postmaterialist index). This suggests that in the past,

Inglehart and colleagues may have underestimated the importance of changing gender roles when they set out to measure the cultural changes linked with the emergence of postindustrial society. During the past few decades, these changes have transformed the entire way of life for over half the world's population. Throughout history, women in virtually all societies have had their life options restricted to the roles of wife and mother. Increasingly today, in postindustrial societies, almost any career and almost any lifestyle is opening up to them. These cultural changes have been important for men, but the transformation in the lives of women is far more dramatic, moving them from narrow subordination toward full equality. A radical change is altering women's education, career opportunities, fertility rates, sexual behavior, and worldviews. With this in mind, it is not surprising to find that gender issues constitute such a central component – arguably, the single most central component – of value change in postindustrial societies.

The Rising Tide of Gender Equality

The opening chapters of this book considered alternative explanations for the growing equality of men and women, arguing that if this were due to the process of modernization, then evidence should be available showing substantial contrasts in cultural attitudes between more developed and less developed societies, and, within each type, between older and younger generations. Chapter 2 went on to operationalize and measure attitudes and values with respect to the growing equality in sex roles and developed the Gender Equality Scale, including items on the family, work, and politics. The results of the comparison using this scale revealed that, far from showing a random distribution, attitudes toward gender equality form coherent and predictable patterns. In particular, there are clearly established contrasts between countries at different levels of societal modernization, with agrarian nations being the most traditional in emphasizing sharply divided sex roles, industrial societies in the early stages of transition, and postindustrial societies the most egalitarian in their beliefs about the roles of women and men. Moreover, we demonstrated that this is not just a matter of *economic* development, because a wide range of other indicators of human development, from levels of energy use to average life expectancy, are about equally good predictors of support for gender equality. A comparision of birth cohorts also showed predictable patterns, with younger generations in postindustrial societies being far more egalitarian than their parents and grandparents. This indication of generational change was bound in industrial nations; within poorer agrarian societies there was no evidence of any significant generational shifts. Within societies, we found significant differences between women and men, but in postindustrial nations younger men have shifted their values in the same direction as younger women. Support for gender equality was also stronger among the well-educated, the less religious, the un-married, and postmaterialists. Nevertheless, the gap that has emerged *between* traditional agrarian societies and postindustrial societies is far greater than the gap between women and men *within* each type of society.

Building on these findings, we hypothesized that the process of so-cietal modernization is path-specific, with the pace of change in any given society conditioned by cultural legacies and religious traditions. Chapter 3 demonstrated that a process of secularization has gradu-ally accompanied societal modernization, weakening religious values among the younger generation in postindustrial societies, and fueling the rising tide of gender equality. Generational comparisons suggest that postindustrial societies have experienced a parallel liberalization of moral values toward sexuality among the younger generation, ex-emplified by attitudes toward the issues of abortion, homosexuality, prostitution, and divorce. At the same time, in agrarian societies re-ligiosity continues to exert a strong influence on social norms about the appropriate division of sex roles in the home, the workforce, and in the public sphere. Attitudes toward women vary among adherents of different religious sects and denominations; in particular, an Islamic religious heritage was one of the most powerful barriers to the rising tide of gender equality.

To explore the political consequences of these developments, the study went on to consider how far this process has altered the so-cial basis of party politics and voting behavior, there by giving rise to gender dealignment or realignment. The analysis found that in many nations today, women hold more left-leaning values than men in their attitudes toward the appropriate role of the state versus the market, favoring active government intervention in social protection and public ownership. Although an extensive body of evidence indicates that from the 1950s to the 1980s, women tended to be more conservative than men in their ideology and voting behavior, this pattern has now changed, with women becoming more left-leaning than men in many societies. In explaining why women are now more left-leaning in their values, we demonstrated that the modern gender gap persists in many nations even after introducing a battery of social controls, but that the size of the gap diminishes substantially when we take cultural values into account. This suggests that the modern gender gap reflects differences in the value orientations of women and men, especially in their orientations toward postmaterialism, the role of government, and gender equality, more than differences in their lifestyles or social backgrounds. Lastly, generational comparisons provide indirect evidence of value change in postindustrial societies, showing that the *modern* gender gap in ideology is strongest among the younger age groups, while the *traditional* gender gap persists among the elderly. If this reflects a generational change rather than a life-cycle effect, as seems likely, it implies that the process of generational population replacement will continue to move women leftward. In the long term, as younger voters gradually replace older generations, the shift towards left-leaning values among women should become stronger in affluent nations.

On this basis, we reviewed the evidence in many countries to see whether gender differences in political activism have diminished or whether they continue to remain significant in contemporary societies. The study compared patterns of traditional political activism via elections and parties; civic activism through voluntary organizations, new social movements, and community associations; and protest politics, including by demonstrations, petitions, strikes, and boycotts. We established that, despite the rising tide of gender equality transforming many other aspects of men's and women's lives and cultural values, in the public sphere there was a lagged effect, as women continue to remain less politically active in most nations. The gender gap is usually modest, but consistent across all major dimensions of civic life. Nevertheless, we demonstrated that the gender gap in political activism was often greatest in poorer developing nations and that it usually diminished – and in one case (associational activism) even reversed – in postindustrial societies. The analysis also showed that the gender gap in civic and protest activism is largest among certain social groups that are contracting in size – namely, among women in the oldest generation, those not in paid work, the less educated, and those holding traditional views of gender equality – suggesting that long-term social trends, such as secularization and female labor force participation, that are transforming women's lifestyles and values will tend to close the gap in future decades. The demographic process of generational turnover, in particular, can be expected to contribute long-term change.

But what is the role of political culture in women's leadership at the apex of politics? Do traditional attitudes toward women as political leaders function as a significant barrier to their empowerment? And how important is culture in comparison to alternative structural and institutional factors? The evidence indicates that there are substantial differences in egalitarian attitudes toward women's leadership among postindustrial, post-Communist, and agrarian societies. In particular, traditional attitudes toward gender equality remain a major obstacle to the election of women to parliament. Culture continues to influence the proportion of women in parliament, even controlling for social structural and political institutions. Yet there is also evidence that as a result of modernization, these cultural barriers have been fading among the younger generation in postindustrial societies. Trying to alter deep-seated attitudes toward sex roles in public life may prove difficult in the short term, but in the longer term the secular trends in value change associated with the process of modernization, especially among younger generations of women and men, seems likely to facilitate the entry of more women into positions of power in advanced industrialized nations. The combination of cultural shifts in attitudes and institutional reforms in recruitment processes within parties holds considerable promise for structural change, that will help women to move toward political parity in elected and appointed office. It seems clear that social values have shifted further and faster than the reality of women's power in democratic societies.

Contrasting conclusions could be drawn from the analysis presented here. One response could be that social change appears to be largely deterministic, so that, left by itself, the rising tide will eventually sweep aside the traditional barriers to women's full participation in the public sphere; women will eventually gain entry into the boardroom and professions in the workplace and achieve equal responsibility for child care and family in the home, without needing activists to change the policy agenda or government initiatives to expand equal opportunities. At the same time, a fatalistic interpretation could assume that in poorer societies the lives of women and men are determined by global processes of societal modernization, so that there is little or nothing that political actors, women's movements, or government policies can do to alter the broad sweep of human history. This is not our view. We believe that long-term cultural shifts are important in bringing greater equality between women and men, but that both basic investment in human development in poorer nations, and structural policy reforms designed to reduce sex discrimination and expand opportunities for women, can accelerate the pace of change in the lives of men and women. Moreover, tides can ebb and flow, with reverses in opportunities for women – such as substantial cuts in welfare state spending, which can disproportionately affect women as the main caregivers responsible for children and the elderly, or downturns in the economy, which result in rising levels of female unemployment and lower pay. Even more importantly, there is often a lengthy time lag between shifts in public opinion and the response of institutions. Cultural change, while important for consolidating and reinforcing social change, is not enough by itself. The cultural changes we have examined tend to generate support for the women's movement, as well as encouraging a climate sympathetic to legal and administrative public policies designed to achieve equal opportunities, affirmative action, and positive discrimination for women. "Top-down" policy initiatives can be introduced by government, even if they run ahead of public opinion, as exemplified by the common use by Communist regimes of gender quotas to get women into parliaments, a process that was discarded with the first free and fair elections in Central and Eastern Europe. But without widespread public support, the danger is that these public policy initiatives to secure equality can prove to be transient and can eventually generate a backlash. They may also prove to be merely symbolic gestures, such as formal declarations of support for equal opportunities that fail to be implemented in practice. But if human development is combined with legal and structural reforms, and if public opinion is also gradually shifting in a more egalitarian direction, it will help to consolidate and entrench substantial gains for women, ratcheting up the pace of social change. Moving further toward achieving equality for women – in the home and family, in the workplace, and in positions of political power – remains one of the most important challenges facing governments in the twenty-first century.

Appendix A

TABLE A.1. *Classification of types of society*

| | Included in WVS/EVS | | | | HDI | |
	1980 Wave	1990 Wave	1995 Wave	2000 Wave	1998	Type of State
Postindustrial						
1 Australia	Yes	.	Yes	.	.929	Older democracy
2 Austria	.	Yes	.	Yes	.908	Older democracy
3 Belgium	Yes	Yes	.	Yes	.925	Older democracy
4 Canada	Yes	Yes	.	Yes	.935	Older democracy
5 Denmark	Yes	Yes	.	Yes	.911	Older democracy
6 Finland	Yes	Yes	Yes	Yes	.917	Older democracy
7 France	Yes	Yes	.	Yes	.917	Older democracy
8 Germany[a]	Yes	Yes	Yes	Yes	.911	Older democracy
9 Iceland	Yes	Yes	.	Yes	.927	Older democracy
10 Ireland	Yes	Yes	.	Yes	.907	Older democracy
11 Italy	Yes	Yes	.	Yes	.903	Older democracy
12 Japan	Yes	Yes	Yes	Yes	.924	Older democracy
13 Luxembourg	.	.	.	Yes	.908	Older democracy
14 Netherlands	Yes	Yes	.	Yes	.925	Older democracy
15 New Zealand	.	.	Yes	.	.903	Older democracy
16 Norway	Yes	Yes	Yes	.	.934	Older democracy
17 Spain	Yes	Yes	Yes	Yes	.899	Older democracy
18 Sweden	Yes	Yes	Yes	Yes	.926	Older democracy
19 Switzerland	.	Yes	Yes	.	.915	Older democracy

(continued)

TABLE A.I *(continued)*

	Included in WVS / EVS					
	1980 Wave	1990 Wave	1995 Wave	2000 Wave	HDI 1998	Type of State
Postindustrial						
20 United Kingdom[a]	Yes	Yes	Yes	Yes	.918	Older democracy
21 United States	Yes	Yes	Yes	Yes	.929	Older democracy
Industrial						
1 Argentina	Yes	Yes	Yes	Yes	.837	Newer democracy
2 Belarus	.	Yes	Yes	Yes	.781	Non-democracy
3 Bosnia and Herzegovina	.	.	Yes	.	.	Non-democracy
4 Brazil	.	Yes	Yes	.	.747	Semi-democracy
5 Bulgaria	.	Yes	Yes	Yes	.772	Newer democracy
6 Chile	.	Yes	Yes	Yes	.826	Newer democracy
7 Colombia	.	.	Yes	.	.764	Semi-democracy
8 Croatia	.	.	Yes	Yes	.795	Semi-democracy
9 Czech Republic	.	Yes	Yes	Yes	.843	Newer democracy
10 Estonia	.	Yes	Yes	Yes	.801	Newer democracy
11 Georgia	.	.	Yes	.	.762	Semi-democracy
12 Greece	.	.	.	Yes	.875	Older democracy
13 Hungary	Yes	Yes	Yes	Yes	.817	Newer democracy
14 Korea, Rep.	Yes	Yes	Yes	.	.854	Newer democracy
15 Latvia	.	Yes	Yes	Yes	.771	Newer democracy
16 Lithuania	.	Yes	Yes	Yes	.789	Newer democracy
17 Macedonia	.	.	Yes	.	.763	Semi-democracy
18 Malta				Yes	.865	Older democracy
19 Mexico	Yes	Yes	Yes	Yes	.784	Semi-democracy
20 Philippines	.	.	.	Yes	.744	Newer democracy
21 Poland	.	Yes	Yes	Yes	.814	Newer democracy
22 Portugal	.	Yes	.	Yes	.864	Older democracy
23 Romania	.	Yes	Yes	Yes	.770	Newer democracy
24 Russian Federation	.	Yes	Yes	Yes	.771	Semi-democracy
25 Slovakia	.	Yes	Yes	Yes	.825	Newer democracy
26 Slovenia	.	Yes	Yes	Yes	.861	Newer democracy
27 Taiwan	.	.	Yes	.	.	Newer democracy
28 Turkey	.	Yes	Yes	Yes	.732	Semi-democracy
29 Ukraine	.	.	Yes	Yes	.744	Semi-democracy
30 Uruguay	.	.	Yes	.	.825	Newer democracy
31 Venezuela	.	.	Yes	Yes	.770	Semi-democracy
32 Yugoslavia, Fed. Rep.[a]		Yes				Non-democracy

| | Included in WVS / EVS | | | | | |
	1980 Wave	1990 Wave	1995 Wave	2000 Wave	HDI 1998	Type of State
Agrarian						
1 Albania	.	.	Yes	.	.713	Semi-democracy
2 Armenia	.	.	Yes	.	.721	Semi-democracy
3 Azerbaijan	.	.	Yes	.	.722	Non-democracy
4 Bangladesh	.	.	Yes	Yes	.461	Semi-democracy
5 China	.	Yes	Yes	.	.706	Non-democracy
6 Dominican Rep	.	.	Yes	.	.729	Newer democracy
7 Egypt	.	.	.	Yes	.623	Non-democracy
8 El Salvador	.	.	.	Yes	.696	Newer democracy
9 India	.	Yes	Yes	.	.563	Older democracy
10 Iran	.	.	.	Yes	.709	Non-democracy
11 Jordan	.	.	.	Yes	.721	Semi-democracy
12 Moldova, Rep.	.	.	.	Yes	.700	Semi-democracy
13 Morocco				Yes	.589	Semi-democracy
14 Nigeria	.	Yes	Yes	Yes	.439	Semi-democracy
15 Pakistan	.	.	Yes	.	.522	Non-democracy
16 Peru	.	.	Yes	.	.737	Semi-democracy
17 South Africa	Yes	Yes	Yes	Yes	.697	Newer democracy
18 Tanzania				Yes	.415	Semi-democracy
19 Uganda	.	.	.	Yes	.409	Non-democracy
20 Vietnam	.	.	.	Yes	.671	Non-democracy
21 Zimbabwe	.	.	.	Yes	.555	Non-democracy
74						

Note: The classification of societies is based on categorizing the UNDP Human Development Index (1998), based on longevity (as measured by life expectancy at birth), educational achievement, and standard of living (as measured by per capita GDP [PPP $US]).

The classification of states is based on the Freedom House estimates of political rights and civil liberties (mean 1980–2000).

[a] It should be noted that certain nation-states are subdivided into societies for analysis because of their distinctive political legacies, historical traditions, and social cleavages, including Germany (subdividing West and East Germany), the United Kingdom (Northern Ireland and Great Britain), and the Federal Republic of Yugoslavia (Serbia and Montenegro after 1992). Therefore, in total there are seventy-four nation states but seventy-seven societies compared within the study.

Source: UNDP. *UNDP Human Development Report 2000.* New York: UNDP/Oxford University Press.

TABLE A.2. *Types of nation-state included in any wave of the World Values Survey / European Values Survey*

	Total number of Nation-States in the World	Number of States in Any Wave of the WVS/EVS	% of States included in the WVS/EVS
Size of state			
Small (population of one million or less)	41	2	5
Moderate (population from 1 million to 30 million)	116	44	38
Large (population over 30 million)	33	28	85
Type of society			
Postindustrial	21	21	100
Industrial	64	32	50
Agrarian	106	21	20
Type of government regime			
Older democracy	39	25	64
Newer democracy	43	19	44
Semi-democracy	47	19	40
Non-democracy	62	11	18
World region			
Asia-Pacific	38	12	32
Central and Eastern Europe	26	21	81
Middle East	19	5	26
North America	3	3	100
Scandinavia	5	5	100
South America	32	9	28
Sub-saharan Africa	49	5	10
Western Europe	19	14	70
All	191	74	39

For details of the classification of government regimes and types of societies, see Table A.1.

Appendix B

TABLE B.1. *Concepts and measures*

Variable	Definitions, Coding, and Sources
Human development indicators	
Human Development Index	The Human Development Index (HDI) is based on longevity, as measured by life expectancy at birth; educational achievement; and standard of living, as measured by per capita GDP (PPP $US). UNDP. *Human Development Report 2000.*
Type of society	"Postindustrial societies" are defined as the twenty most affluent states around the world, ranking with an HDI score over .900 and mean per capita GDP of $29,585. "Industrial societies" are classified as the 58 nations with a moderate HDI (ranging from .740 to .899) and a moderate per capita GDP of $6,314. Lastly, "agrarian societies" are the 97 nations with lower levels of development (HDI of .739 or below) and mean per capita GDP of $1,098.
Per capita GDP	Measured in $US in Purchasing Power Parity, 1998. UNDP. *Human Development Report 2000.*
Economic equality	The Gini Index measures the extent to which the distribution of income within an economy deviates from a perfectly equal distribution. The index has been reversed so that 1 represents perfect equality. World Bank. *World Development Indicators 2001.*

(continued)

TABLE B.1 *(continued)*

Variable	Definitions, Coding, and Sources
Lower infant mortality	The number of infants dying before the age of one year, per 1,000 live births, 1999. The indicator has been reversed so that a higher figure represents lower infant mortality. World Bank. *World Development Indicators 2001.*
Public health expenditure	Public health expenditure consists of recurrent and capital spending from government budgets, external borrowings, and grants, as a percentage of GDP, 1997–99. World Bank. *World Development Indicators 2001.*
Life expectancy	Life expectancy at birth (years), 1995–2000. UNDP. *Human Development Report 2000.*
Adult literacy rate	Literacy as a percentage of adults (age fifteen and above), 1998. UNDP. *Human Development Report 2000.*
% Secondary education	Secondary age group enrolment as a percentage of the relevant age group, 1997. UNDP. *Human Development Report 2000.*
Contraceptive prevalence rate	The percentage of married women of childbearing age (15–49) who are using any form of contraception. UNDP. *Human Development Report 2000.*
Dependency ratio	The ratio of the population defined as dependent – those under fifteen and over sixty-four years old – to the working-age population. UNDP. *Human Development Report 2000.*
Gender-related Development Index	A composite index using the same variables as the Human Development Index but adjusting life expectancy, educational attainment, and income in accordance with the disparity in achievement between women and men in each country. UNDP. *Human Development Report 2000.*
Gender Empowerment Measure	A composite index combining indices for economic participation and decision making, for political participation and decision making, and for power over economic resources. UNDP. *Human Development Report 2000.*
Political indicators	
Level of democracy	The Gastil index, a seven-point scale used by Freedom House, measuring political rights and civil liberties every year. <www.Freedomhouse.com>
Type of state	Based on the Gastil index, we define older democracies as states with at least twenty years' continuous experience of democracy from 1980 to

Variable	Definitions, Coding, and Sources
	2000 and a Freedom House rating of 5.5 to 7.0 in the latest available estimate (1999–2000). States classified as newer democracies have less than twenty years' experience with democracy and a current Gastil index rating of 5.5 to 7.0. Semi-democracies have been democratic for less than twenty years and have current Gastil index ratings of 3.5 to 5.5. Non-democracies are the remaining states, with a Gastil index score from 1.0 to 3.0; they include military-backed dictatorships, authoritarian states, elitist oligarchies, and absolute monarchies.
Women in elected office	The percentage of women elected to the lower house of parliament, 2000, is from Inter-Parliamentary Union. March 2001. *Percentage of Women in the Lower House of Parliament, 2001.* Geneva: IPU. <www.ipu.org>
Civic activism	Belong: "Please look carefully at the following list of voluntary organizations and activities and say which, if any, do you belong to?" Active: (If belong) "And for which, if any, are you currently doing unpaid voluntary work?" Political parties or groups; sports or recreation; peace movement; professional associations; labor unions; local community action groups; youth work (e.g., scouts, guides, youth clubs); conservation, environmental, or animal rights; third world development or human rights; education, arts, music, or cultural activities; religious or church organizations; voluntary organizations concerned with health; social welfare for the elderly, handicapped, or deprived people; women's groups.
Protest activism	A summary five-point scale based on the following items: "Now I'd like you to look at this card. I'm going to read out some different forms of political action that people can take, and I'd like you to tell me, for each one, whether you have actually done any of these things, whether you might do it, or would never, under any circumstances, do it." Signing a petition, joining in boycotts, attending lawful demonstrations, joining unofficial strikes, occupying buildings or factories. % "Have actually done."

(continued)

TABLE B.I *(continued)*

Variable	Definitions, Coding, and Sources
Left-Right Voting Scale	V210. "If there were a national election tomorrow, for which party on this list would you vote?" The ten-point left-right voting scale is coded by classifying responses according to the Inglehart-Huber (1995) expert party location scale. *Source:* WVS/EVS.
Left-Right Ideology Scale	V123. "In political matters people talk of 'the left' and 'the right'. How would you place your views on this scale, generally speaking?" The ten-point scale is coded from 1 = most left to 10 = most right. *Source:* WVS/EVS.
Political Discussion Scale	V37. "When you get together with friends, would you say you discuss political matters frequently (3), occasionally (2), or never (1)?" *Source:* WVS/EVS.
Cultural indicators	
Gender Equality Scale	The combined 100-point Gender Equality Scale is based on the following 5 items: MENPOL Q118: "On the whole, men make better political leaders than women do." (agree coded low); MENJOBS Q78: "When jobs are scarce, men should have more right to a job than women." (agree coded low); BOYEDUC Q119: "A university education is more important for a boy than a girl." (agree coded low); NEEDKID Q110: "Do you think that a woman has to have children in order to be fulfilled or is this not necessary?" (agree coded low); SGLMUM Q112: "If a woman wants to have a child as a single parent but she doesn't want to have a stable relationship with a man, do you approve or disapprove?" (disapprove coded low). *Source:* Pooled WVS/EVS, 1995–2001.
Gender equality categories	The Gender Equality Scale is dichotomized into low (traditional) and high (egalitarian).
Religiosity scale	The combined 6-item Strength of Religiosity Scale, standardized to 100 points, consists of the following items: Identify: V186. "Independently of whether you go to church or not, would you say you are ... a religious person, not a religious person, or a convinced atheist?" (% religious) Attend: V185. "Apart from weddings, funerals and christenings, about how often do you attend

Variable	Definitions, Coding, and Sources
	religious services these days?" (% once a week or more) Importance: V196. "How important is God in your life?" (% "Very" scaled 6–10). Believe: V191 "Do you believe in God?" (% Yes) Life: V192. "Do you believe in life after death?" (% Yes) Comfort: V.197. "Do you find that you get comfort and strength from religion?" *Source:* Pooled WVS/EVS, 1995–2001.
Type of religion	V184: "Do you belong to a religious denomination?" (If yes). "Which one?" Coded: No, not a member; Roman Catholic; Protestant; Orthodox (Russian/Greek/etc.); Jewish; Muslim; Hindu; Buddhist; Other. *Source:* Pooled WVS/EVS, 1995–2001.
Type of predominant religion worldwide	The classification of the major religion (adhered to by the largest population) in all 193 states around the world is based on CIA. *The World Factbook, 2001.* Washington, DC: Central Intelligence Agency. *Source:* <http://www.cia.gov/cia/publications/factbook>
Traditional versus secular-rational values	The traditional values scale is measured by support for the following items: God is very important in respondent's life; it is more important for a child to learn obedience and religious faith than independence and determination; autonomy index; abortion is never justifiable; respondent has strong sense of national pride; respondent favors respect for authority. Support for secular-rational values is measured by the opposite position on all of the above. *Source:* WVS/EVS.
Survival versus self-expression values	The survival values scale is measured by support for the following items: respondent gives priority to economic and physical security over self-expression and quality of life (four-item Materialist/Postmaterialist Values Index); respondent describes self as not very happy; homosexuality is never justifiable; respondent has not and would not sign a petition; you have to be very careful about trusting people. Support for self-expression values is measured by the opposite position on all of the above. *Source:* WVS/EVS.

(continued)

TABLE B.I *(continued)*

Variable	Definitions, Coding, and Sources
Sexual liberalization scale	"Please tell me for each of the following statements whether you think it can always be justified (10), never justified (1), or somewhere in-between, using this card...abortion, homosexuality, prostitution, divorce." *Source:* WVS/EVS.
Demographic indicators	
Occupational class	Coded for the respondent's occupation. "In which profession/occupation do you, or did you, work?" The nine-point scale is coded from employer/manager with ten or more employees (1) to unskilled manual worker (9). *Source:* WVS/EVS.
Paid work status	V220. "Are you employed now or not?" Coded full-time, part-time, or self-employed (1), other (0). *Source:* WVS/EVS.
Education	V217. "What is the highest educational level that you have ever attained?" Coded on a nine-point scale from no formal education (1) to university level with degree (9). *Source:* WVS/EVS.
Age	Coded by date of birth in continuous years. *Source:* WVS/EVS.
Age group	Young = under 30 years old; Middle-aged = 30–59 years old; Older = 60 years old and above. *Source:* WVS/EVS.
Cohort	Coded into cohorts by year of birth: 1900–1916, 1917–1926, 1927–1936, 1937–1946, 1947–1956, 1957–1966, 1967–1976, 1977–1984. *Source:* WVS/EVS.

Note: Full details of the WVS/EVS codebooks and questionnaires can be found at <www.worldvaluessurvey.com>.

Appendix C

Technical Note on the Major Scales

Given the central importance of the five-item Gender Equality Scale and the 6-item religiosity scale, additional diagnostic tests were run to examine the reliability and consistency of these scales among, and within, different types of society.

Gender Equality Scale

The five-item Gender Equality Scale from the pooled 1995–2001 WVS/EVS, standardized to 100 points, included the following items:

- MENPOL Q118: "On the whole, men make better political leaders than women do." (Agree coded low) (1990–2001 WVS)
- MENJOBS Q78: "When jobs are scarce, men should have more right to a job than women." (Agree coded low) (1990–2001 WVS)
- BOYEDUC Q119: "A university education is more important for a boy than a girl." (Agree coded low) (1990–2001 WVS)
- NEEDKID Q110: "Do you think that a woman has to have children in order to be fulfilled or is this not necessary?" (Agree coded low) (1981–2001 WVS)
- SGLMUM Q112: "If a woman wants to have a child as a single parent but she doesn't want to have a stable relationship with a man, do you approve or disapprove?" (1981–2001 WVS)

The coefficients from the factor analysis for the five-item scale fell into one consistent dimension across all societies, although the

TABLE C.1. *Factor analysis of the Gender Equality Scale (five-item) by type of society*

	Agrarian	Industrial	Postindustrial	All
Men make better political leaders than women.	.71	.68	.71	.71
Men should have more right to a job than women.	.67	.67	.71	.67
University education is more important for a boy.	.59	.63	.70	.64
Necessary for woman to have children to be fulfilled	.46	.47	.55	.56
Women wants to have children as single parent	.43	.44	.39	.39
% of total variance	.34	.34	.39	37

Note: Principal component factor analysis with varimax rotation.
Source: Pooled WVS/EVS, 1995–2001.

TABLE C.2. *Reliability analysis of the Gender Equality Scale*

	Cronbach's Alpha if the Item Is Deleted			
	Agrarian	Industrial	Postindustrial	All
Men make better political leaders than women.	.40	.47	.53	.45
Men should have more right to a job than women.	.39	.47	.52	.45
University education is more important for a boy.	.41	.47	.49	.49
Necessary for woman to have children to be fulfilled	.48	.58	.55	.55
Women wants to have children as single parent	.48	.62	.58	.54
Cronbach's Alpha	.50	.50	.57	.56

Source: Pooled WVS/EVS, 1995–2001.

coefficients proved to be slightly stronger in the postindustrial than in the other types of society (see Table C.1). The same pattern was evident when the reliability analysis broken down by type of society (see Table C.2).

Additional models, where the results of the factor analysis were broken down by each of the sixty-one nations where the items could be compared, showed that in some industrial and agrarian societies two dimensions emerged from the battery of items, loading the two items NEEDKID and SGLMUM separately from the three items MENPOL, BOYEDUC, and MENJOBS. For comparison, therefore, a shorter three-item Gender Equality Scale was constructed to see if this made any substantive difference to the analysis of cross-national variations. The scale included just the items MENPOL, BOYEDUC, and MENJOBS. The simple Pearson correlation between the national scores on the five-item and the three-item Gender Equality Scales was extremely strong (R = 0.96, P.000) as was the Spearman Rank Order correlation in the relative order of countries on both scales (R = .95, P.000). The results in Figure C.1 show the order of nations ranked by the three-item Gender Equality Scale for comparison with Figure 2.1 in Chapter 2. Again, the Scandinavian societies rank highest in gender equality on this measure, while Jordan, Egypt, and Morocco fall at the bottom of the ranking.

Therefore, even if the items concerning the sex roles in the family and child care are excluded, and we restrict the comparison to egalitarian attitudes toward sex roles in politics, the paid workforce, and education, the primary contrasts between the different types of society remain. The items concerning gender equality in politics, the paid workforce, and education can be regarded as reflecting some of the most basic demands that have long been articulated by feminists and by the women's movement in many countries around the globe; moreover, they reflect the standards for gender equality established by international conventions such as CEDAW and the United Nations declarations for women's rights, and by indicators included in the UNDP Gender Empowerment Scale. Many other important demands are commonly made in order to promote full equality for women and men, and a fuller and more comprehensive attitudinal scale could capture some of these dimensions, if data were available. The Gender Equality Scale should not be regarded as reflecting the *actual* conditions of equality experienced in women's and men's lives; rather, it reflects cultural attitudes towards gender equality. These tests suggest that the five-item scale provides reliable indicators of cultural attitudes toward gender equality.

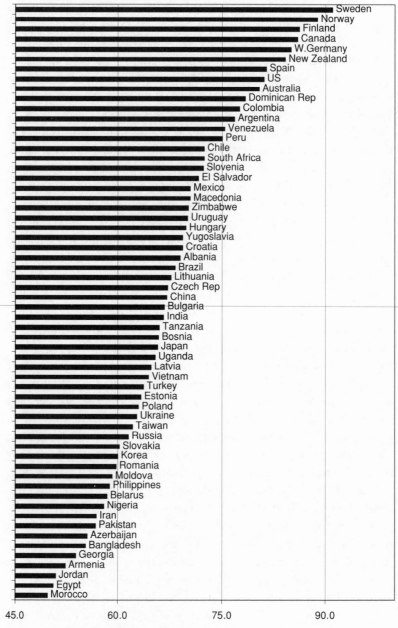

FIGURE C.1. Gender equality (three-item scale).

TABLE C.3. *Factor analysis of the Strength of Religiosity Scale (six-item) by religious regions*

	Western Christianity	Islamic	Orthodox	Central Europe	Latin America	Sinic	Hindu	Japanese	Sub-Saharan Africa	All
Importance of God	.90	.81	.87	.91	.77	.84	.82	.82	.85	.88
Comfort in religion	.84	.80	.86	.90	.74	.84	.78	.79	.85	.85
Belief in God	.81	.70	.84	.87	.72	.76	.76	.78	.78	.84
Religious identity	.80	.66	.84	.86	.69	.75	.73	.74	.69	.79
Attend religious services	.75	.54	.69	.81	.60	.56	.50	.63	.61	.72
Life after death	.66	.35	.65	.71	.43	.54	.40	.56	.30	.65
% of total variance	.63	.44	.63	.71	.44	.52	.47	.52	.50	63

Note: Principal component factor analysis with varimax rotation.
Source: WVS/EVS, pooled sample 1981–2001.

Religiosity scale

Similar procedures were used to test the reliability and consistency of the religiosity scale used in Chapter 3 in different world regions. The combined six-item Strength of Religiosity Scale, standardized to 100 points, consists of the following items:

- Importance: V196. *"How important is God in your life?"* (% "Very," scaled 6–10)
- Comfort: V.197. *"Do you find that you get comfort and strength from religion?"*
- Identify: V186. *"Independently of whether you go to church or not, would you say you are . . . a religious person, not a religious person, or a convinced atheist?"* (% Religious)
- Believe: V191 *"Do you believe in God?"* (%Yes)
- Attend: V185. *"Apart from weddings, funerals and christenings, about how often do you attend religious services these days?"* (% Once a week or more)
- Life: V192. *"Do you believe in life after death?"* (% Yes)

Models were run for major world regions to see whether the scale proved to be reliable for different religious cultures. Countries were classified into regions by the predominant religion in each, using categories developed elsewhere[1]. The results in Table C.3 show that all the items in the scale fell into a single dimension in all religious regions except for sub-Saharan Africa, where two dimensions emerged, the second of which was strongly related to beliefs in life after death. The consistency of these scales in each region was given further confirmation when they were tested by reliability analysis (details not reproduced here).

Notes

1. Introduction: Explaining the Rising Tide of Gender Equality

1. Mary K. Meyer and Elisabeth Prugl, Eds. 1999. *Gender Politics and Global Governance*. Lanham, MD: Rowman and Littlefield; J. True and M. Mintrom. 2001. "Transnational networks and policy diffusion: The case of gender mainstreaming." *International Studies Quarterly* 45 (1): 27–57; L. Reanda. 1999. "Engendering the United Nations – The changing international agenda." *European Journal of Women's Studies* 6 (1): 49–61.
2. United Nations. *Women 2000: Gender Equality, Development and Peace*. Special session of the General Assembly, June 5–9. <http://www.un.org/womenwatch/daw/followup/beijing+5.htm>
3. United Nations. 2000. *The World's Women 2000: Trends and Statistics*. New York: United Nations; United Nations. 2001. *Human Development Report 2001*. New York: United Nations/Oxford University Press; World Bank. 2001. *Engendering Development*. New York: Oxford University Press.
4. Mary Buckley. 1997. *Post-Soviet Women: From the Baltic to Central Asia*. New York: Cambridge University Press; Deborah Ellis. 2000. *Women of the Afghan War*. Westport, CT: Praeger.
5. See, for example, World Bank. 2001. *Engendering Development*. New York: World Bank/Oxford University Press.
6. Isabella Baaker, Ed. 1994. *Strategic Silence: Gender and Economic Policy*. London: Zed Books.
7. For more details, see Lauri Karvonen and Per Selle. 1995. *Women in Nordic Politics*. Aldershot: Dartmouth.
8. Walt Whitman Rostow. 1960. *The Stages of Economic Growth*. Cambridge: Cambridge University Press.

9. For a discussion, see World Bank. 2001. *Engendering Development*. New York: World Bank/Oxford University Press; Lourdes Beneria with Savitri Bisnath, Eds. 2001. *Gender and Development: Theoretical, Empirical, and Practical Approaches*. London: Edwards Elgar.

10. Valentine M. Moghadam. 1993. *Modernizing Women: Gender and Social Change in the Middle East*. Boulder, CO: Lynne Reinner; Margaret L. Meriwether and Judith E. Tucker, Eds. 2000. *Social History of Women and Gender in the Modern Middle East*. Boulder, CO: Westview; Lila Abu-Lughod, Ed. 1998. *Remaking Women: Feminism and Modernity in the Middle East*. Princeton, NJ: Princeton University Press; Suad Joseph and Susan Slyomovics. 2001. *Women and Power in the Middle East*. Philadelphia: University of Pennsylvania Press; Samira A. S. Omar. 1995. "Constraints that hinder women's participation in development: The case of Kuwait." *Pakistan Journal of Women's Studies* 2 (2): 17–26.

11. L. Kasturi. 1998. "Greater political representation for women: The case of India." *Asian Journal of Women's Studies* 4 (4): 9–38; Kiran Sakesena, Ed. 2000. *Women and Politics*. New Delhi: Gyan Publishing; Sangeetha Purushothaman. 1998. *The Empowerment of Women in India: Grassroots Women's Networks and the State*. New Delhi: Sage.

12. Jane Jacquette and Sharon Wolchik, Eds. 1998. *Women and Democracy: Latin America and Central and Eastern Europe*. Baltimore, MD: Johns Hopkins University Press; Nikki Craske. 1999. *Women and Politics in Latin America*. New Brunswick, NJ: Rutgers University Press.

13. Inter-Parliamentary Union. *Women in National Parliaments*. April 10, 2002. <www.ipu.org>Geneva: IPU.

14. For a fuller discussion, see N. Forsythe, R. P. Korzeniewicz, and V. Durrant. 2000. "Gender inequalities and economic growth: A longitudinal evaluation." *Economic Development and Cultural Change* 48 (3): 573–617.

15. E. Riddell-Dixon. 1999. "Mainstreaming women's rights: Problems and prospects within the centre for human rights." *Global Governance* 5 (2): 149–171.

16. See Ester Boserup. 1971. *Women's Role in Economic Development*. London: Allen and Unwin; Amartya Sen. 1999. *Development as Freedom*. New York: Anchor Books, Chapter 8.

17. Charles Humana. 1992. *World Human Rights Guide*, 3rd ed. New York: Oxford University Press; UNDP. 1995. *United Nations Development Report 1995*. New York: Oxford University Press/UNDP.

18. UNDP. 2000. *United Nations Development Report 2000*. New York: Oxford University Press/UNDP.

19. Joni Lovenduski and Pippa Norris, Eds. 1993. *Gender and Party Politics*. London: Sage; Jyette Klausen and Charles S. Maier, Eds. 2001. *Has Liberalism Failed Women? Parity, Quotas and Political Representation*. New York: St Martin's Press; Mala N. Htun and Mark P. Jones. 1999. "Engendering the right to participate in decision-making: Electoral quotas

and women's leadership in Latin America." Paper presented at the ninety-fifth annual meeting of the American Political Science Association.

20. Martha Fetherolf Loutfi. 2001. *Women, Gender and Work: What Is Equality and How Do We Get There?* Geneva: International Labour Office; Dorothy Stetson and Amy Mazur. 1995. *Comparative State Feminism.* Thousand Oaks, CA: Sage; Nira Yuval-Davis and Floya Anthias. 1989. *Woman, Nation, State.* New York: St. Martin's Press.

21. See, for example, IDEA. 1998. *Women in Parliament: Beyond Numbers.* Stockholm: International IDEA; Rebecca Davis. 1997. *Women and Power in Western Democracies.* Lincoln: University of Nebraska Press.

22. Linda Wirth. 2001. *Breaking Through the Glass Ceiling: Women in Management.* Geneva: International Labour Office; Morley Gunderson. 1994. *Comparable Worth and Gender Discrimination: An International Perspective.* Geneva: International Labour Office; Jerry A. Jacobs, Ed. 1995. *Gender Inequality at Work.* Thousand Oaks, CA: Sage; Jane Jenson, Jacqueline Laufer, and Margaret Maruani, Eds. 2000. *The Gendering of Inequalities: Women, Men, and Work.* Aldershot: Ashgate; Sandra Fredman. 1997. *Women and the Law.* Oxford: Oxford University Press.

23. For a discussion of the concept of culture, see George Steinmetz, Ed. 1999. *State/Culture: State Formation after the Cultural Turn.* New York: Cornell University Press. For a broader discussion, see also Lawrence E. Harrison and Samuel P. Huntington. 2000. *Culture Matters: How Values Shape Human Progress.* New York: Basic Books.

24. For a discussion, see Sonia Alvarez. *Engendering Democracy in Brazil.* Princeton, NJ: Princeton University Press; Karen Beckwith. 2000. "Beyond compare? Women's movements in comparative perspective." *European Journal of Political Research* 37 (4): 431–468.

25. Martha Nussbaum and Jonathan Glover. 1995. *Women, Culture and Development.* Oxford: Clarendon Press; Serena Nanda. 2000. *Gender Diversity: Cross-cultural Variations.* Prospect Heights, IL: Waveland Press; Leonore Loeb Adler. 1993. *International Handbook on Gender Roles.* Westport, CT: Greenwood Press; Burton Pasternak, Carol R. Ember, and Melvin Ember. 1997. *Sex, Gender, and Kinship: A Cross-cultural Perspective.* Englewood Cliffs, NJ: Prentice Hall; Shawn Meghan Burn. 2000. *Women across Cultures: A Global Perspective.* Palo Alto, CA: Mayfield; P. Chua, K. K. Bhavnani, and J. Foran. 2000. "Women, culture, development: A new paradigm for development studies?" *Ethnic and Racial Studies* 23 (5): 820–841; Alaka Basu. 1992. *Culture, the Status of Women and Demographic Behavior.* Oxford: Clarendon Press; Christopher Clague and Shoshana Grossbard-Shechtman, Eds. 2001. "Culture and development: international perspectives." *Annals of the American Academy of Political and Social Science* 573: 8–15; Lars Gule and Oddvar Storebo, Eds. 1993. *Development and Modernity: Perspectives on Western Theories of Modernisation.* Bergen, Norway: Ariadne.

26. Bonnie G. Smith, Ed. 2000. *Global Feminisms since 1945*. New York: Routledge; Amrita Basu, Ed. 1995. *The Challenge of Local Feminisms: Women's Movements in Global Perspective*. Boulder, CO: Westview Press; Valentine M. Moghadam. 1994. *Identity politics and women: cultural reassertions and feminisms in international perspective*. Boulder, CO: Westview.

27. See, for example, Bernadette C. Hayes, Ian Mcallister, and Donley Studlar. 2000. "Gender, postmaterialism, and feminism in comparative perspective." *International Political Science Review* 21 (4): 425–439; Clyde Wilcox. 1991. "The causes and consequences of feminist consciousness among Western European women." *Comparative Political Studies* 23 (4): 519–545; Janeen Baxter and Emily W. Kane. 1995. "Dependence and independence – A cross-national analysis of gender inequality and gender attitudes." *Gender & Society* 9 (2): 193–215; Duane F. Alwin, Michael Braun, and Jacqueline Scott. 1993. "The separation of work and family: Attitudes towards women's labour-force participation in Germany, Great Britain, and the United States." *European Sociological Review* 8: 13–37; Nancy J. Davis and Robert Robinson. 1991. "Men and women's consciousness of gender inequality: Austria, West Germany, Great Britain, and the United States." *American Sociological Review* 56: 72–84.

28. Daniel Lerner. 1958. *The Passing of Traditional Society: Modernizing the Middle East*. New York: Free Press; Seymour Martin Lipset. 1959. "Some social requisites of democracy: Economic development and political legitimacy." *American Political Science Review* 53: 69–105; Seymour Martin Lipset. 1960. *Political Man: The Social Basis of Politics*. New York: Doubleday; Walt W. Rostow. 1952. *The Process of Economic Growth*. New York: Norton; Walt W. Rostow. 1960. *The Stages of Economic Growth*. Cambridge: Cambridge University Press; Karl W. Deutsch. 1964. "Social mobilization and political development." *American Political Science Review* 55: 493–514; Daniel Bell. 1999. *The Coming of Post-Industrial Society: A Venture in Social Forecasting*. New York: Basic Books; Seymour Martin Lipset, Kyoung-Ryung Seong, and John Charles Torres. 1993. "A comparative analysis of the social requisites of democracy." *International Social Science Journal* 45 (2): 154–175.

29. Daniel Bell. 1999. *The Coming of Post-Industrial Society: A Venture in Social Forecasting*. New York: Basic Books (first edition 1973).

30. For the key texts, see Ronald Inglehart. 1977. *The Silent Revolution: Changing Values and Political Styles among Western Publics*. Princeton, NJ: Princeton University Press; Ronald Inglehart. 1990. *Culture Shift in Advanced Industrial Society*. Princeton, NJ: Princeton University Press; Ronald Inglehart. 1997. *Modernization and Postmodernization: Cultural, Economic and Political Change in 43 Societies*. Princeton, NJ: Princeton University Press. For other works, see the Select Bibliography.

31. World Bank. 2001. *World Development Indicators, 2001.* Washington, DC: World Bank, p. 4.

32. Ibid., p. 6.

33. Deepa Narayan. 2000. *Voices of the Poor: Can Anyone Hear Us?* New York: Oxford University Press/World Bank; Hans-Peter Blossfeld and Sonja Drobnic, Eds. 2001. *Careers of Couples in Contemporary Societies: A Cross-national Comparison of the Transition from Male Breadwinner to Dual-Earner Families.* New York: Oxford University Press; Judith Frankel. 1997. *Families of Employed Mothers: An International Perspective.* New York: Garland Press.

34. Adam Przeworski and Henry Teune. 1970. *The Logic of Comparative Social Inquiry.* New York: Wiley–Interscience.

35. C. Buchmann. 1996. "The debt crisis, structural adjustment and women's education – Implications for status and social development." *International Journal Of Comparative Sociology* 37 (1–2): 5–30.

36. Marilyn Rueschemeyer, Ed. 1998. *Women and the Politics of Postcommunist Eastern Europe.* New York: M. E. Sharpe.

37. For discussion of the theoretical and policy relevance of the Human Development Index, its validity, and the reliability of the data used in constructing the index, see UNDP. *UNDP Human Development Report 1995.* New York: Oxford University Press/UNDP; Mark McGillivray and Howard White. 1993. "Measuring development? The UNDP's Human Development Index." *Journal of International Development.* 5 (2): 183–192.

38. See Appendix A at the end of this book for the detailed classification of all nations. Note that this classification differs from that used by the UNDP, which uses a different distinction between medium and low levels of human development.

39. A. Geske Dijkstra and Lucia C. Hanmer. 2000. "Measuring socio-economic gender inequality: Toward an alternative to the UNDP Gender-Related Development Index." *Feminist Economics* 6 (2): 41–75.

40. See Adam Przeworski et al. 2000. *Democracy and Development: Political Institutions and Well-Being in the World, 1950–1990.* New York: Cambridge University Press. See also G. L. Munck and J. Verkuilen. 2002. "Conceptualizing and measuring democracy – Evaluating alternative indices." *Comparative Political Studies* 35 (1): 5–34.

41. Societies are defined based on the annual ratings provided by Freedom House since 1972. The *level of freedom* is classified according to the combined mean score for political rights and civil liberties in Freedom House's 1972–2000 annual surveys, Freedom in the World. <www.freedomhouse.org>

42. Full methodological details about the World Values Surveys, including the questionnaires, sampling procedures, fieldwork procedures, principle investigators, and organization can be found at <http://wvs.isr.umich.edu/wvs-samp.html>.

43. These countries are ranked as equally "free" according to the 2000–01 Freedom House assessments of political rights and civil liberties. Freedom House. 2000. *Freedom in the World 2000–2001.* <www.freedomhouse.org>

2. From Traditional Roles toward Gender Equality

1. For an excellent summary of trends around the world, see United Nations. 2000. *The World's Women 2000: Trends and Statistics.* New York: United Nations.
2. Burton Pasternak, Carol R. Ember, and Melvin Ember. 1997. *Sex, Gender, and Kinship: A Cross-cultural Perspective.* Englewood Cliffs, NJ: Prentice Hall; Nancy Bonvillain. 1995. *Women and Men: Cultural Constructs of Gender.* Englewood Cliffs, NJ: Prentice Hall; Serena Nanda. 2000. *Gender Diversity: Cross-cultural Variations.* Prospect Heights, IL: Waveland Press.
3. K. Mason and A-M. Jenson, Eds. 1995. *Gender and Family Change in Industrialized Countries.* Oxford: Clarendon Press; Bron B. Ingoldsby and Suzanna Smith, Eds. 1995. *Families in Multicultural Perspective.* New York: Guilford Press; Stevan Harrell. 1997. *Human Families.* Boulder, CO: Westview.
4. Hans-Peter Blossfeld and Sonja Drobnic, Eds. 2001. *Careers of Couples in Contemporary Societies: A Cross-national Comparison of the Transition from Male Breadwinner to Dual-Earner Families.* New York: Oxford University Press; Judith Frankel. 1997. *Families of Employed Mothers: An International Perspective.* New York: Garland Press; Jane C. Hood, Ed. 1993. *Men, Work, and Family.* Newbury Park, CA: Sage.
5. Janneen Baxter. 1997. "Gender equality and participation in housework: A cross-national perspective." *Journal Of Comparative Family Studies* 28 (3): 220.
6. Jyette Klausen and Charles S. Maier, Eds. 2001. *Has Liberalism Failed Women? Parity, Quotas and Political Representation.* New York: St. Martin's Press.
7. John E. Williams and Deborah L. Best. 1990. *Measuring Sex Stereotypes: A Multination Study.* Newbury Park, CA: Sage; N. E. Downing and K. L. Roush. 1985. "From passive acceptance to active commitment – A model of feminist identity development for women." *Counseling Psychologist* 13 (4): 695–709; E. A. Gerstmann and D. A. Kramer. 1997. "Feminist identity development: Psychometric analyses of two feminist identity scales." *Sex Roles* 36 (5–6): 327–348; A. R. Fischer, D. M. Tokar, M. M. Mergl, G. E. Good, M. S. Hill, and S. A. Blum. 2000. "Assessing women's feminist identity development – Studies of convergent, discriminant, and structural validity." *Psychology of Women Quarterly* 24 (1): 15–29; M. Liss, C. O'Connor, E. Morosky, and M. Crawford. 2001. "What makes a feminist? Predictors and correlates of feminist social identity in college

women." *Psychology of Women Quarterly* 25 (2): 124–133; A. Bargad and J. S. Hyde. 1991. "Women's Studies – A study of feminist identity development in women." *Psychology of Women Quarterly* 15 (2): 181–201; I. H. Frieze and M. C. McHugh. 1998. "Measuring feminism and gender role attitudes." *Psychology of Women Quarterly* 22 (3): 349–352; N. M. Henley and W. J. McCarthy. 1998. "Measuring feminist attitudes – Problems and prospects." *Psychology of Women Quarterly* 22 (3): 363–369.

8. Clyde Wilcox. 1991. "The causes and consequences of feminist consciousness among Western European women." *Comparative Political Studies* 23 (4): 519–545; Lee Ann Banaszak and Eric Plutzer. 1993. "The social bases of feminism in the European Community." *Public Opinion Quarterly* 57 (1): 29–53; Jacqueline Scott, Michael Braun, and Duane Alwin. 1993. "The family way." In *International Social Attitudes: The Tenth Report*, ed. Roger Jowell, Lindsay Brook, and Lizanne Dowds, with Daphne Ahrendt. Aldershot, Hants: SCPR; Jacqueline Scott, Michael Braun, and Duane Alwin. 1998. "Partner, parent, worker: Family and gender roles." In *British – and European – Social Attitudes: The Fifteenth Report*. Aldershot, Hants: Ashgate/SCPR.

9. Other items in the WVS/EVS were tested for incorporation into the Gender Equality Scale, including approval of marriage, the division of household income, and the fulfillment of being a housewife; these items were subsequently dropped as tapping other distinct value dimensions.

10. For the detailed evidence, see Ronald Inglehart. 1997. *Modernization and Postmodernization: Cultural, Economic and Political Change in 43 Societies.* Princeton, NJ: Princeton University Press; Ronald Inglehart and Wayne Baker. 2000. "Modernization, globalization and the persistence of tradition: Empirical evidence from 65 societies." *American Sociological Review* 65:19–55.

11. To test this further, a four-point Gender Equality Scale was developed, dropping the item on men in politics, facilitating comparison of sixty-four societies that included all survey items from 1990 to 2000. The comparison confirmed a very similar rank order across this broader range of nations.

12. Amartya Sen. 1999. *Development as Freedom.* New York: Anchor Books.

13. UNDP. 2000. *Human Development Report 2000.* New York: Oxford University Press/UNDP.

14. Mark Casson and Andrew Godley, Eds. 2000. *Cultural Factors in Economic Growth.* New York: Springer.

15. Jacqueline Scott, Michael Braun, and Duane Alwin. 1993. "The family way." In *International Social Attitudes: The Tenth Report*, ed. Roger Jowell, Lindsay Brook, and Lizanne Dowds, with Daphne Ahrendt. Aldershot, Hants: SCPR, p. 44.

16. T. Ciabattari. 2001. "Changes in men's conservative gender ideologies – Cohort and period influences." *Gender & Society* 15 (4): 574–591. See

also Nancy J. Davis and Robert Robinson. 1991. "Men and women's consciousness of gender inequality: Austria, West Germany, Great Britain, and the United States." *American Sociological Review* 56: 72–84.

17. Lee Ann Banaszak and Eric Plutzer. 1993. "The social bases of feminism in the European Community." *Public Opinion Quarterly* 57 (1): 29–53; Bernadette C. Hayes, Ian Mcallister, and Donley Studlar. 2000. "Gender, post-materialism, and feminism in comparative perspective." *International Political Science Review* 21 (4): 425–439; Beth Reingold and H. Foust. 1998. "Exploring the determinants of feminist consciousness in the United States." *Women & Politics* 19 (3):19–48.

18. For full details, see Ronald Inglehart. 1997. *Modernization and Postmodernization: Cultural, Economic and Political Change in 43 Societies.* Princeton, NJ: Princeton University Press.

3. Religion, Secularization, and Gender Equality

1. Ria Kloppenborg and Wouter J. Hanegraaff, Eds. 1995. *Female Stereotypes in Religious Traditions.* Leiden: E.J. Brill; William H. Swatos, Jr., Ed. 1996. *Gender and Religion.* New Brunswick, NJ: Transaction; Majella Franzmann. 2000. *Women and Religion.* Oxford: Oxford University Press; Jacob Neusner, Ed. 1999. *Women and Families.* Cleveland: Pilgrim Press; Arvind Sharma and Katherine K. Young, Eds. 1999. *Feminism and World Religions.* Albany: State University of New York Press.

2. Pamela Johnston Conover and Virginia Gray. 1983. *Feminism and the New Right: Conflict over the American Family.* New York: Praeger; Pamela Johnston Conover. 1988. "Feminists and the gender gap." *Journal of Politics* 50: 985–1010; Daniel Bell, Ed. 2002. *The Radical Right*, 3rd ed. New Brunswick, NJ: Transaction; Mark A. Noll. 2001. *American Evangelical Christianity: An Introduction.* Oxford: Blackwell.

3. Maurice Duverger. 1955. *The Political Role of Women.* Paris: UNESCO; Lawrence Mayer and Roland E. Smith. 1985. "Feminism and religiosity: Female electoral behavior in Western Europe." In *Women and Politics in Western Europe*, ed. Sylvia Bashevkin. London: Frank Cass.

4. Lane Kenworthy and Melissa Malami. 1999. "Gender inequality in political representation: A worldwide comparative analysis." *Social Forces* 78 (1): 235–269. See also Wilma Rule. 1987. "Electoral systems, contextual factors and women's opportunities for parliament in 23 democracies." *Western Political Quarterly* 40: 477–98; Wilma Rule. 1994. "Parliaments of, by, and for the people: Except for women?" In *Electoral Systems in Comparative Perspective: Their Impact on Women and Minorities*, ed. Wilma Rule and Joseph Zimmerman. Westport, CT: Greenwood Press; Andrew Reynolds. 1999. "Women in the legislatures and executives of the world: Knocking at the highest glass ceiling." *World Politics* 51 (4): 547–572;

Richard E. Matland. 1998. "Women's representation in national legislatures: Developed and developing countries ." *Legislative Studies Quarterly* 23 (1): 109–125.

5. Courtney W. Howland. 1999. *Religious Fundamentalisms and the Human Rights of Women.* Basingstoke, Hampshire: Macmillan; T. Saliba. 2000. "Arab feminism at the millennium." *Signs* 25 (4): 1087–1092; A. Majid. 2000. "The politics of feminism in Islam." *Signs.* 23 (2): 321–361; S. Khan. 1998. "Muslim women: Negotiations in the third space." *Signs* 23 (2): 463–494; F. Kazemi. 2000. "Gender, Islam and politics." *Social Research* 67 (2): 453–474; Y. Arat. 2000. "Feminists, Islamists, and political change in Turkey." *Political Psychology* 19 (1): 117–131; A. R. Norton. 1997. "Gender, politics and the state: What do Middle Eastern women want?" *Middle East Policy* 5 (3): 155–165; N. Berkovitch and V. M. Moghadam. 1999. "Middle East politics and women's collective action: Challenging the status quo." *Social Politics* 6 (3): 273–291; K. Meyer, H. Rizzo, and Y. Ali. 1998. "Islam and the extension of citizenship rights to women in Kuwait." *Journal for the Scientific Study of Religion* 37 (1): 131–144; L. Ahmed. 1992. *Women and Gender in Islam – Historical Roots of a Modern Debate;* Asghar Ali Engineer, Ed. 2001. *Islam, Women and Gender Justice.* New Delhi: Gyan Publishing; Shirin M. Rai, Ed. 2000. *International Perspectives on Gender and Democratization.* Basingstoke: Macmillan; Haideh Moghissi. 1999. *Feminism and Islamic Fundamentalism: The Limits of Postmodern Analysis.* New York: Zed Books.

6. For a summary of the debate about secularization theory, see W. H. Swatos and K. J. Christiano. 2001. "Secularization theory: The course of a concept." *Sociology of Religion* 60 (3): 209–228.

7. See O. Tschannen. 1991. "The secularization paradigm." *Journal for the Scientific Study of Religion* 30: 395–415; Samuel P. Huntington. 1996. *The Clash of Civilizations and the Remaking of World Order.* New York: Simon and Schuster; Peter L. Berger, Ed. 1999. *The Desecularization of the World.* Washington, DC: Ethics and Public Policy Center; Rodney Stark. 1999. "Secularization, RIP." *Sociology of Religion* 60 (3): 249–273; W. H. Swatos, Jr., Ed. 1989. *Religious Politics in Global and Comparative Perspective.* New York: Greenwood Press.

8. Samuel P. Huntington. 1993. "The clash of civilizations?" *Foreign Affairs* 72 (3): 22–49; Samuel P. Huntington. 1996. *The Clash of Civilizations and the Remaking of World Order.* New York: Simon and Schuster.

9. Max Weber. 1930. *The Protestant Ethic and the Spirit of Capitalism.* New York: Scribner. For a discussion, see Steve Bruce, Ed. 1992. *Religion and Modernization.* Oxford: Oxford University Press.

10. W. H. Swatos and K. J. Christiano. 2001. "Secularization theory: The course of a concept." *Sociology of Religion* 60 (3): 209–228.

11. Daniel Bell. 1999. *The Coming of Post-Industrial Society.* New York: Basic Books.

12. Steve Bruce. 1996. *Religion in the Modern World: From Cathedrals to Cults.* Oxford: Oxford University Press; Sheena Ashford and Noel Timms. 1992. *What Europe Thinks: A Study of Western European Values.* Aldershot: Dartmouth; Wolfgang Jagodzinski and Karel Dobbelaere. 1995. "Secularization and church religiosity." In *The Impact of Values,* ed. Jan W. van Deth and Elinor Scarbrough. Oxford: Oxford University Press; L. Voye. 1999. "Secularization in a context of advanced modernity." *Sociology of Religion* 60 (3): 275–288.

13. For further details, see Pippa Norris. 2002. *Democratic Phoenix: Political Activism Worldwide.* New York: Cambridge University Press, Chapter 9. See also Anthony M. Abela. 1993. "Post-secularisation: The social significance of religious values in four Catholic European countries." *Melita Theolgica* 44: 39–58; Pierre Brechon. 1997. *Religions et politique en Europe.* Paris: Documentation Francaise; Karel Dobbelaere. 1993. "Church involvement and secularization: Making sense of the European case." In *Secularization, Rationalism and Sectarism,* ed. E. Barker, J. A. Beckford, and K. Dobbelaere. Oxford: Clarendon Press; Karel Dobbelaere and Wolfgang Jagodzinski. 1995. "Religious cognitions and beliefs." In *The Impact of Values,* ed. Jan W. van Deth and Elinor Scarbrough. Oxford: Oxford University Press.

14. R. Stark and W. S. Bainbridge. 1985. "A supply-side reinterpretation of the 'secularization' of Europe." *Journal for the Scientific Study of Religion* 33: 230–52.

15. The Gallup Organization. "*Did you, yourself, happen to attend church or synagogue in the last seven days, or not?*" 1939: 41% Yes; 2001: 41% Yes. Similar levels are evident in the latest available Gallup poll on the subject (May 2001). < www.gallup.com/poll/indicators/indreligion.asp > For a more detailed analysis, see Robert Wuthnow. 1999. "Mobilizing civic engagement: The changing impact of religious involvement." In *Civic Engagement in American Democracy,* ed. Theda Skocpol and Morris P. Fiorina. Washington, DC: Brookings Institution Press.

16. For a detailed discussion, see Andrew Greeley. 1980. *Religious Change in America.* Cambridge, MA: Harvard University Press; Andrew Greeley. 1995. "The persistence of religion." *Cross Currents* 45: 24–41; Karel Dobbelaere. 1995. "Religion in Europe and North America." In *Values in Western Societies,* ed. Ruud de Moor. Tilburg: Tilburg University Press.

17. David B. Barrett, George T. Kurian, and Todd M. Johnson. 2001. *World Christian Encyclopedia: A Comparative Survey of Churches and Religions in the Modern World.* Oxford: Oxford University Press. For details, see Table 1.1. See also Philip M. Parker. 1997. *Religious Cultures of the World: A Statistical Reference.* Westport, CT: Greenwood Press; David B. Barrett and Todd M. Johnson. 2001. *World Christian Trends AD 30–2200.* Pasedena, CA: William Carey Library; Global Evangelization Movement. 2001. *Status of Global Mission 2001.*

18. Samuel P. Huntington. 1996. *The Clash of Civilizations and the Remaking of World Order*. New York: Simon and Schuster. See also Peter L. Berger, Ed. 1999. *The Desecularization of the World*. Washington, DC: Ethics and Public Policy Center; Rodney Stark. 1999. "Secularization, RIP." *Sociology of Religion* 60 (3): 249–273; W. H. Swatos, Jr., Ed. 1989. *Religious Politics in Global and Comparative Perspective*. New York: Greenwood Press

19. For further discussion of this issue, see Pippa Norris and Ronald Inglehart. 2002. "Islam and the West: Testing the clash of civilizations thesis." *Comparative Sociology* 1 (3): forthcoming.

20. For further discussion, see ibid.

4. The Gender Gap in Voting and Public Opinion

1. Jeff Manza and Clem Brooks. 1998. "The gender gap in U.S. presidential elections: When? Why? Implications?" *American Journal of Sociology* 103 (5): 1235–1266.

2. For a general discussion of the way that U.S. political culture and institutions are distinctive, see Seymour Martin Lipset. 1996. *American Exceptionalism: A Double Edged Sword*. New York: Norton.

3. Herbert L. G. Tingsten, 1937. *Political Behavior: Studies in Election Statistics*. London: P. S. King, pp. 37–65.

4. Seymour M. Lipset and Stein Rokkan. 1967. *Party Systems and Voter Alignments*. New York: Free Press.

5. Maurice Duverger. 1955. *The Political Role of Women*. Paris: UNESCO. pp. 65–66; Seymour M. Lipset. 1960. *Political Man: The Social Bases of Politics*. Garden City, New York: Doubleday, p. 143; David Butler and Donald E. Stokes. 1974. *Political Change in Britain*. New York: St. Martin's Press, p. 160; Angus Campbell et al. 1960. *The American Voter*. New York: Wiley, p. 493.

6. Seymour M. Lipset. 1960. *Political Man: The Social Bases of Politics*. Garden City, New York: Doubleday, p. 260; Jean Blondel. 1970. *Votes, Parties and Leaders*. London: Penguin, pp. 55–56.

7. For a critical summary of the assumptions in the early literature, however, see Murray Goot and Elizabeth Reid. 1984. "Women: If not apolitical, then conservative." In *Women and the Public Sphere*, ed. Janet Siltanen and Michelle Stanworth. London: Hutchinson.

8. Gabriel A. Almond and Sidney Verba. 1963. *The Civic Culture: Political Attitudes and Democracy in Five Nations*. Princeton, NJ: Princeton University Press, p. 325

9. Ronald Inglehart. 1977. *The Silent Revolution: Changing Values and Political Styles among Western Publics*. Princeton, NJ: Princeton University Press, p. 229.

10. Sandra Baxter and Marjorie Lansing. 1983. *Women and Politics*. Ann Arbor: University of Michigan Press; Bernadette Hayes. 1997. "Gender,

feminism and electoral behaviour in Britain." *Electoral Studies* 16 (2): 203–216; Richard Rose and Ian McAllister. 1986. *Voters Begin to Choose: From Closed Class to Open Elections in Britain.* London: Sage.

11. Frank L. Rusciano. 1992. "Rethinking the gender gap: The case of West German elections, 1949–87." *Comparative Politics* 24 (3): 335–357.

12. Lawrence Mayer and Roland E. Smith. 1985. "Feminism and religiosity: Female electoral behavior in Western Europe." In *Women and Politics in Western Europe*, ed. Sylia Bashevkin. London: Frank Cass.

13. Jack Vowles. 1993. "Gender and electoral behaviour in New Zealand." In *Women and Politics in New Zealand*, ed Helena Catt and Elizabeth McLeay. Wellington: Victoria University Press.

14. Ola Listhaug, Arthur H. Miller, and Henry Vallen. 1985. "The gender gap in Norwegian voting behavior." *Scandinavian Political Studies* 83: 187–206; Maria Oskarson. 1995. "Gender gaps in Nordic voting behavior." In *Women in Nordic Politics*, ed. Lauri Karvonen and Per Selle. Aldershot: Dartmouth.

15. Lawrence Mayer and Roland E. Smith. 1985. "Feminism and religiosity: Female electoral behavior in Western Europe." In *Women and Politics in Western Europe*, ed. Sylia Bashevkin. London: Frank Cass; Pippa Norris. 1988. "The impact of parties." In *Women, Equality and Europe*, ed. M. Buckley and M. Anderson. London: Macmillan, pp. 142–159; Maria Oskarson. 1995. "Gender gaps in Nordic voting behavior." In *Women in Nordic Politics*, ed. Lauri Karvonen and Per Selle. Aldershot: Dartmouth; Richard E. Matland and Donley Studlar. 1998. "The electoral opportunity structure for women in the Canadian provinces." *Political Research Quarterly* (forthcoming).

16. David DeVaus and Ian McAllister. 1989. "The changing politics of women: Gender and political alignments in 11 nations." *European Journal of Political Research* 17: 241–262.

17. Russell J. Dalton, Scott C. Flanagan, Paul A. Beck, and James E. Alt. 1984. *Electoral Change in Advanced Industrial Democracies: Realignment or Dealignment?* Princeton, NJ: Princeton University Press; Ivor Crewe and D. T. Denver. 1985. *Electoral Change in Western Democracies: Patterns and Sources of Electoral Volatility.* New York: St. Martin's Press; Mark Franklin, Thomas T. Mackie, Henry Valen, and Clive Bean. 1992. *Electoral Change: Responses to Evolving Social and Attitudinal Structures in Western Countries.* Cambridge: Cambridge University Press.

18. Jerome M. Clubb, William H. Flanigan, and Nancy H. Zingale. 1990. *Partisan Realignment: Voters, Parties and Government in American History.* Boulder, CO: Westview.

19. Eleanor Smeal. 1984. *Why and How Women Will Elect the Next President.* New York: Harper and Row; Ethel Klein. 1984. *Gender Politics.* Cambridge, MA: Harvard University Press; Carol Mueller, Ed. 1988. *The Politics of the Gender Gap.* London: Sage; Mary Bendyna and Celinda Lake.

1998. "Gender and voting in the 1992 presidential election." In *The Year of the Woman: Myths and Realities*, ed. Elizabeth Adell Cook et al. Boulder, CO: Westview Press; Warren E. Miller and Merril Shankes. 1996. *The New American Voter*. Cambridge, MA: Harvard University Press; Richard Seltzer et al. 1997. *Sex as a Political Variable*. Boulder, CO: Lynne Rienner.

20. Pippa Norris. 1999. "The gender–generation gap." In *Critical Elections: British Parties and Voters in Long-term Perspective*, ed. Geoffrey Evans and Pippa Norris. London: Sage.

21. Stephen P. Erie and Rein Martin. 1988. "Women and the welfare state." In *The Politics of the Gender Gap*, ed. Carol M. Mueller. Newbury Park, CA: Sage; Robert Shapiro and Harpreet Mahajan. 1986. "Gender differences in policy preferences." *Public Opinion Quarterly* 50:42–61; Martin Gilens. 1988. "Gender and support for Reagan." *American Journal of Political Science* 32:19–49; Benjamin I. Page and Robert Y. Shapiro. 1993. *The Rational Public*. Chicago: University of Chicago Press; Richard A. Seltzer, Jody Newman, and Melissa V. Leighton. 1997. *Sex as a Political Variable*. Boulder, CO: Lynne Reinner.

22. Ronald Inglehart and Hans-Dieter Klingemann. 1976. "Party identification, ideological preference and the left-right dimension among Western publics." In *Party Identification and Beyond*, ed. Ian Budge et al. New York: Wiley.

23. Jon Huber and Ronald Inglehart. 1995. "Expert interpretations of party space and party locations in 42 societies." *Party Politics* 1 (1): 71–111

24. To test for reliability, this measure was correlated with another survey item asking people to place themselves on a ten-point left-right ideological scale. Overall, these scales were closely associated ($r = .46$), increasing confidence in their use.

25. For more details, see Ronald Inglehart and Pippa Norris. 2000. "The developmental theory of the gender gap: Women's and men's voting behavior in global perspective." *International Political Science Review.* 21 (4): 441–462.

26. Seymour M. Lipset and Stein Rokkan. 1967. *Party Systems and Voter Alignments*. New York: Free Press.

27. Russell J. Dalton, Scott C. Flanagan, Paul A. Beck, and James E. Alt. 1984. *Electoral Change in Advanced Industrial Democracies: Realignment or Dealignment?* Princeton, NJ: Princeton University Press; Ivor Crewe and D. T. Denver. 1985. *Electoral Change in Western Democracies: Patterns and Sources of Electoral Volatility*. New York: St. Martin's Press; Mark Franklin, Thomas T. Mackie, Henry Valen, and Clive Bean. 1992. *Electoral Change: Responses to Evolving Social and Attitudinal Structures in Western Countries*. Cambridge: Cambridge University Press.

28. Seymour M.Lipset. 1960. *Political Man: The Social Bases of Politics*. Garden City, New York: Doubleday.

29. Ronald Inglehart. 1997. *Modernization and Postmodernization: Cultural, Economic and Political Change in 43 Societies.* Princeton, NJ: Princeton University Press.

30. Arthur Miller. 1988. "Gender and the vote: 1984." In *The Politics of the Gender Gap: The Social Construction of Political Influence,* ed. Carol M. Mueller. Beverly Hills, CA: Sage, p. 264.

31. Susan J. Carroll. 1988. "Women's autonomy and the gender gap: 1980 and 1982." In *The Politics of the Gender Gap: The Social Construction of Political Influence,* ed. Carol M. Mueller. Beverly Hills, CA: Sage, pp. 236–257.

32. Cal Clark and Janet Clark. 1993. "The gender gap 1988: Compassion, pacifism and indirect feminism." In *Women in Politics: Outsiders or Insiders?,* ed. Lois Lovelace Duke. Englewood Cliffs, NJ: Prentice Hall.

33. See Ethel Klein. 1984. *Gender Politics.* Cambridge, MA: Harvard University Press; Arland Thornton, Duane F. Alwin, and Donald Camburn. 1983. "Causes and consequences of sex-role attitudes and attitudes change." *American Sociological Review* 48: 211–227.

34. Ethel Klein. 1984. *Gender Politics.* Cambridge, MA: Harvard University Press.

35. Richard Anker. 1998. *Gender and Jobs: Sex Segregation of Occupations in the World.* Geneva: International Labour Office.

36. Morley Gunderson. 1994. *Comparable Worth and Gender Discrimination: An International Perspective.* Geneva: International Labour Office; Jerry A. Jacobs, Ed. 1995. *Gender Inequality at Work.* Thousand Oaks, CA: Sage; Jane Jenson, Jacqueline Laufer, and Margaret Maruani, Eds. 2000. *The Gendering of Inequalities: Women, Men, and Work.* Aldershot: Ashgate; United Nations, 2000. *The World's Women 2000: Trends and Statistics.* New York: United Nations.

37. International Labour Organization. 1997. *World Employment Report 1996–97.* Geneva: ILO <www.ilo.org/public/english/bureau/inf/pkits/wlr97.htm>; B. Radcliff and P. Davis. 2000. "Labor organization and electoral participation in industrial democracies." *American Journal of Political Science* 44 (1): 132–141.

38. Martin Plissner. 1983. "The marriage gap." *Public Opinion* 53: 2; Eric Plutzer. 1988. "Work life, family life and women's support for feminism." *American Sociological Review* 53: 640–49.

39. See, for example, David DeVaus and Ian McAllister. 1989. "The changing politics of women: Gender and political alignments in 11 nations." *European Journal of Political Research* 17: 241–262; Donley Studlar, Ian McAllister, and Bernadette Hayes. 1998. "Explaining the gender gap in voting: A cross-national analysis." *Social Science Quarterly* 79: 779–798; Clyde Wilcox. 1991. "The causes and consequences of feminist consciousness among Western European women." *Comparative Political*

Studies 23 (4): 519–545; Lee Ann Banaszak and Eric Plutzer. 1993. "The social bases of feminism in the European Community." *Public Opinion Quarterly* 57 (1): 29–53; Lee Ann Banaszak and Eric Plutzer. 1993. "Contextual determinants of feminist attitudes – National and subnational influences in Western Europe." *American Political Science Review* 87(1): 147–157; Frank L Rusciano. 1992. "Rethinking the gender gap: The case of West German elections, 1949–87." *Comparative Politics* 24 (3): 335–357.

40. Ronald Inglehart, 1977. *The Silent Revolution: Changing Values and Political Styles among Western Publics*. Princeton, NJ: Princeton University Press; Ronald Inglehart. 1997. *Modernization and Postmodernization: Cultural, Economic and Political Change in 43 Societies*. Princeton, NJ: Princeton University Press.

41. Ronald Inglehart, 1990. *Culture Shift in Advanced Industrial Society*. Princeton, NJ: Princeton University Press, pp. 177–211; Ronald Inglehart. 1997. *Modernization and Postmodernization: Cultural, Economic and Political Change in 43 Societies*. Princeton, NJ: Princeton University Press, pp. 267–292.

42. Pamela Johnston Conover. 1988. "Feminists and the gender gap." *Journal of Politics* 50: 985–1010.

43. For a critical discussion, however, see Elizabeth A. Cook and Clyde Wilcox. 1991. "Feminism and the gender gap: A second look." *Journal of Politics* 53: 1111–1122.

44. Stephen P. Erie and Rein Martin. 1988. "Women and the welfare state." In *The Politics of the Gender Gap*, ed. Carol M. Mueller. Newbury Park, CA: Sage; Robert Shapiro and Harpreet Mahajan. 1986. "Gender differences in policy preferences." *Public Opinion Quarterly* 50:42–61; Martin Gilens. 1988. "Gender and support for Reagan." *American Journal of Political Science* 32:19–49; Benjamin I. Page and Robert Y. Shapiro. 1993. *The Rational Public*. Chicago: University of Chicago Press; Richard A. Seltzer, Jody Newman, and Melissa V. Leighton. 1997. *Sex as a Political Variable*. Boulder, CO: Lynne Reinner.

45. Jyette Klausen and Charles S. Maier, Eds. 2001. *Has Liberalism Failed Women? Parity, Quotas and Political Representation*. New York: St. Martin's Press.

46. David DeVaus and Ian McAllister. 1989. "The changing politics of women: Gender and political alignments in 11 nations." *European Journal of Political Research* 17: 241–262.

47. As Studlar and colleagues noted in their comparison of the U.S., Australia, and Britain. Donley Studlar, Ian McAllister, and Bernadette Hayes. 1998. "Explaining the gender gap in voting: A cross-national analysis." *Social Science Quarterly* 79.

48. Carol Mueller, Ed. 1988. *The Politics of the Gender Gap: The Social Construction of Political Influence*. London: Sage.

49. Ronald Inglehart, 1977. *The Silent Revolution: Changing Values and Political Styles among Western Publics.* Princeton, NJ: Princeton University Press, p. 229.

50. Pippa Norris, 1988. "The gender gap: A cross national trend?" In *The Politics of the Gender Gap: The Social Construction of Political Influence,* ed. Carol Mueller. Beverley Hills, CA: Sage.

5. Political Activism

1. Herbert Tingsten. 1937. *Political Behavior: Studies in Election Statistics.* Totowa, NJ: Bedminster Press (1963); Gabriel A. Almond and Sidney Verba. 1963. *The Civic Culture: Political Attitudes and Democracy in Five Nations.* Princeton, NJ: Princeton University Press; Giuseppe DiPalma. 1970. *Apathy and Participation.* New York: Free Press; Seymour Martin Lipset. 1960. *Political Man: The Social Basis of Politics.* New York: Doubleday.

2. Sidney Verba, Norman Nie, and Jae-on Kim. 1978. *Participation and Political Equality: A Seven-Nation Comparison.* New York: Cambridge University Press.

3. Samuel Barnes and Max Kaase. 1979. *Political Action: Mass Participation in Five Western Democracies.* Beverley Hills, CA: Sage, pp. 107–110.

4. Inter-Parliamentary Union. 1997. *Men and Women in Politics.* (Reports and Documents Series 28.) Geneva: IPU; Inter-Parliamentary Union. 2000. *Participation of Women in Public Life.* Geneva: IPU.

5. For more details, see Pippa Norris. 2002. *Democratic Phoenix: Political Activism Worldwide.* New York: Cambridge University Press.

6. See, for example, Margaret Conway, Gertrude A. Steuernagel, and David Ahern. 1997. *Women and Political Participation.* Washington, DC: CQ Press.

7. Sidney Verba, Norman H. Nie, and Jae-on Kim. 1971. *The Modes of Democratic Participation: A Cross-National Analysis.* Beverly Hills, CA: Sage; Sidney Verba and Norman Nie. 1972. *Participation in America: Social Equality and Political Participation.* New York: Harper Collins; Sidney Verba, Norman Nie, and Jae-on Kim. 1978. *Participation and Political Equality: A Seven-Nation Comparison.* New York: Cambridge University Press.

8. See, for example, Seymour Martin Lipset. 1960. *Political Man: The Social Basis of Politics.* New York: Doubleday.

9. Carol Christy. 1987. *Sex Differences in Political Participation: Processes of Change in Fourteen Nations.* New York: Praeger; David DeVaus and Ian McAllister. 1989. "The changing politics of women: Gender and political alignments in 11 nations." *European Journal of Political Research* 17: 241–262; Margaret Conway, Gertrude A. Steuernagel, and David Ahern. 1997. *Women and Political Participation.* Washington, DC: CQ Press, p. 79.

10. CAWP. 2000. "Sex differences in voting turnout." <www.cawp.org>

11. Pippa Norris. 1999. "A gender-generation gap?" In *Critical Elections: British Parties and Voters in Long-term Perspective*, ed. Geoffrey Evans and Pippa Norris. London: Sage.

12. For some evidence along these lines, see Pippa Norris. 2001. "Women's power at the ballot box." In IDEA. *Voter Turnout from 1945 to 2000: A Global Report on Political Participation*, 3rd ed. Stockholm: IDEA.

13. Nancy Burns, Kay Lehman Schlozman, and Sidney Verba. 2001. *The Private Roots of Public Action*. Cambridge, MA: Harvard University Press.

14. Joni Lovenduski and Pippa Norris, Eds. 1993. *Gender and Party Politics*. London: Sage; Inter-Parliamentary Union. 1997. *Men and Women in Politics*. (Reports and Documents Series 28.) Geneva: IPU; Inter-Parliamentary Union. 2000. *Participation of Women in Public Life*. Geneva: IPU; Paul Whiteley, Patrick Seyd, and Jeremy Richardson. 1994. *True Blues: The Politics of Conservative Party Membership*. Oxford: Clarendon Press.

15. Richard Katz and Peter Mair, Eds. 1994. *How Parties Organize: Change and Adaptation in Party Organizations in Western Democracies*. London: Sage; Jyette Klausen and Charles S. Maier, Eds. 2001. *Has Liberalism Failed Women? Parity, Quotas and Political Representation*. New York: St Martin's Press; Miki Caul. 1999. "Women's representation in parliament." *Party Politics* 5 (1): 79–98.

16. Jan Willem Van Deth, Ed. 1997. *Private Groups and Public Life: Social Participation, Voluntary Associations and Political Involvement in Representative Democracies*. London: Routledge; Carole Uhlaner. 1989. "Rational turnout: The neglected role of groups." *American Journal of Political Science* 33: 390–422; Mark Gray and Miki Caul. 2000. "Declining voter turnout in advanced industrial democracies, 1950 to 1997." *Comparative Political Studies* 33 (9): 1091–1122.

17. International Confederation of Free Trade Unions. 1998. "European trade unions step up organizing activities." <www.iftu.org>

18. Margaret Inglehart. 1979. "Political interest in West European women." *Comparative Political Studies* 14: 299–336.

19. Ronald Inglehart. 1997. *Modernization and Postmodernization: Cultural, Economic and Political Change in 43 Societies*. Princeton, NJ: Princeton University Press, pp. 308–11.

20. For the detailed argument, see Pippa Norris. 2002. *Democratic Phoenix: Political Activism Worldwide*. New York: Cambridge University Press.

21. See Sidney Tarrow. 1994. *Power in Movement*. Cambridge: Cambridge University Press; Charles Tilly. 1978. *From Mobilization to Revolution*. Reading, MA: Addison-Wesley; Doug McAdam, John D. McCarthy, and Mayer N. Zald, Eds. 1996. *Comparative Perspectives on Social Movements*. New York: Cambridge University Press; Russell J. Dalton and Manfred Kuechler, Eds. 1990. *Challenging the Political Order: New*

Social and Political Movements in Western Democracies. New York: Oxford University Press; Donnatella Della Porta and Mario Diani. 1999. *Social Movements: An Introduction*. Oxford: Blackwell.

22. See Margaret E Keck and Kathryn Sikkink. 1998. *Activists beyond Borders – Advocacy Networks in International Politics*. Ithaca, New York: Cornell University Press; J. Smith, C. Chatfield, and R. Pagnucco, Eds. 1997. *Transnational Social Movements and Global Politics: Solidarity beyond the State*. Syracuse, New York: Syracuse University Press; H. Kriesi, Donnatella Della Porta, and Dieter Riucht, Eds. 1998. *Social Movements in a Globalizing World*. London: Macmillan.

23. Mayer Zald and John McCarthy, Eds. 1987. *Social Movements in an Organizational Society*. New Brunswick, NJ: Transaction; Anthony Oberschall. 1993. *Social Movements: Ideologies, Interests and Identities*. New Brunswick, NJ: Transaction; David Meyer and Sidney Tarrow, Eds. 1998. *The Social Movement Society: Contentious Politics for a New Century*. Lanham, MD: Rowman and Littlefield; Enrique Larana, Hank Johnston, and Joseph R. Gudfield, Eds. 1994. *New Social Movements: From Ideology to Identity*. Philadelphia: Temple University Press; Douglas McAdam, John D. McCarthy, and Mayer N. Zald. 1996. *Comparative Perspectives on Social Movements*. New York: Cambridge University Press.

24. See Jonathan Baker. 1999. *Street-Level Democracy: Political Settings at the Margins of Global Power*. Connecticut: Kumarian Press.

25. For a literature review, see Karen Beckwith. 2000. "Beyond compare? Women's movements in comparative perspective." *European Journal of Political Research* 37: 431–468.

26. Clyde Wilcox. 1991. "The causes and consequences of feminist consciousness among Western European women." *Comparative Political Studies* 23 (4): 519–545; Lee Ann Banaszak and Eric Plutzer. 1993. "The social bases of feminism in the European Community." *Public Opinion Quarterly* 57 (1): 29–53; Lee Ann Banaszak and Eric Plutzer. 1993. "Contextual determinants of feminist attitudes – National and subnational influences in Western Europe." *American Political Science Review* 87 (1): 147–157.

27. The primary works on social capital are Robert D. Putnam. 1993. *Making Democracy Work: Civic Traditions in Modern Italy*. Princeton, NJ: Princeton University Press; Robert D. Putnam. 1996. "The strange disappearance of civic America." *The American Prospect* 24: 34–48; Robert D. Putnam. 2000. *Bowling Alone: The Collapse and Revival of American Community*. New York: Simon and Schuster. More recent comparative research is presented in Susan Pharr and Robert Putnam, Eds. 2000. *Disaffected Democracies: What's Troubling the Trilateral Countries?* Princeton, NJ: Princeton University Press; Robert D. Putnam, Ed. 2002. *The Dynamics of Social Capital*. Oxford: Oxford University Press.

28. The analysis is limited to the final (2000) wave of the WVS because the wording of the items measuring "belonging" and "activism" within civic associations changed over successive waves.

29. Pippa Norris. 2002. *Democratic Phoenix: Political Activism Worldwide.* New York: Cambridge University Press, Chapter 10; Ronald Inglehart. 1997. *Modernization and Postmodernization: Cultural, Economic and Political Change in 43 Societies.* Princeton, NJ: Princeton University Press, pp.311–315.

30. Samuel Barnes and Max Kaase. 1979. *Political Action: Mass Participation in Five Western Democracies.* Beverly Hills, CA: Sage, pp.107–110. See also Alan Marsh.1977. *Protest and Political Consciousness.* Beverly Hills, CA: Sage.

31. Peter Van Aelst and Stefaan Walgrave. 2001. "Who is that (wo)man in the street? From the normalization of protest to the normalization of the protester." *European Journal of Political Research* 39: 461–486.

32. Samuel Barnes and Max Kaase. 1979. *Political Action: Mass Participation in Five Western Democracies.* Beverly Hills, CA: Sage.

33. For a fuller discussion, see Christopher A. Rootes. 1981. "On the future of protest politics in Western democracies: A critique of Barnes, Kaase et al., *Political Action.*" *European Journal of Political Research* 9: 421–432.

34. Sidney Verba, Kay Schlozman, and Henry E. Brady. 1995. *Voice and Equality: Civic Voluntarism in American Politics.* Cambridge, MA: Harvard University Press.

35. Ray Wolfinger and Steven Rosenstone. 1980. *Who Votes?* New Haven, CT: Yale University Press.

36. Nancy Burns, Kay Lehman Schlozman, and Sidney Verba. 2001. *The Private Roots of Public Action.* Cambridge, MA: Harvard University Press, p. 35.

37. Steven J. Rosenstone and John Mark Hansen. 1993. *Mobilization, Participation and Democracy in America.* New York: Macmillan, p. 5.

38. For American accounts of this process, see John Aldrich. 1996. *Why Parties? The Origins and Transformation of Political Parties in America.* Chicago: University of Chicago Press; Robert Huckfelt and John Sprague. 1995. *Citizens, Politics and Social Communication: Information and Influence in an Election Campaign.* New York: Cambridge University Press.

6. Women as Political Leaders

1. United Nations. *Women 2000: Gender Equality, Development and Peace.* Special Session of the General Assembly, June 5–9. <http://www.un.org/womenwatch/daw/followup/beijing+5.html>

2. United Nations. 2000. *The World's Women 2000: Trends and Statistics.* New York: United Nations.

3. Inter-parliamentary Union. 2000. *Women in National Parliaments.* <www.ipu.org>

4. For recent overviews of the literature, see Azza Karam, Ed. 1998. *Women in Politics beyond Numbers.* Stockholm: IDEA. <http://www.int-idea.se/women/>; Andrew Reynolds. 1999. "Women in the legislatures and executives of the world: Knocking at the highest glass ceiling." *World Politics* 51 (4): 547–572; Lane Kenworthy and Melissa Malami. 1999. "Gender inequality in political representation: A worldwide comparative analysis." *Social Forces* 78 (1): 235–269; Alan Siaroff. 2000. "Women's representation in legislatures and cabinets in industrial democracies." *International Political Science Review* 21 (2): 197–215.

5. Reynolds measured socioeconomic development by the UN gender-related development index. Andrew Reynolds. 1999. "Women in the legislatures and executives of the world: Knocking at the highest glass ceiling." *World Politics* 51 (4).

6. Wilma Rule. 1987. "Electoral systems, contextual factors and women's opportunities for parliament in 23 democracies." *Western Political Quarterly* 40: 477–98; Wilma Rule. 1988. "Why women don't run: The critical contextual factors in women's legislative recruitment." *Western Political Quarterly* 34: 60–77; Pippa Norris. 1985. "Women in European legislative elites." *West European Politics* 8 (4): 90–101; Pippa Norris. 1987. *Politics and Sexual Equality.* Boulder, CO: Rienner; Robert Darcy, Susan Welsh, and Janet Clark. 1994. *Women, Elections and Representation.* Lincoln: University of Nebraska Press.

7. United States Census Bureau. 2000. *Statistical Abstract of the United States, 1999.* <www.census.gov>

8. See, for example, the discussion in Azza Karam, Ed. 1998. *Women in Politics beyond Numbers.* Stockholm: IDEA. <http://www.int-idea.se/women/>

9. Andrew Reynolds. 1999. "Women in the legislatures and executives of the world: Knocking at the highest glass ceiling." *World Politics* 51 (4): 547–572.

10. Pippa Norris. 2000. "Women's representation and electoral systems." In *The International Encyclopedia of Elections*, ed. Richard Rose. Washington, DC: CQ Press, pp. 348–351; Richard E Matland. 1993. "Institutional variables affecting female representation in national legislatures: The case of Norway." *Journal of Politics* 55 (3): 737–755.

11. Joni Lovenduski and Pippa Norris. 1993. *Gender and Party Politics.* London: Sage; Pippa Norris and Joni Lovenduski. 1995. *Political Recruitment: Gender, Race and Class in the British Parliament.* Cambridge: Cambridge University Press; Miki Caul. 1999. "Women's representation in parliament." *Party Politics* 5 (1): 79–98.

12. Maurice Duverger. 1955. *The Political Role of Women.* Paris: UNESCO.

13. See the relevant chapters in Pippa Norris, Ed. 1998. *Passages to Power*. Cambridge: Cambridge University Press; Pippa Norris and Joni Lovenduski. 1995. *Political Recruitment: Gender, Race and Class in the British Parliament*. Cambridge: Cambridge University Press.

14. Inter-parliamentary Union. 2000. *Politics: Women's Insight*. (IPU Reports and Documents No. 36.) Geneva: IPU

15. Lauri Karvonen and Per Selle. 1995. *Women in Nordic Politics*. Aldershot: Dartmouth.

16. This patterns holds despite including the election as prime minister of Benazir Bhutto in Pakistan, Tansu Ciller in Turkey, and Begum Khaleda Zia and Sheikh Hasina Wajed in Bangladesh. Gehan Abu-Zayd. 1998. "In search of political power: Women in parliament in Egypt, Jordan and Lebanon." In *Women in Parliament: Beyond Numbers*, ed. Azza Karam. IDEA: Stockholm.

17. Wilma Rule. 1987. "Electoral systems, contextual factors and women's opportunities for parliament in 23 democracies." *Western Political Quarterly* 40: 477–498.

18. Margaret Inglehart. 1979. "Political interest in West European women." *Comparative Political Studies* 14: 299–336.

19. Andrew Reynolds. 1999. "Women in the legislatures and executives of the world: Knocking at the highest glass ceiling." *World Politics* 51 (4): 547–572.

20. Lawrence Mayer and Roland E. Smith. 1985. "Feminism and religiosity: Female electoral behavior in Western Europe." In Sylia Bashevkin. 1985. *Women and Politics in Western Europe*. London: Frank Cass; Clyde Wilcox. 1991. "The causes and consequences of feminist consciousness among Western European women." *Comparative Political Studies* 23 (4): 519–545.

21. Ronald Inglehart and Pippa Norris. 2000. "The developmental theory of the gender gap: Women's and men's voting behavior in global perspective." *International Political Science Review* 21 (4): 441–462.

22. Ronald Inglehart and Wayne E. Baker. 2000. "Modernization, cultural change and the persistence of traditional values." *American Sociological Review* 65: 19–51.

23. Kendall Baker, Russell Dalton, and Kai Hildebrandt. 1981. *Germany Transformed*. Cambridge, MA: Harvard University Press; Ronald Inglehart. 1977. *The Silent Revolution: Changing Values and Political Styles among Western Publics*. Princeton, NJ: Princeton University Press; Ronald Inglehart. 1997. *Modernization and Postmodernization: Cultural, Economic and Political Change in 43 Societies*. Princeton, NJ: Princeton University Press.

24. Mark Jones. 1996. "Increasing women's representation via gender quotas: The Argentine Ley de Cupos." *Women & Politics* 16 (4): 75–98; Mark Jones. 1998. "Gender quotas, electoral laws, and the election of women – Lessons from the Argentine provinces." *Comparative Political Studies*

31 (1): 3–21; Mark Jones. 1999. "Assessing the effectiveness of gender quotas in open-list proportional representation electoral systems." *Social Science Quarterly* 80 (2): 341–355.

25. Drude Dahlerup. 1998. "Using quotas to increase women's political representation." In Azza Karam, Ed. 1998. *Women in Politics beyond Numbers.* Stockholm: IDEA. <http://www.int-idea.se/women/>

26. Inter-parliamentary Union. 1999. *Participation of Women in Political Life.* (IPU Reports and Documents No 35.) Geneva: IPU.

7. Conclusions: Gender Equality and Cultural Change

1. Ronald Inglehart. 1997. *Modernization and Postmodernization: Cultural, Economic and Political Change in 43 Societies.* Princeton, NJ: Princeton University Press.

2. Ronald Inglehart and Wayne Baker. 2000. "Modernization, cultural change and the persistence of traditional values." *American Sociological Review* 65: 19–51. The study provides full details on how these dimensions were measured, together with factor analyses at both the individual level and the national level, demonstrating that the same dimensional structure emerges at both levels.

3. Ronald Inglehart and Wayne Baker. 2000. "Modernization, cultural change and the persistence of traditional values." *American Sociological Review* 65.

4. Max Weber. 1904/1958. *The Protestant Ethic and the Spirit of Capitalism.* New York: Charles Scribner's Sons.

Appendix C: Technical Note on the Major Scales

1. See Pippa Norris and Ronald Inglehart. 2002. "Islam and the West: Testing the clash of civilizations thesis." <www.pippanorris.com> Paper presented at the APSA political communication conference, Terrorism, the Media, and Public Affairs, at the John F. Kennedy School of Government, August.

Select Bibliography

Abramson, Paul R., and Ronald Inglehart. 1995. *Value Change in Global Perspective*. Ann Arbor: University of Michigan Press.

Abzug, Bella, and M. Kelber. 1983. *Gender Gap*. Boston: Houghton Mifflin.

Abu-Lughod, Lila, Ed. 1998. *Remaking Women: Feminism and Modernity in the Middle East*. Princeton, NJ: Princeton University Press.

Adler, M.A., and A. Brayfield. 1996. "East-West differences in attitudes about employment and family in Germany." *Sociological Quarterly* 37 (2): 245–260.

Adler, Leonore Loeb. 1993. *International Handbook on Gender Roles*. Westport, CT: Greenwood Press.

Almond, Gabriel A., and Sidney Verba. 1963. *The Civic Culture: Political Attitudes and Democracy in Five Nations*. Princeton, NJ: Princeton University Press.

Alwin, Duane F., Michael Braun, and Jacqueline Scott. 1992. "The separation of work and family: Attitudes towards women's labour-force participation in Germany, Great Britain, and the United States." *European Sociological Review* 8: 13–37.

Andersen, Kristi. 1996. *After Suffrage*. Chicago: University of Chicago Press.

Anker, Richard. 1998. *Gender and Jobs: Sex Segregation of Occupations in the World*. Geneva: International Labor Office.

Arat, Y. 2000. "Feminists, Islamists, and political change in Turkey." *Political Psychology* 19 (1): 117–131.

Asghar, Ali Engineer, Ed. 2001. *Islam, Women and Gender Justice*. New Delhi: Gyan Publishing.

Banaszak, Lee Ann, and Eric Plutzer. 1993. "Contextual determinants of feminist attitudes – National and sub-national influences in Western Europe." *American Political Science Review* 87 (1): 147–157.

Banaszak, Lee Ann, and Eric Plutzer. 1993. "The social bases of feminism in the European Community." *Public Opinion Quarterly* 57 (1): 29–53.

Banducci, S. A., and Jeff A. Karp. 2000. "Gender, leadership and choice in multiparty systems." *Political Research Quarterly* 53 (4): 815–848.

Bargad, A., and J. S. Hyde. 1991. "Women's studies - A study of feminist identity development in women." *Psychology of Women Quarterly* 15 (2): 181–201.

Barnes, Samuel, and Max Kaase. 1979. *Political Action: Mass Participation in Five Western Democracies*. Beverly Hills, CA: Sage.

Barrett, H. 1995. "Women in Africa - The neglected dimension in development." *Geography* 80 (348): 215–224.

Basu, Amrita, Ed. 1995. *The Challenge of Local Feminisms: Women's Movements in Global Perspective*. Boulder, CO: Westview Press.

Baxter, Janeen, and Emily W. Kane. 1995. "Dependence and independence - A cross-national analysis of gender inequality and gender attitudes." *Gender & Society* 9 (2): 193–215.

Baxter, Janeen. 1997. "Gender equality and participation in housework: A cross-national perspective." *Journal of Comparative Family Studies* 28 (3): 220.

Baxter, Sandra, and Marjorie Lansing. 1983. *Women and Politics*. Ann Arbor: University of Michigan Press.

Beckwith, Karen. 2000. "Beyond compare? Women's movements in comparative perspective." *European Journal of Political Research* 37: 431–68.

Bell, Daniel. 1999. *The Coming of Post-Industrial Society: A Venture in Social Forecasting*. New York: Basic Books.

Bennett, Linda, and Stephen Bennett. 1989. "Enduring gender differences in political interest." *American Politics Quarterly* 17: 105–22.

Bennett, Stephen Earl, and Linda Bennett. 1992. "From traditional to modern conceptions of gender equality in politics." *Western Political Quarterly* 451: 93–111.

Berkman, Michael, and Robert O'Connor. 1993. "Do women legislators matter? Female legislators and state abortion policy." *American Politics Quarterly* 21: 102–124.

Berkovitch, N., and V. M. Moghadam. 1999. "Middle East politics and women's collective action: Challenging the status quo." *Social Politics* 6 (3): 273–291.

Black, Earl, and Merle Black. 1987. *Politics and Society in the South*. Cambridge, MA: Harvard University Press.

Blackburn, Robin, J. Jarman, and B. Brooks. 2000. "The puzzle of gender segregation and inequality: A cross-national analysis." *European Sociological Review* 16 (2): 119–135.

Blondel, Jean. 1970. *Votes, Parties and Leaders*. London: Penguin.

Boserup, Ester. 1971. *Women's Role in Economic Development*. New York: St. Martin's Press.

Braun, Michael, Jacqueline Scott, and Duane Alwin. 1994. "Economic necessity or self-actualization? Attitudes towards women's labour-force participation in East and West Germany." *European Sociological Review* 10: 29–47.

Brettell, Caroline, and Carolyn F. Sargent, Eds. 2001. *Gender in Cross-cultural Perspective*. Englewwod Cliffs, NJ: Prentice Hall.

Brill, Alida, Ed. 1995. *A Rising Public Voice: Women in Politics Worldwide*. New York: Feminist Books.

Buchmann, C. 1996. "The debt crisis, structural adjustment and women's education - Implications for status and social development." *International Journal of Comparative Sociology* 37 (1–2): 5–30.

Burn, Shawn Meghan. 2000. *Women across Cultures: A Global Perspective*. Palo Alto, CA: Mayfield.

Butler, David, and Donald E. Stokes. 1974. *Political Change in Britain: The Evolution of Electoral Choice*, 2nd ed. London: Macmillan.

Buvinic, M. 1999. "Promoting gender equality." *International Social Science Journal* 51 (4): 567.

Campbell, Angus, Philip Converse, Warren E. Miller, and Donald E. Stokes. 1960. *The American Voter*. New York: Wiley.

Caprioli, M., and M. A. Boyer. 2001. "Gender, violence, and international crisis." *Journal of Conflict Resolution* 45 (4): 503–518.

Caul, Miki. 1999. "Women's representation in parliament." *Party Politics* 5 (1): 79–98.

Carroll, Susan J. 1988. "Women's autonomy and the gender gap: 1980 and 1982." In *The Politics of the Gender Gap: The Social Construction of Political Influence*, ed. Carol M. Mueller. Beverly Hills, CA: Sage, pp. 236–257.

Carroll, Susan J., and Pippa Norris. 1997. "The dynamics of the news framing process: From Reagan's gender gap to Clinton's soccer moms." Paper presented at the annual meeting of the Southern Political Science Association, Norfolk, VA.

Carroll, Susan J. 1999. "The disempowerment of the gender gap: Soccer moms and the 1996 elections." *PSOnline*, pp. 7–11. <http://www.apsanet.org/ps/>

CAWP. 2000. <http://www.rci.rutgers.edu/~cawp/ggap.html>

Chang M, I. 2000. "The evolution of sex segregation regimes." *American Journal of Sociology* 105 (6): 1658–1701.

Chang, L. 1999. "Gender role egalitarian attitudes in Beijing, Hong Kong, Florida, and Michigan." *Journal of Cross-Cultural Psychology* 30 (6): 722–741.

Chaney, Carol K., Michael Alvarez, and Jonathan Nagler. 1998. "Explaining the gender gap in US presidential elections, 1980–1992." *Political Research Quarterly* 51 (2): 311–340.

Charlton, Sue Ellen M., Jana Everett, and Kathleen Staudt, Eds. 1989. *Women, the State, and Development*. Albany: State University of New York Press.

Christie, Carol. 1987. *Sex Differences in Political Participation*. New York: Praeger.

Clubb, Jerome M., William H. Flanigan, and Nancy H. Zingale. 1990. *Partisan Realignment: Voters, Parties and Government in American History*. Boulder, CO: Westview Press.

Chua, P., K. K. Bhavnani, and J. Foran. 2000. "Women, culture, development: A new paradigm for development studies?" *Ethnic and Racial Studies* 23 (5): 820–841.

Ciabattari, T. 2001. "Changes in men's conservative gender ideologies - Cohort and period influences." *Gender & Society* 15 (4): 574–591.

Clark, Cal, and Rose J. Lee, Eds. 2000. *Democracy and the Status of Women in East Asia*. Boulder, CO: Lynne Rienner.

Clark, R., T. W. Ramsbey, and E. S. Adler. 1991. "Culture, gender, and labor-force participation - A cross-national study." *Gender & Society* 5 (1): 47–66.

Clubb, Jerome M., William H. Flanigan, and Nancy H. Zingale. 1990. *Partisan Realignment: Voters, Parties and Government in American History*. Boulder, CO: Westview Press.

Cole, E. R., A. N. Zucker, and J. M. Ostrove. 1998. "Political participation and feminist consciousness among women activists of the 1960s." *Political Psychology* 19 (2): 349–371.

Conover, Pamela Johnston. 1988. "Feminists and the gender gap." *Journal of Politics* 50: 985–1010.

Conway, Margaret, Gertrude A. Steuernagel, and David Ahern. 1997. *Women and Political Participation*. Washington, DC: CQ Press.

Cook, Elizabeth A., and Clyde Wilcox. 1991. "Feminism and the gender gap: A second look." *Journal of Politics* 53: 1111–1122.

Cook, Elizabeth Adell, Sue Thomas, and Clyde Wilcox, Eds. 1998. *The Year of the Woman: Myths and Realities*. Boulder, CO: Westview Press.

Craske, Nikki. 1999. *Women and Politics in Latin America*. New Brunswick, NJ: Rutgers University Press.

Crewe, Ivor, and D. T. Denver. 1985. *Electoral Change in Western Democracies: Patterns and Sources of Electoral Volatility*. New York: St. Martin's Press.

Dahlerup, Drude. 1986. *The New Women's Movements: Feminism and Political Power in Europe and the USA*. London: Sage.

Dalton, Russell J., Scott C. Flanagan, Paul A. Beck, and James E. Alt. 1984. *Electoral Change in Advanced Industrial Democracies: Realignment or Dealignment?* Princeton, NJ: Princeton University Press.

Danner, M., L. Fort, and G. Young. 1999. "International data on women and gender: Resources, issues, critical use." *Women's Studies International Forum* 22 (2): 249–259.

Darcy, Robert, Susan Welsh, and Janet Clark. 1994. *Women, Elections and Representation*. Lincoln: University of Nebraska Press.

Davis, Nancy J., and Robert Robinson. 1991. "Men and women's consciousness of gender inequality: Austria, West Germany, Great Britain, and the United States." *American Sociological Review* 56: 72–84.

Davis, Rebecca. 1997. *Women and Power in Western Democracies*. Lincoln: University of Nebraska Press.

Deutsch, Karl W. 1964. "Social mobilization and political development." *American Political Science Review* 55: 493–514.

DeVaus, David, and Ian McAllister. 1989. "The changing politics of women: Gender and political alignments in 11 nations." *European Journal of Political Research* 17: 241–262.

Dijkstra, A. Geske, and Lucia C. Hanmer. 2000. "Measuring socio-economic gender inequality: Toward an alternative to the UNDP gender-related development index." *Feminist Economics* 6 (2): 41–75.

Dogan, Mattei, and Richard Rose, 1971. *European Politics: A Reader*. London: Macmillan.

Downing, N. E., and K. L. Roush. 1985. "From passive acceptance to active commitment - A model of feminist identity development for women." *Counseling Psychologist* 13 (4): 695–709.

Durant, Henry W. 1949. *Political Opinion*. London: BFI Publishers.

Durant, Henry. 1969. "Voting behavior in Britain 1945–1966." In *Studies in British Politics*, ed. Richard Rose. London: Macmillan.

Duverger, Maurice. 1955. *The Political Role of Women*. Paris: UNESCO.

Erie, Stephen P., and Rein Martin. 1988. "Women and the welfare state." In *The Politics of the Gender Gap*, ed. Carol M. Mueller. Newbury Park, CA: Sage.

Fassinger R. E. 1994. "Development and testing of the Attitudes Toward Feminism and the Women's Movement (FWM) Scale." *Psychology of Women Quarterly* 18 (3): 389–402.

Fischer, A. R., D. M. Tokar, M. M. Mergl, G. E. Good, M. S. Hill, and S. A. Blum. 2000. "Assessing women's feminist identity development - Studies of convergent, discriminant, and structural validity." *Psychology of Women Quarterly* 24 (1): 15–29.

Forsythe, N., R. P. Korzeniewicz, and V. Durrant 2000. "Gender inequalities and economic growth: A longitudinal evaluation." *Economic Development and Cultural Change* 48 (3): 573–617.

Franklin, Mark, Thomas T. Mackie, Henry Valen, and Clive Bean. 1992. *Electoral Change: Responses to Evolving Social and Attitudinal Structures in Western Countries*. Cambridge: Cambridge University Press.

Fredman, Sandra. 1997. *Women and the Law*. Oxford: Oxford University Press.

Frieze, I. H., and M. C. McHugh. 1998. "Measuring feminism and gender role attitudes." *Psychology of Women Quarterly* 22 (3): 349–352.

Gelb, Joyce. 1989. *Feminism and Politics: A Comparative Perspective*. Berkeley: University of California Press.

Gerstmann, E. A., and D. A. Kramer. 1997. "Feminist identity development: Psychometric analyses of two feminist identity scales." *Sex Roles* 36 (5–6): 327–348.

Gerstmann, E. A., and D. A. Kramer. 1997. "Feminist identity development: Psychometric analyses of two feminist identity scales." *Sex Roles* 36 (5–6): 327–348.

Gilens, Martin. 1988. "Gender and support for Reagan." *American Journal of Political Science* 32: 19–49.

Goot, Murray, and Elizabeth Reid. 1984. "Women: If not apolitical, then conservative." In *Women and the Public Sphere*, ed. Janet Siltanen and Michelle Stanworth. London: Hutchinson.

Granato, James, Ronald Inglehart, and David Leblang. 1996. "Cultural values, stable democracy and economic development: A reply." *American Journal of Political Science* 40 (3): 680–696.

Granato, James, Ronald Inglehart, and David Leblang. 1996. "The effect of culture on economic development: Theory, hypotheses and some empirical tests." *American Journal of Political Science* 40 (3): 607–631.

Gunderson, Morley. 1994. *Comparable Worth and Gender Discrimination: An International Perspective*. Geneva: International Labour Office.

Haavio-Mannila, Elina, et al., Eds. 1985. *Unfinished Democracy: Women in Nordic Politics*. Oxford: Pergamon Press.

Hayes, Bernadette C., and Clive S. Bean. 1993. "Gender and local political interest: Some international comparisons." *Political Studies* 41: 672–682.

Hayes, Bernadette C., and Ian McAllister. 1997. "Gender, party leaders and election outcomes in Australia, Britain and the United States." *Comparative Political Studies* 30: 3–26.

Hayes, Bernadette C., Ian Mcallister, and Donley Studlar. 2000. "Gender, postmaterialism, and feminism in comparative perspective." *International Political Science Review* 21 (4): 425–439.

Hayes, Bernadette. 1997. "Gender, feminism and electoral behaviour in Britain." *Electoral Studies* 16 (2): 203–216.

Heath, Anthony, and Dorren McMahon. 1992. "Changes in values." In *British Social Attitudes: The 9th Report*, ed. Roger Jowell et al. Aldershot, Hants: Dartmouth/SCPR.

Heath, Anthony, Roger Jowell, and John Curtice. 1985. *How Britain Votes*. Oxford: Pergamon Press.

Henig, Ruth, and Simon Henig. 2001. *Women and Political Power: Europe since 1945*. London: Routledge.

Henley, N. M., and W. J. McCarthy. 1998. "Measuring feminist attitudes – Problems and prospects." *Psychology of Women Quarterly* 22 (3): 363–369.

Henley, N. M., K. Meng, W. J. Mccarthy, and R. J. Sockloskie. 1998. "Developing a scale to measure the diversity of feminist attitudes." *Psychology of Women Quarterly* 22 (3): 317–348.

Hewitt, Patricia, and Deborah Mattinson. 1987. *Women's Votes: The Keys to Winning*. (Fabian Pamphlet.) London: Fabian Society.

Htun, Mala N., and Mark P. Jones. 1999. "Engendering the right to participate in decision-making: electoral quotas and women's leadership in

Latin America." Paper presented at the ninety-fifth annual meeting of the American Political Science Association.

Huber, Jon, and Ronald Inglehart. 1995. "Expert interpretations of party space and party locations in 42 societies." *Party Politics* 1 (1): 71–111.

Huddy, Leony, F. K. Neely, and M. R. Lafay. 2000. "The polls - Trends - Support for the women's movement." *Public Opinion Quarterly* 64 (3): 309–350.

Humana, Charles. 1992. *World Human Rights Guide*, 3rd ed. New York: Oxford University Press.

Humphries, Jane. 1995. *Gender and Economics*. Cheltenham: Edward Elgar.

Hunter, A. G., and S. L. Sellers. 1998. "Feminist attitudes among African American women and men." *Gender & Society* 12 (1): 81–99.

Inglehart, Margaret. 1979. "Political interest in West European women." *Comparative Political Studies* 14: 299–336.

Inglehart, Ronald, and Paul Abramson. 1999. "Measuring Postmaterialism." *American Political Science Review* 93 (3): 665–677.

Inglehart, Ronald, and Pippa Norris. 2000. "The developmental theory of the gender gap: Women's and men's voting behavior in global perspective." *International Political Science Review* 21 (4): 441–462.

Inglehart, Ronald, and Wayne E. Baker. 2000. "Modernization, globalization and the persistence of tradition: Empirical evidence from 65 societies." *American Sociological Review* 65: 19–55.

Inglehart, Ronald, and Wayne E. Baker. 2001. "Modernization's challenge to traditional values: Who's afraid of Ronald McDonald?" *Futurist* 35 (2): 16–21.

Inglehart, Ronald. 1990. *Culture Shift in Advanced Industrial Society*. Princeton, NJ: Princeton University Press.

Inglehart, Ronald. 1977. *The Silent Revolution: Changing Values and Political Styles among Western Publics*. Princeton, NJ: Princeton University Press.

Inglehart, Ronald. 1997. "The trend toward Postmaterialist values continues." In *Citizen Politics in Post-Industrial Societies*, ed. Terry Clark and Michael Rempel. Boulder, CO: Westview Press.

Inglehart, Ronald. 1997. *Modernization and Postmodernization: Cultural, Economic and Political Change in 43 Societies*. Princeton, NJ: Princeton University Press.

Inglehart, Ronald. 1999. "Trust, well-being and democracy." In *Democracy and Trust*, ed. Mark Warren. Cambridge: Cambridge University Press.

Inglehart, Ronald. 2000. "Culture and democracy." In *Culture Matters*, ed. Samuel Huntington and Lawrence Harrison. New York: Basic Books.

Inglehart, Ronald. 2000. "Globalization and postmodern values." *Washington Quarterly* 23 (2): 215–228.

Inter-parliamentary Union. 1999. *Participation of Women in Political Life*. (IPU Reports and Documents No. 35.) Geneva: IPU.

Inter-parliamentary Union. 2000. *Politics: Women's Insight*. (IPU Reports and Documents No. 36.) Geneva: IPU.

Inter-parliamentary Union. 2000. *Women in National Parliaments.* Geneva: IPU. <www.ipu.org>

Jacobs, Jerry A., Ed. 1995. *Gender Inequality at Work.* Thousand Oaks, CA: Sage.

Jacquette, Jane, and Sharon Wolchik, Eds. 1998. *Women and Democracy: Latin America and Central and Eastern Europe.* Baltimore, MD: Johns Hopkins University Press.

Jelen, Ted G., Sue Thomas, and Clyde Wilcox. 1994. "The gender gap in comparative perspective." *European Journal of Political Research* 25: 171–186.

Jenson, Jane, Jacqueline Laufer, and Margaret Maruani, Eds. 2000. *The Gendering of Inequalities: Women, Men, and Work.* Aldershot: Ashgate.

Jones, Mark. 1996. "Increasing women's representation via gender quotas: The Argentine Ley de Cupos." *Women & Politics* 16 (4): 75–98.

Jones, Mark. 1998. "Gender quotas, electoral laws, and the election of women – Lessons from the Argentine provinces." *Comparative Political Studies* 31 (1): 3–21.

Jones, Mark. 1999. "Assessing the effectiveness of gender quotas in open-list proportional representation electoral systems." *Social Science Quarterly* 80 (2): 341–355.

Joseph, Suad, and Susan Slyomovics. 2001. *Women and Power in the Middle East.* Philadelphia: University of Pennsylvania Press.

Karam, Azza, Ed. 1998. *Women in Politics beyond Numbers.* Stockholm: IDEA. <http://www.int-idea.se/women/>

Karvonen, Lauri, and Per Selle. 1995. *Women in Nordic Politics.* Aldershot: Dartmouth.

Kazemi, F. 2000. "Gender, Islam and politics." *Social Research* 67 (2): 453–474.

Kelly, Rita Mae, et al. 2001. *Gender, Globalization and Democratization.* Lanham, MD: Rowman and Littlefield.

Kenworthy, Lane, and Melissa Malami. 1999. "Gender inequality in political representation: A worldwide comparative analysis." *Social Forces* 78 (1): 235–269.

Khan, S. 1998. "Muslim women: Negotiations in the third space." *Signs* 23 (2): 463–494.

Kiernan, Kathleen. 1992. "Men and women at work and at home." In *British Social Attitudes: The 9th Report,* ed. Roger Jowell et al. Aldershot, Hants: Dartmouth/SCPR.

Klausen, Jyette, and Charles S. Maier, Eds. 2001. *Has Liberalism Failed Women? Parity, Quotas and Political Representation.* New York: St. Martin's Press.

Klein, Ethel. 1984. *Gender Politics.* Cambridge, MA: Harvard University Press.

Koczberski, G. 1998. "Women in development: a critical analysis." *Third World Quarterly* 19 (3): 395–409.

Lantican, C. P., C. H. Gladwin, and J. L. Seale. 1996. "Income and gender inequalities in Asia: Testing alternative theories of development." *Economic Development and Cultural Change* 44 (2): 235–263.

Lerner, Daniel. 1958. *The Passing of Traditional Society: Modernizing the Middle East*. New York: Free Press.

Lipset, Seymour M. 1960. *Political Man: The Social Bases of Politics*. Garden City, New York: Doubleday.

Lipset, Seymour M., and Stein Rokkan. 1967. *Party Systems and Voter Alignments*. New York: Free Press.

Lipset, Seymour Martin, Kyoung-Ryung Seong, and John Charles Torres. 1993. "A comparative analysis of the social requisites of democracy." *International Social Science Journal* 45 (2): 154–175.

Lipset, Seymour Martin. 1959. "Some social requisites of democracy: Economic development and political legitimacy." *American Political Science Review* 53: 69–105.

Liss, M., C. O'Connor, E. Morosky, and M. Crawford. 2001. "What makes a feminist? Predictors and correlates of feminist social identity in college women." *Psychology of Women Quarterly* 25 (2): 124–133.

Listhaug, Ola, Arthur H. Miller, and Henry Vallen. 1985. "The gender gap in Norwegian voting behavior." *Scandinavian Political Studies* 83: 187–206.

Lovenduski, Joni, and Pippa Norris, Eds. 1993. *Gender and Party Politics*. London: Sage.

Lovenduski, Joni, and Pippa Norris, Eds. 1996. *Women in Politics*. Oxford: Oxford University Press.

Lovenduski, Joni. 1986. *Women and European Politics*. Sussex: Wheatsheaf.

Lynott, P. P., and N. J. McCandless. 2000. "The impact of age vs. life experience on the gender role attitudes of women in different cohorts." *Journal of Women & Aging* 12 (1–2): 5–21.

Majid A. 2000. "The politics of feminism in Islam." *Signs* 23 (2): 321–361.

Manza, Jeff, and Clem Brooks. 1998. "The gender gap in U.S. presidential elections: When? Why? Implications?" *American Journal of Sociology* 103 (5): 1235–1266.

Mason, K., and A-M. Jenson, Eds. 1995. *Gender and Family Change in Industrialized Countries*. Oxford: Clarendon Press.

Matland, Richard E. 1993. "Institutional variables affecting female representation in national legislatures: The case of Norway." *Journal of Politics* 55 (3): 737–755.

Matland, Richard E. 1998. "Women's representation in national legislatures: Developed and developing countries." *Legislative Studies Quarterly* 23 (1): 109–125.

Mayer, Lawrence, and Roland E. Smith. 1985. "Feminism and religiosity: Female electoral behavior in Western Europe." In *Women and Politics in Western Europe*, ed. Sylia Bashevkin. London: Frank Cass.

Meriwether, Margaret L., and Judith E. Tucker, Eds. 2000. *Social History of Women and Gender in the Modern Middle East.* Boulder, CO: Westview Press.

Mattei, Laura, R. Winsky, and Franco Mattei. 1998. "If men stayed home... The gender gap in recent congressional elections." *Political Research Quarterly* 51: 411–436.

Meyer, K., Rizzo, and Y. Ali. 1998. "Islam and the extension of citizenship rights to women in Kuwait." *Journal for the Scientific Study of Religion* 37 (1): 131–144.

Meyer, Mary K., and Elisabeth Prugl, Eds. 1999. *Gender Politics and Global Governance.* Lanham, MD: Rowman and Littlefield.

Miller, Warren, and Merrill Shanks. 1996. *The New American Voter.* Ann Arbor: University of Michigan Press.

Moghadam, Valentine M. 1993. *Modernizing Women: Gender and Social Change in the Middle East.* Boulder, CO: Lynne Reinner.

Moghadam, Valentine M. 1994. *Identity Politics and Women: Cultural Reassertions and Feminisms in International Perspective.* Boulder, CO: Westview Press.

Moghissi, Haideh. 1999. *Feminism and Islamic Fundamentalism: The Limits of Postmodern Analysis.* New York: Zed Books.

Moore, G., and G. Shackman. 1996. "Gender and authority: A cross-national study." *Social Science Quarterly* 77 (2): 273–288.

Mueller, Carol, Ed. 1988. *The Politics of the Gender Gap.* London: Sage.

Nanda, Serena. 2000. *Gender Diversity: Cross-Cultural Variations.* Prospect Heights, IL: Waveland Press.

Nelson, Barbara, and Najma Chowdhury, Eds. 1994. *Women and Politics Worldwide.* New Haven, CT: Yale University Press.

Nijeholt, Geertje Lyucklama, et al. 1998. *Women's Movements and Public Policy in Europe, Latin America and the Caribbean.* New York: Garland.

Norris, Pippa, and Joni Lovenduski. 1995. *Political Recruitment: Gender, Race and Class in the British Parliament.* Cambridge: Cambridge University Press.

Norris, Pippa, and Ronald Inglehart. 2001. "Cultural obstacles to equal representation." *The Journal of Democracy* 12 (3): 126–140.

Norris, Pippa. 1985. "The gender gap in America and Britain." *Parliamentary Affairs* 38: 192–201.

Norris, Pippa. 1986. "Conservative attitudes in recent British elections: An emerging gender gap?" *Political Studies* 34: 120–128.

Norris, Pippa. 1993. "The gender-generation gap in British elections." *British Elections and Parties Yearbook 1993*, ed. David Denver, Pippa Norris, David Broughton, and Colin Rallings. London: Harvester Wheatsheaf.

Norris, Pippa. 1996. "Mobilising the women's vote: The gender-generation gap in voting behaviour." *Parliamentary Affairs* 49 (1): 333–42.

Norris, Pippa. 1999. "The gender-generation gap." In *Critical Elections: British Parties and Voters in Long-term Perspective*, ed. Geoffrey Evans and Pippa Norris. London: Sage.

Norris, Pippa. 1985. "Women in European legislative elites." *West European Politics* 8 (4): 90–101.

Norris, Pippa. 1987. *Politics and Sexual Equality.* Boulder, CO: Rienner.

Norris, Pippa. 1988. "The gender gap: A cross national trend?" In *The Politics of the Gender Gap*, ed. Carol Mueller. Beverly Hills, CA: Sage.

Norris, Pippa. 1996. "Gender realignment in comparative perspective." In *The Paradox of Parties*, ed. Marian Simms. St. Leonards, Australia: Allen and Unwin.

Norris, Pippa. 1996. "Legislative recruitment." In *Comparing Democracies*, ed. Lawrence LeDuc, Richard G. Niemi, and Pippa Norris. Newbury Park, CA: Sage.

Norris, Pippa, Ed. 1997. *Passages to Power.* Cambridge: Cambridge University Press.

Norris, Pippa. 2000. "Women's representation and electoral systems." In *The International Encyclopedia of Elections*, ed. Richard Rose. Washington, DC: CQ Press, pp. 348–351.

Norris, Pippa. 2001. "Breaking the barriers: Positive discrimination policies for women." In *Has Liberalism Failed Women? Parity, Quotas and Political Representation*, ed. Jyette Klausen and Charles S. Maier. New York: St. Martin's Press.

Norris, Pippa. 2002. *Democratic Phoenix: Political Activism Worldwide.* New York: Cambridge University Press.

Norton, A. R. 1997. "Gender, politics and the state: What do Middle Eastern women want?" *Middle East Policy* 5 (3): 155–165.

Nuss, S., and L. Majka. 1983. "The economic integration of women - a cross-national investigation work and occupations." *Work and Occupations* 10 (1): 29–48.

Nussbaum, Martha, and Jonathan Glover. 1995. *Women, Culture and Development.* Oxford: Clarendon Press.

Nyamu, C. I. 2000. "How should human rights and development respond to cultural legitimization of gender hierarchy in developing countries?" *Harvard International Law Journal* 41 (2): 381–418.

Oskarson, Maria. 1995. "Gender gaps in Nordic voting behavior." In *Women in Nordic Politics*, ed. Lauri Karvonen and Per Selle. Aldershot: Dartmouth.

Page, Benjamin I., and Robert Y. Shapiro. 1993. *The Rational Public.* Chicago: University of Chicago Press.

Pasternak, Burton, Carol R. Ember, and Melvin Ember. 1997. *Sex, Gender, and Kinship: A Cross-Cultural Perspective.* Englewood Cliffs, NJ: Prentice Hall.

Pateman, Carole. 1998. *The Sexual Contract.* Stanford, CA: Stanford University Press.

Paxton, P. 2000. "Women's suffrage in the measurement of democracy: Problems of operationalization." *Studies In Comparative International Development* 35 (3): 92–111.

Perry, S. 1998. "Holding up half the sky: Women in China." *Current History* 97 (620): 279–284.

Pillai, V. K., and G. Z. Wang. 1999. "Social structural model of women's reproductive rights: A cross-national study of developing countries." *Canadian Journal Of Sociology – Cahiers Canadiens De Sociologie* 24 (2): 255–281.

Plissner, Martin. 1983. "The marriage gap." *Public Opinion* 53: 23–30.

Plutzer, Eric. 1988. "Work life, family life and women's support for feminism." *American Sociological Review* 53: 640–649.

Poole, Keith T., and L. Harmon Zeigler. 1985. *Women, Public Opinion and Politics: The Changing Political Attitudes of American Women.* New York, Longman.

Pulzer, Peter G. J. 1967. *Political Representation and Elections in Britain.* London: Allen and Unwin.

Rai, Shirin M., and Geraldine Lievesley, Eds. 1997. *Women and the State: International Perspectives.* London: Taylor and Francis.

Rai, Shirin M., Ed. 2000. *International Perspectives on Gender and Democratization.* Basingstoke: Macmillan.

Ramirez, F. O., Y. Soysal, and S. Shanahan. 1997. "The changing logic of political citizenship: Cross-national acquisition of women's suffrage rights, 1890 to 1990." *American Sociological Review* 62 (5): 735–745.

Randall, Vicky. 1987. *Women and Politics.* London: Macmillan, pp. 68–78.

Reingold, Beth, and H. Foust. 1998. "Exploring the determinants of feminist consciousness in the United States." *Women & Politics* 19 (3): 19–48.

Renfrow, Patty. 1994. "The gender gap in the 1993 election." *Australian Journal of Political Science* 29: 118.

Reynolds, Andrew, and Ben Reilly. 1997. *The International IDEA Handbook of Electoral System Design.* Stockholm: IDEA. <http://www.idea.int>

Reynolds, Andrew. 1999. "Women in the legislatures and executives of the world: Knocking at the highest glass ceiling." *World Politics* 51 (4): 547–572.

Riddell-Dixon, E. 1999. "Mainstreaming women's rights: Problems and prospects within the centre for human rights." *Global Governance* 5 (2): 149–171.

Rinehart, Sue T. 1992. *Gender Consciousness and Politics.* New York: Routledge.

Roded, Ruth. 1999. *Women in Islam and the Middle East: A Reader.* London and New York: IB Tauris Publishers.

Rokkan, Stein. 1970. *Citizens, Elections, Parties: Approaches to the Comparative Study of the Processes of Development.* Oslo: Universitetsforlaget.

Rose, Richard, and Ian McAllister. 1986. *Voters Begin to Choose: From Closed Class to Open Elections in Britain.* London: Sage.

Rose, Richard, and Ian McAllister. 1990. *The Loyalties of Voters.* London: Sage.

Rose, Richard. 1974. *Electoral Behavior: A Comparative Handbook.* New York: Free Press.

Rosenthal, Cindy Simon. 1998. *When Women Lead.* Oxford: Oxford University Press.

Ross, James F. S. 1955. *Elections and Electors: Studies in Democratic Representation.* London: Eyre and Spottiswoode.

Rostow, Walt Whitman. 1952. *The Process of Economic Growth.* New York: Norton.

Rostow, Walt Whitman. 1960. *The Stages of Economic Growth.* Cambridge: Cambridge University Press.

Rozell, Mark, and Clyde Wilcox. 1998. "A GOP gender gap? Motivations, policy, and candidate choice." *Women & Politics* 19 (1): 91–106.

Rueschemeyer, Marilyn, Ed. 1998. *Women and the Politics of Postcommunist Eastern Europe.* New York: M. E. Sharpe.

Rule, Wilma. 1987. "Electoral systems, contextual factors and women's opportunities for parliament in 23 democracies." *Western Political Quarterly* 40: 477–498.

Rule, Wilma. 1988. "Why women don't run: The critical contextual factors in women's legislative recruitment." *Western Political Quarterly* 34: 60–77.

Rusciano, Frank L. 1992. "Rethinking the gender gap: The case of West German elections, 1949–87." *Comparative Politics* 24 (3): 335–357.

Saliba, T. 2000. "Arab feminism at the millennium." *Signs* 25 (4): 1087–1092.

Saxonberg, S. 2000. "Women in East European parliaments." *Journal Of Democracy* 11 (2): 145–158.

Scott, Jacqueline, Duane Alwin, and Michael Braun. 1996. "Generational changes in gender role attitudes: Britain in cross-national perspective." *Sociology* 30 (3): 471–492.

Scott, Jacqueline, Michael Braun, and Duane Alwin. 1993. "The family way." In *International Social Attitudes: The Tenth Report*, ed. Roger Jowell, Lindsay Brook, and Lizanne Dowds, with Daphne Ahrendt. Aldershot, Hants: SCPR.

Scott, Jacqueline, Michael Braun, and Duane Alwin. 1998. "Partner, parent, worker: Family and gender roles." In *British – and European – Social Attitudes: the Fifteenth Report.* Aldershot, Hants: Ashgate/SCPR.

Seltzer, Richard A., Jody Newman, and Melissa V. Leighton. 1997. *Sex as a Political Variable.* Boulder, CO: Lynne Reinner.

Semyonov, M., and F. L. Jones. 1999. "Dimensions of gender occupational differentiation in segregation and inequality: A cross-national analysis." *Social Indicators Research* 46 (2): 225–247.

Sen, Amartya. 1999. *Development as Freedom.* New York: Anchor Books.

Shapiro, Robert, and Harpreet Mahajan. 1986. "Gender differences in policy preferences." *Public Opinion Quarterly* 50: 42–61.

Sharma, Arvind, and Katherine K. Young, Eds. 1999. *Feminism and World Religions.* Albany: State University of New York Press.

Siaroff, A. 2000. "Women's representation in legislatures and cabinets in industrial democracies." *International Political Science Review* 21 (2): 197–215.

Simon, Rita J., and Jean M. Landis. 1989. "Women's and men's attitudes about a woman's place and role." *Public Opinion Quarterly* 53: 265–276.

Smeal, Eleanor. 1984. *Why and How Women Will Elect the Next President.* New York: Harper and Row.

Smith, Bonnie G., Ed. 2000. *Global Feminisms since 1945.* New York: Routledge.

Smith, Tom. 1984. "The polls: Gender and attitudes towards violence." *Public Opinion Quarterly* 48: 384–396.

Stetson, Dorothy, and Amy Mazur. 1995. *Comparative State Feminism.* Thousand Oaks, CA: Sage.

Stoper, Emily. 1989. "The gender gap concealed and revealed: 1936–1984." *Journal of Political Science* 17 (1,2): 50–62.

Studlar, Donley, Ian McAllister, and Bernadette Hayes. 1998. "Explaining the gender gap in voting: A cross-national analysis." *Social Science Quarterly* 79.

Thomas, Sue, and Susan Welch. 1991. "The impact of gender on activities and priorities of state legislators." *Western Political Quarterly* 442: 445–456.

Thomas, Sue. 1991. "The impact of women on state legislative policies." *Journal of Politics* 53 (4): 958–976.

Thomas, Sue. 1996. *How Women Legislate.* Oxford: Oxford University Press.

Thornton, Arland, Duane F. Alwin, and Donald Camburn. 1983. "Causes and consequences of sex-role attitudes and attitudes change." *American Sociological Review* 48: 211–227.

Tingsten, Herbert L. G. 1937. *Political Behavior: Studies in Election Statistics.* London: P. S. King.

Togeby, Lise. 1994. "The disappearance of a gender gap: Tolerance and liberalism in Denmark from 1971–1990." *Scandinavian Political Studies* 14 (1): 47–68.

Trevor, M. C. 1999. "Political socialization, party identification and the gender gap." *Public Opinion Quarterly* 63 (1): 62–89.

Tripp, Aili Mari. 2000. *Women and Politics in Uganda.* Madison: University of Wisconsin Press.

True, J. and M. Minstrom. 2001. "Transnational networks and policy diffusion: The case of gender mainstreaming." *International Studies Quarterly* 45 (1): 27–57.

Twenge, J. M. 1997. "Attitudes towards women, 1970–1995 – A meta analysis." *Psychology of Women Quarterly* 21 (1): 35–51.

Twenge, J., and M. Zucker. 1999. "What is a feminist? Evaluations and stereotypes in closed- and open-ended responses." *Psychology of Women Quarterly* 23 (3): 591–605.

United Nations. 2000. *The World's Women 2000: Trends and Statistics.* New York: United Nations.

United Nations. 2001. *Human Development Report 2001.* New York: United Nations/Oxford University Press.

United Nations. *Women 2000: Gender Equality, Development and Peace.* Special session of the General Assembly, 5–9 June. <http://www.un.org/womenwatch/daw/followup/beijing+5.html>

United States Census Bureau. 2000. *Statistical Abstract of the United States, 1999.* < www.census.gov>

Verba, Sidney, and Norman Nie. 1972. *Participation in America: Political Democracy and Social Equality.* New York: Harper and Row.

Vianello, Mino, and Renata Siemienska, Eds. 1990. *Gender Inequality.* London: Sage.

Vollebergh, W. A. M., J. Iedema, and W. Meeus. 1999. "The emerging gender gap: Cultural and economic conservatism in the Netherlands, 1970–1992." *Political Psychology* 20 (2): 291–321.

Vowles, Jack. 1993. "Gender and electoral behaviour in New Zealand." In *Women and Politics in New Zealand,* ed. Helena Catt and Elizabeth McLeay. Wellington: Victoria University Press.

Wangnerud, Lena. 1994. "Male and female party images in Sweden." *Scandinavian Political Studies* 172: 143–170.

Wangnerud, Lena. 2000. "Testing the politics of presence: Women's representation in the Swedish Riksdag." *Scandinavian Political Studies* 23 (1): 67–91.

Welch, Susan, and Susan Thomas. 1988. "Explaining the gender gap in British public opinion." *Women and Politics* 8: 25–44.

Wilcox, Clyde. 1991. "The causes and consequences of feminist consciousness among Western European women." *Comparative Political Studies* 23 (4): 519–545.

Williams, John E., and Deborah L. Best. 1990. *Measuring Sex Stereotypes: A Multination Study.* Newbury Park, CA: Sage.

Williams, R., and M. A. Wittig. 1997. " 'I'm not a feminist, but...': Factors contributing to the discrepancy between pro-feminist orientation and feminist social identity." *Sex Roles* 37 (11–12): 885–904.

Wirls, Donald. 1986. "Reinterpreting the gender gap." *Public Opinion Quarterly* 50: 316–30.

Wirth, Linda. 2001. *Breaking Through the Glass Ceiling: Women in Management.* Geneva: International Labour Office.

Young, G., L. Fort, and M. Danner. 1994. "Moving from the status of women to gender inequality – Conceptualization, social-indicators and an empirical application." *International Sociology* 9 (1): 55–85.

Yuval-Davis, Nira, and Floya Anthias. 1989. *Woman, Nation, State.* New York: St. Martin's Press.

Index